Design Patterns in TypeScript

Common GoF (Gang of Four) Design Patterns
Implemented in TypeScript

Sean Bradley

Copyright © 2019-2022 Sean Bradley

Table of contents

1. Design Patterns in TypeScript — 4
   - 1.1 Pattern Types — 5
   - 1.2 Class Scope and Object Scope Patterns — 6
2. Development Environment Setup — 7
   - 2.1 Course Code — 8
3. TypeScript Basics — 11
   - 3.1 Getting Started — 11
   - 3.2 Common Types — 19
   - 3.3 Classes — 28
   - 3.4 Interfaces — 32
   - 3.5 Extending Classes — 37
   - 3.6 Abstract Classes — 45
   - 3.7 Access Modifiers — 49
   - 3.8 Static Members — 53
   - 3.9 ES6 Imports/Exports — 56
4. UML Diagrams — 58
   - 4.1 A Basic Class — 58
   - 4.2 Directed Association — 58
   - 4.3 A Class That Extends/Inherits A Class — 59
   - 4.4 A Class That Implements an Interface — 60
   - 4.5 Aggregates — 60
   - 4.6 Composition — 61
   - 4.7 Pseudocode Annotation — 61
5. Creational — 63
   - 5.1 Factory Design Pattern — 63
   - 5.2 Abstract Factory Design Pattern — 70
   - 5.3 Builder Design Pattern — 82
   - 5.4 Prototype Design Pattern — 89
   - 5.5 Singleton Design Pattern — 96

6. Structural ... 103
    6.1 Decorator Design Pattern ... 103
    6.2 Adapter Design Pattern ... 110
    6.3 Facade Design Pattern ... 119
    6.4 Bridge Design Pattern ... 131
    6.5 Composite Design Pattern ... 139
    6.6 Flyweight Design Pattern ... 148
    6.7 Proxy Design Pattern ... 157
7. Behavioral ... 164
    7.1 Command Design Pattern ... 164
    7.2 Chain of Responsibility Design Pattern ... 173
    7.3 Observer Pattern ... 181
    7.4 Interpreter Design Pattern ... 192
    7.5 Iterator Design Pattern ... 206
    7.6 Mediator Design Pattern ... 211
    7.7 Memento Design Pattern ... 218
    7.8 State Design Pattern ... 228
    7.9 Strategy Design Pattern ... 235
    7.10 Template Method Design Pattern ... 241
    7.11 Visitor Design Pattern ... 249
8. Summary ... 258

1. Design Patterns in TypeScript

Hello, I'm Sean Bradley, and welcome to my book on Design Patterns in TypeScript.

You may have bought this book because you find it more relaxing to read from a book, rather than from a computer screen. Well that's how it works for me. However, as part of the purchase of this book, I have also provided you with the ability to view for free, all the videos which are part of my official **Design Patterns in TypeScript** courses on Udemy, Skillshare and through YouTube Memberships.

To view the videos, in each section of this book, you will find several **SBCODE Video IDs**. Visit https://sbcode.net/typescript/ and at the beginning of each instructional page on the accompanying documentation website, there are options to enter the video code ID and view the related video for free without needing to register on one of the course platforms first. Press the **SBCODE** button in the **Video Lecture** sections on the website and then enter the video code ID that you found for each related section within this book. So please watch the videos after you read each section, since they will give you an alternative perspective compared to what you may have understood from just reading it.

Now, a little about me, for over 20 years I have been an IT engineer building and managing real time, low latency, high availability, asynchronous, multithreaded, remotely managed, fully automated, monitored solutions in the education, aeronautical, banking, drone, gaming and telecommunications industries.

I have also created and written hundreds of Open-Source GitHub Repositories, Medium Articles and video tutorials on YouTube, Udemy and Skillshare.

This book focuses on the 23 famous GoF (Gang of Four) Design Patterns but implemented in TypeScript. The first part of the book is about familiarizing yourself with TypeScript in case you've never used it before. And then when we get into each design pattern, you should be able to understand better each line of code in the examples and why I have written it that way.

A Design Pattern is a description or template that can be repeatedly applied to a commonly recurring problem in software design.

A familiarity of Design Patterns will be very useful when planning, discussing, managing and documenting your applications from now on and into the future.

So, in this book, you will learn about these 23 Design Patterns,

- Creational
    - Factory
    - Abstract Factory

- Builder
- Prototype
- Singleton
- Structural
  - Decorator
  - Adapter
  - Facade
  - Bridge
  - Composite
  - Flyweight
  - Proxy
- Behavioral
  - Command
  - Chain of Responsibility
  - Observer Pattern
  - Interpreter
  - Iterator
  - Mediator
  - Memento
  - State
  - Strategy
  - Template Method
  - Visitor

1.1 Pattern Types

In the list of patterns above, there are Creational, Structural and Behavioral patterns.

- **Creational** : Abstracts the instantiation process so that there is a logical separation between how objects are composed and finally represented.
- **Structural** : Focuses more on how classes and objects are composed using the different structural techniques, and to form structures with more or altered flexibility.
- **Behavioral** : Are concerned with the inner algorithms, process flow, the assignment of responsibilities and the intercommunication between objects.

1.2 Class Scope and Object Scope Patterns

Each pattern can be further specified whether it relates more specifically to classes or instantiated objects.

Class scope patterns deal more with relationships between classes and their subclasses.

Object scope patterns deal more with relationships that can be altered at runtime

Pattern	Description	Scope	Type
Factory, Abstract Factory	Defers object creation to subclasses	Class	Creational
Builder, Prototype, Singleton	Defers object creation to objects	Object	Creational
Adapter, Bridge, Composite, Decorator, Facade, Flyweight, Proxy	Describes a way to assemble objects	Object	Structural
Interpreter, Template	Describes algorithms and flow control	Class	Behavioral
Chain of Responsibility, Command, Iterator, Mediator, Memento, Observer, State, Strategy, Visitor	Describes how groups of objects co-operate	Object	Behavioral

2. Development Environment Setup

SBCODE Video ID #d29be7

All the examples in this course will be run using the Node.js runtime. All the code is written in TypeScript first and then converted into JavaScript that the Node.js runtime will further interpret and execute.

So, to get started, install Node.js first.

Open a browser and visit https://nodejs.org/en/download/

I am using Windows 10 64-bit, so I will use the 64-bit Windows Installer (.msi). Be sure to use the correct installer for your operating system.

After the installation has finished, depending on your operating system, whether Windows, Linux or Mac OSX, open a terminal/bash/cmd or PowerShell prompt and type

```
node -v
```

If the installation completed without issue, you should see a response similar to

```
v16.13.2
```

All the code written in this book should work for versions of Node.js above v10.

Node.js also comes with another program called NPM. We will use NPM to install the TypeScript compiler (TSC).

Check that NPM exists and works, by typing

```
npm -v
```

Output should be a version number and not an error. E.g.,

```
8.11.10
```

Now that Node.js and NPM work, we can install the TypeScript compiler (TSC) globally on our system.

```
npm install -g typescript
```

And then verify that the installation is successful by checking the version number.

```
tsc -v
```

Output should be a version number and not an error. E.g.,

```
4.7.2
```

If you are using PowerShell, you may see an error concerning execution policy.

```
tsc.ps1 cannot be loaded because running scripts is
disabled on this system
```

You have several options, such as run your commands using the classic Windows CMD prompt, Git Bash or use the `tsc.cmd` option instead.

```
tsc.cmd -v
```

When I was writing the code in this book, I was using Visual Studio Code and executing TSC using PowerShell in the VSCode integrated terminal.

I recommend to use VSCode, it is free and provides many useful features when coding.

Download VSCode from https://code.visualstudio.com/

When running PowerShell in the VSCode integrated terminal, you may also see the execution policy error.

You can use `tsc.cmd` in place of `tsc`.

You can even use a different terminal prompt in the VSCode integrated terminal such as the classic Windows CMD, Git Bash and there are many others that you may want to set up.

2.1 Course Code

SBCODE Video ID #29949d

All the code examples in this book can be viewed from my GitHub repository at https://github.com/Sean-Bradley/Design-Patterns-In-TypeScript

If you have Git installed, you can download a copy locally using the command

```
git clone https://github.com/Sean-Bradley/Design-Patterns-In-
TypeScript.git
```

You can install Git for Windows from https://gitforwindows.org/.

Linux will normally have git preinstalled.

Or,

you can download a zip of all the code, using the link

https://sbcode.net/typescript/zips/Design-Patterns-In-TypeScript.zip

or using `wget` on Linux

```
wget https://sbcode.net/typescript/zips/Design-Patterns-In-TypeScript.zip
sudo apt install unzip
unzip Design-Patterns-In-TypeScript.zip
cd Design-Patterns-In-TypeScript/
```

After extracting the zip, go to where you extracted it, and in the main folder where `package.json` exists, run `npm install` to set up the project.

You can then experiment with the code at your own pace and try out different variations.

If you would rather build the project manually and type the code from the book, then follow these further instructions.

On my system, I have created a working folder on one of my spare drives, `E:\`, and then created a new folder in it named `Design-Patterns-In-TypeScript`, and then `cd` into it. You can use a different folder name and drive if you prefer.

```
C:\> e:
E:\> mkdir Design-Patterns-In-TypeScript
E:\> cd .\Design-Patterns-In-TypeScript
```

The `Design-Patterns-In-TypeScript` folder is now also known as your projects root folder.

Throughout the documentation I will also refer to the project root folder as `./`

Now while in your projects root folder, create two extra sub folders named `src` and `dist`

```
mkdir src
mkdir dist
```

So that your folder structure appears as below.

```
|-- Design-Patterns-In-TypeScript
    |-- dist
    |-- src
```

Then type `npm init`, accept all defaults by pressing enter/return for each question.

```
npm init
```

This would have created a new file in your project root named `package.json`.

Now since we are writing TypeScript that will use some inbuilt Node.js functionality, we will need to also install the Node.js types.

So, run

```
npm install --save @types/node
```

This will add a new dependency to your existing `package.json` for the Node.js types that some example code in this book will directly reference.

Your folder structure should now match

```
|-- Design-Patterns-In-TypeScript
    |-- dist
    |-- node_modules
        |-- @types
            |-- node (A folder including many *.d.ts files)
    |-- src
    package.json
    package-lock.json
```

The basic project setup is now complete.

As each design pattern is introduced, it will be within its own sub folder named after the design pattern.

So, for example, all the TypeScript source code for the Factory pattern, will be in the `./src/factory` folder, and when `tsc` compiles the code, it will create the JavaScript equivalent versions of it in the `./dist/factory` folder.

We will type the TypeScript source code in the `./src/*` folder hierarchy and the Node.js runtime will execute the outputted JavaScript that TSC saved in the `./dist/*` folder equivalent hierarchy.

Remember that if all the manual setup of the project becomes over whelming, there is the official GitHub project that you can refer to at https://github.com/Sean-Bradley/Design-Patterns-In-TypeScript.

3. TypeScript Basics

3.1 Getting Started

SBCODE Video ID #117f2b

TypeScript is a tool to help you write type-safe JavaScript. JavaScript is a weakly typed language which means that types are assigned implicitly as they are used at runtime. While this can be considered a feature, it can be dangerous if your code needs to be treating types precisely at all times. Enforcing type safety ensures that all usage of the properties, functions and classes are consistent within your application and as a result makes your application more robust.

When writing TypeScript, it will appear in many ways very similar to JavaScript. TypeScript is a subset of JavaScript. So, you can write JavaScript in a TypeScript file first, but the IDE, VSCode in my case, will indicate many suggestions on how to modify your code to be more type safe.

In this next section on TypeScript basics, we will go through many concepts which may be JavaScript first, but you will see the TypeScript equivalent so that you can get a better understanding between the languages.

3.1.1 Create Our First TypeScript File

The first example is that we will create a basic TypeScript file that we will compile/transpile into JavaScript that Node.js will run.

Note

The terminology of whether TypeScript is **compiling** or **transpiling** is an ongoing argument that you can look up on the internet if you want to take part in it. I will use the term **compile**, since **transpile** is not currently a real word in the Oxford Dictionary, and TSC is called the TypeScript **Compiler**.

Go to the `./src` folder in your project and create a new file called `test.ts`

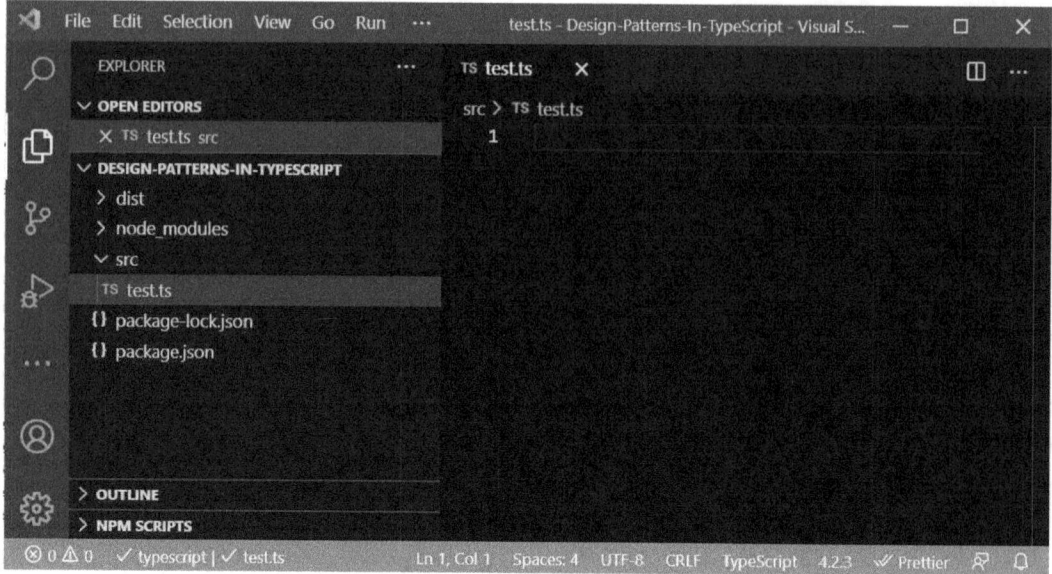

In that file add this script

```
function foo(bar: string) {
    return 'Hello, ' + bar
}

let baz = 'ABC'

console.log(foo(baz))
```

3.1.2 Compile The TypeScript File Into JavaScript

Open the VSCode integrated terminal using the keys `Ctrl+Shift+'`, or using the top menu `Terminal --> New Terminal`.

In the project root folder type

```
tsc ./src/test.ts --outDir ./dist
```

Note

Remember that you don't need to use PowerShell. You can use Git Bash, Windows CMD prompt, or another terminal on your operating system. If you are using PowerShell in the VSCode integrated terminal, and you haven't modified the `settings.json` as outlined in the last section, you may have gotten an execution policy error. You have the option to start the `tsc` compilation process by using the `tsc.cmd` option instead. E.g,
`tsc.cmd ./src/test.ts --outDir ./dist`

So, now if you visit the `./dist` folder there will be a new file in it called `test.js`. It will be almost identical to the `./src/test.ts` file that we just wrote and processed with TSC, but with the new file extension being `.js` instead of `.ts` and the TypeScript type annotations removed. I.e.,

```
//see ./src/test.ts
function foo(bar: string) {
```

becomes

```
//see ./dist/test.js
function foo(bar) {
```

The TypeScript version explicitly declares which type the `bar` arguments must be when passed to the `foo` function and that is a `string`.

 Warning

If you have `./src/test.ts` and `./dist/test.js` open in VSCode at the same time, you may see an error indicated saying that `foo` and `baz` have been re-declared in the other file. This happens when both files are open in the editor at the same time and your project doesn't have a `tsconfig.json` indicating which folders are officially the `rootDir` and `outDir` folders of your project. This will be discussed and setup in the next section. In the meantime, you can close one of the files in the IDE to prevent VSCode from thinking that this is an error.

3.1.3 Run The Compiled JavaScript

We can now run this `./dist/test.js` using Node.js. So from your project root run,

```
node ./dist/test.js
```

You should get the output,

```
Hello, ABC
```

Note

On Windows, using either forward slashes `/` or backslashes `\` as folder and file separators is ok. So, while I have written `node ./dist/test.js` in my documentation, I could also have written `node .\dist\test.js` and executed it in PowerShell or Windows CMD, and it would still work. I prefer to use forward slashes in my documentation since backslashes may cause ambiguity in case of the backslash escape character functionality that can also be utilized when entering commands into a terminal.

Now, to see type safety in action, in the TypeScript file `./src/test.ts` change

```
let baz = 'ABC'
```

to

```
let baz = 123
```

and the VSCode editor will now indicate to you at design time, the error

```
Argument of type 'number' is not assignable to parameter of type
'string'
```

Warning

Don't forget to change the line back to `let baz = 'ABC'` since we will use this file in the next section.

While passing a number to a function that expects a string in JavaScript may not always be a problem for you and will not throw a runtime error; by compiling our JavaScript from a TypeScript source file first it can protect us from those unforeseen potential problems that may occur when writing JavaScript code directly. This protection provided by writing TypeScript in the VSCode IDE/editor happens at design time, rather than at runtime when any problems caused could potentially have been much worse.

Remember that TypeScript is not intended to run in the final environment, such as in Node.js or in a web browser, but it is a tool that developers can use to help write type-safe and more robust JavaScript.

3.1.4 Adding tsconfig.json

SBCODE Video ID #9aac47

Normally, it is best practice to create a `tsconfig.json` file in the base of your TypeScript source folder in your project.

So, create a new file called `tsconfig.json` in the `./src/` folder alongside the existing `test.ts`

./src/tsconfig.json

```
{
    "compilerOptions": {
        "strict": true,
        "target": "ES2015",
        "module": "CommonJS",
        "outDir": "../dist",
        "rootDir": "./",
        "moduleResolution": "node"
    },
    "include": ["**/*.ts"]
}
```

Your project structure should now resemble

```
|-- Design-Patterns-In-TypeScript
    |-- dist
        |-- test.js
    |-- node_modules
        |-- @types
            |-- node (A folder including many *.d.ts files)
    |-- src
        |-- test.ts
        |-- tsconfig.json
    package.json
    package-lock.json
```

Now you can compile your `test.ts` into JavaScript by calling `tsc` and indicating the `tsconfig.json` which is located in the `./src` folder.

```
tsc -p ./src
```

To analyze this `tsconfig.json`,

- `"strict":true` : The strict flag enables a wide range of type checking behavior that results in stronger guarantees of program correctness. I mainly use it to ensure that all class properties are either assigned when first declared, or in the constructor.

- `"target": "ES2015"` : ES stands for ECMAScript which is a documented JavaScript standard. TSC will produce JavaScript that matches the selected standard. Options are `ES3`, `ES5`, `ES2015`, `ES2016`, `ES2017`, `ES2018`, `ES2019`, `ES2020`, `ES2021`, `ES2022` and `ESNEXT`. Each ES version introduces new core JavaScript functionality. I have chosen ES2015 since TSC won't compile earlier versions if the source TypeScript contains private identifiers. Visit https://en.wikipedia.org/wiki/ECMAScript for more information about the ES version differences.

- `"module": "CommonJS"` : In many of the code examples in this book, I am using `ES6` import/export syntax. The `CommonJS` module setting will produce output that relies on the popular `RequireJS` module loader that Node.js supports by default. This means that any JavaScript produced from TSC will work in Node.js in case your source TypeScript code contains any `ES6` import commands.

- `"outDir": "../dist"` : This is the folder where the compiled JavaScript will be placed. Note that it has 2 dots indicating to go back/down one folder, and then up into the `dist` folder. This is relative to the `rootDir` parameter discussed in the next line.

- `"rootDir": "./"` : This is the root directory of the TypeScript project containing all the `*.ts` files, and not the project root directory which was referred to earlier that contains all the projects files including the `src`, `dist`, `node_modules`, `package.json`, etc. It is the folder that TSC should consider to be the root when compiling.

- `"moduleResolution": "node"` : Is the default, and describes the file finding resolution process in which TSC will find dependencies if and when they are referenced in any code.

- `"include": ["**/*.ts"]` : Indicates to compile all files it finds ending in `.ts` in this and any sub folders relative to the `rootDir` setting within this same `tsconfig.json`.

The sample `tsconfig.json` I have provided is minimal and is ideal for this complete course when trying to execute the code examples using Node.js. On the internet you will find many TypeScript projects with varying tsconfig files all written specifically for the purpose of the particular project that they exist in.

 Note

Now that you have a `tsconfig.json` in your TypeScript source root, you can open both the in your TypeScript source root, you can open both the `./src/test.ts` and `./dist/test.js` in the VSCode IDE and no errors describing duplicate declarations should occur.

For documentation on all the options that you can have in a `tsconfig.json` file, visit https://www.typescriptlang.org/tsconfig

3.1.5 TSC Watch

SBCODE Video ID #006bcb

Before running your compiled JavaScript in Node.js, you need to run your TypeScript source files through TSC.

This process of running `tsc -p ./src` and then seeing the output in Node.js using `node ./dist/test.js` for example, can be quite tedious if you need to keep typing the `tsc` and the `node` commands in turn for every change you make.

Instead, you can run TSC in watch mode, which will cause it to continue running and automatically compile and check any changes you make to the TypeScript source files, and then you open a second terminal that you can use specifically for executing the `node` or other commands.

Run

```
tsc -p ./src -w
```

This will keep the first terminal running indefinitely while it watches and re-compiles any changes you make in the `./src` folder and sub folders.

Now open a second console/terminal, or use the `split` option to open a second terminal to the right.

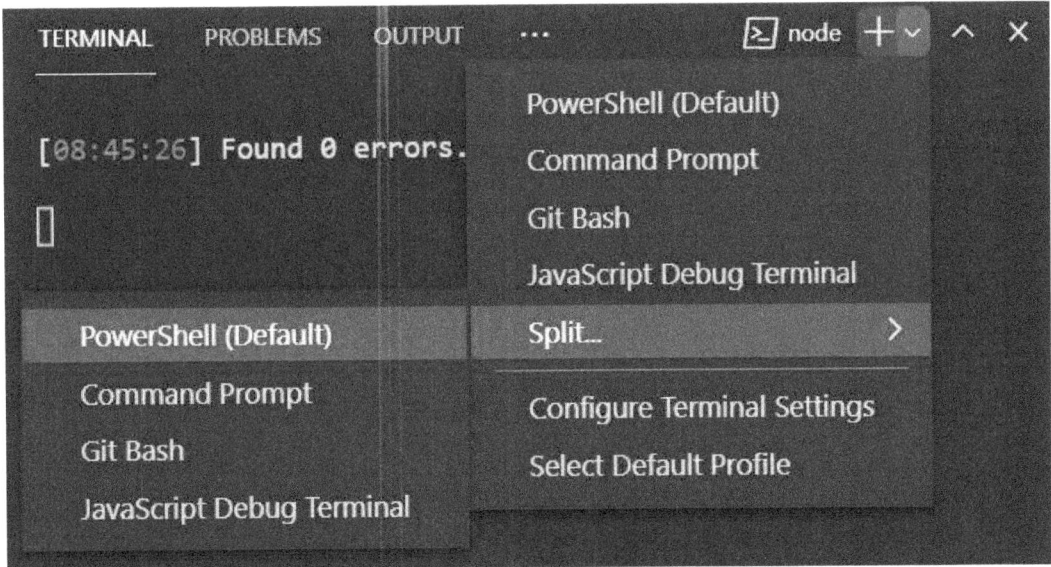

In the second terminal, you can now run your JavaScript, for example `node ./dist/test.js`

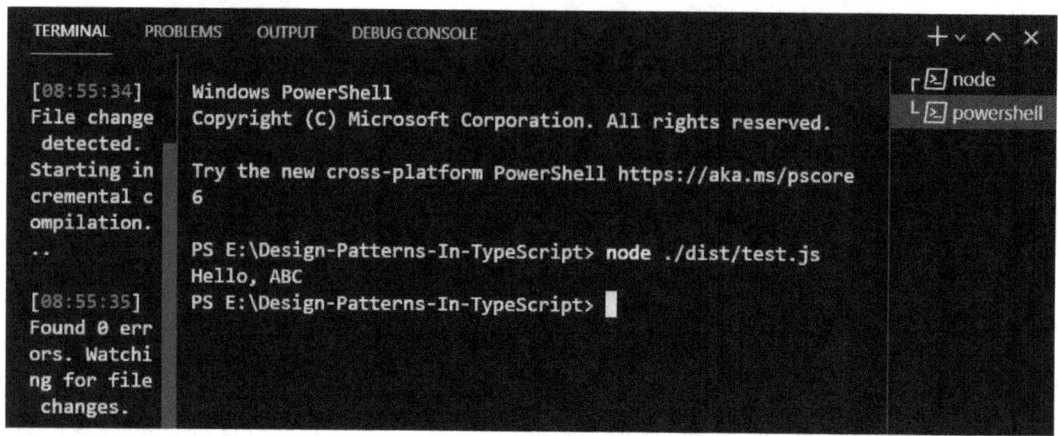

In the above image, the left pane is busy running `tsc -p ./src -w` while the right pane is free to enter any manual commands as needed such as `node ./dist/test.js`

I advise to watch the video for this section to show how I do this if my description is hard to understand.

3.2 Common Types

This section is a basic introduction of the types that you can use in TypeScript. It is useful to help you learn some TypeScript basics in case you are new to TypeScript. Each of the types listed below are used throughout this book.

3.2.1 Let/Const

SBCODE Video ID #fc018b

When declaring any properties in your TypeScript files, you can declare them using the `let` or `const` keywords.

If you declare a property using `let`, e.g.,

```
let a = 1
```

then you can change the value of `a` at a later time.

```
let a = 1
a = 2
```

If you declared `a` as a `const`, then you wouldn't be able to change `a` later. It will stay as a constant value throughout the lifetime of your program.

```
const a = 1
a = 2
```

Changing the value of `a` would indicate an error.

When you declare a `const`, you must also initialize it with a value at the same time. E.g.,

```
const a = 1
```

If you declared it as just,

```
const a
```

Then that would indicate an error that `const` declarations must be initialized with a value.

You can also use the `var` keyword to create properties/variables. But it is better practice using either `let` or `const` since they will be treated as block scope variables when declared within classes or any other code within curly braces {}, rather than global. Variables declared using the `var` keyword may overwrite variables of the same name that are used elsewhere in your program. When using `let` or `const`, TSC errors and warnings will also be much more relevant. If you were to use a linter on your code, such as ESLint, and it found usages of `var` then you would see the error,

```
Unexpected var, use let or const instead
```

3.2.2 Types

SBCODE Video ID #001757

Replace `./src/test.ts` with this script below and recompile using `tsc -p ./src`

```
let foo: string
let bar: boolean
let baz: number
let qux: string[]
let quuz: [number, string]
let corge: { [key: number]: string }
let grault: Set<number>

foo = 'ABC'
bar = true
baz = 123
qux = ['a', 'b', 'c']
quuz = [1, 'abc']
corge = { 123: 'abc', 456: 'def' }
grault = new Set([1, 2, 3])
```

Open the compiled JavaScript version from `./dist/test.js` in the editor.

```
'use strict'
let foo
let bar
let baz
let qux
let quuz
let corge
let grault
foo = 'ABC'
bar = true
baz = 123
qux = ['a', 'b', 'c']
quuz = [1, 'abc']
```

```
corge = { 123: 'abc', 456: 'def' }
grault = new Set([1, 2, 3])
```

You can see that the compiled JavaScript is almost identical. While in the TypeScript version, the types are explicit and must conform when the variables are assigned vales, the JavaScript version does not indicate the type, but will fall back to a type known as `any` which can be anything. Since the source was written in TypeScript, you can trust that the outputted JavaScript will work correctly in regard to the types that you have chosen despite the JavaScript version not actually enforcing it.

So, in the TypeScript version I have demonstrated explicitly setting some types of

- string
- boolean
- number
- array of numbers
- a tuple of two elements consisting of a number and a string
- dictionary if string where the key is a number
- a Set of numbers

As an experiment, try swapping some types of each variable without changing the values. I.e., re-declare `foo` as a `boolean` and you will see that the VSCode IDE will indicate that you are assigning the wrong type of values to each variable. If you were to write this directly in JavaScript, then no such error would be indicated.

3.2.3 Strings

SBCODE Video ID #8456e4

Some more string experiments you can try are,

```
let foo: string
foo = 'ABC'
foo = '123'
foo = 'ABC = 123'
foo = 'quick brown fox, etc'
foo = "It wasn't me"
```

It is common practice, but not essential, to wrap single quotes around string values unless it contains a single quote in it, e.g., "didn't".

3.2.4 Boolean

SBCODE Video ID #2ee9bf

A boolean can either be `true` or `false`.

```
let bar: boolean
bar = true
bar = false
```

3.2.5 Number

SBCODE Video ID #cf0649

A number can be written in many bases or with floating point precision.

```
let baz:number
baz = 123         //decimal
baz = 123.456     //float
baz = 0xffff      //hex
baz = 0b10101     //binary
baz = 0o671       //octal
```

3.2.6 Array

SBCODE Video ID #ba0840

An array is a JavaScript object first that can contain a series of any types, but in TypeScript you can set the types explicitly or even as `unknown`.

```
let a: string[]
a = ['a', 'b', 'd', 'd']
let b: number[]
b = [1, 2, 3, 4]
let c: boolean[]
c = [true, false, true]
let d: unknown[]
d = [1, 'a', true, ['even', 'another', 'internal', 'array']]

// Array items can be retrieved using a zero based index.
console.log(a[1])
console.log(b[0])
console.log(c[1])
console.log(d[2])
```

Outputs

```
b
1
```

```
false
true
```

Some other operations on an Array.

```
const a = ['a', 'b', 'c', 'd']

// log the whole array
console.log(a)

// log how may items in the array
console.log(a.length)

// returns and removes the last item from the array
console.log(a.pop())

// returns and removes the first item from the array
console.log(a.shift())

// log the whole array again
console.log(a)

// add an item to the end
a.push('z')
console.log(a)

// add an item to the beginning
a.unshift('x')
console.log(a)

// remove 1 item starting at the 3rd item (0 based index)
a.splice(2, 1)
console.log(a)

// replace an item (0 based index)
a[1] = 'y'
console.log(a)
```

Outputs

```
[ 'a', 'b', 'c', 'd' ]
4
d
a
[ 'b', 'c' ]
[ 'b', 'c', 'z' ]
[ 'x', 'b', 'c', 'z' ]
```

```
[ 'x', 'b', 'z' ]
[ 'x', 'y', 'z' ]
```

I have used Arrays in various other ways in almost every single pattern example in the book.

Visit https://developer.mozilla.org/en-US/docs/Web/JavaScript/Reference/Global_Objects/Array for more detailed information about the Array.

3.2.7 Dictionary

SBCODE Video ID #641c44

A Dictionary is used as a key/value construct, where you can retrieve a value from the dictionary by using a key.

```
let a: { [key: number]: string }
a = { 123: 'abc', 456: 'def' }
let b: { [key: string]: boolean }
b = { abc: true, def: false, ghi: true }

console.log(a[123])
console.log(b['def'])
```

Outputs

```
abc
false
```

Some other operations on a Dictionary.

```
// The key of a dictionary can be of any type and name
let a: { [key: string]: string }
let b: { [id: number]: string }
a = { a: 'car', b: 'train', c: 'plane', d: 'boat' }
b = { 1: 'car', 2: 'train', 3: 'plane', 4: 'boat' }
// and can be retrieved as such
console.log(a['a'])
console.log(b[2])

// Since Dictionaries are really just objects. You can also retrieve
// a dictionary's value using object notation if the keys are strings
console.log(a.c)
// console.log(b.2) // this doesn't work when the key is a number

// you can add items to a dictionary
a['e'] = 'go-cart'
```

```
console.log(a)

// you can delete
delete b[2]
console.log(b)

// The values of a dictionary can be of any type, even an array.
let c: { [id: number]: number[] }
c = { 1: [1, 2, 3], 2: [4, 5, 6], 3: [7, 8, 9], 4: [10, 11, 12] }
console.log(c)
```

Outputs

```
car
train
plane
{ a: 'car', b: 'train', c: 'plane', d: 'boat', e: 'go-cart' }
{ '1': 'car', '3': 'plane', '4': 'boat' }
{
  '1': [ 1, 2, 3 ],
  '2': [ 4, 5, 6 ],
  '3': [ 7, 8, 9 ],
  '4': [ 10, 11, 12 ]
}
```

The Dictionary is actually a basic object `{}` in JavaScript. But in TypeScript, we can also set the types of the keys and values.

I have used Dictionaries in various other ways in the Command, Facade, Flyweight, Observer and Singleton pattern examples.

3.2.8 Tuple

SBCODE Video ID #2042f9

The Tuple is similar to an array, but you are explicitly indicating how many items are in the Tuple and of which type they are when you instantiate it. The Tuple type is not directly supported in JavaScript as a Tuple, but as an array instead. The rules of the Tuple are enforced in TypeScript only when it is created. After the Tuple is created, it behaves the same as an array. You can add/remove/edit items.

```
let a: [number, string]
a = [1, 'abc']
let b: [string, boolean, number]
b = ['abc', false, 123]
```

```
console.log(a[1])
console.log(b[2])
```

Outputs

```
abc
123
```

I have used Tuples in various other ways in the pattern examples for the Adapter and Facade (as the `getHistory` dictionary values).

3.2.9 Set

SBCODE Video ID #e53f42

The Set object lets you store unique values of any type. Any duplicate items added to the Set won't be added.

```
let a: Set<number>
a = new Set([1, 2, 3, 4])
let b: Set<string>
b = new Set(['a', 'b', 'c', 'd', 'a']) // the second `a` is not added
let c: Set<unknown>
c = new Set([1, 'b', true])

console.log(a)
console.log(b)
console.log(c)
```

Outputs

```
Set(4) { 1, 2, 3, 4 }
Set(4) { 'a', 'b', 'c', 'd' }
Set(3) { 1, 'b', true }
```

Some other operations on a Set.

```
const a: Set<string> = new Set()
// adding items
a.add('cat')
a.add('dog')
a.add('bird')
console.log(a)

// remove an item
a.delete('dog')
```

```
console.log(a)

// Retrieve an individual item.
console.log(Array.from(a)[1])

// The great thin about a set compared to an array, is that all
// items are guaranteed to be unique. No duplicates allowed.
a.add('bird')
a.add('bird')
console.log(a)

// Get the length of the Set
console.log(a.size)

// Check if a Set has a value
console.log(a.has('cat'))
```

Outputs

```
Set(3) { 'cat', 'dog', 'bird' }
Set(2) { 'cat', 'bird' }
bird
Set(2) { 'cat', 'bird' }
2
true
```

Sets are a JavaScript concept first, but the types within the Set can be assigned using TypeScript.

I have used Sets in various other ways in the Mediator, Memento and Observer pattern examples.

Note that this book does not cover all the types and all the many features that can be found when using TypeScript. You can visit https://www.typescriptlang.org/docs/handbook/2/everyday-types.html for a more detailed explanation of each type and also many more of types if you want to explore them further.

3.3 Classes

SBCODE Video ID #0b8a41

Every design pattern in this book uses classes, so it is appropriate to get a basic understanding of them.

Simply, they are a template that can be used when creating custom objects.

3.3.1 Class Example 1

Update `./src/test.ts` with this script

```
class Cat {
    constructor() {}

    walk(): void {
        console.log('Cat is walking')
    }
}

const CAT = new Cat()
CAT.walk()
```

Re compile and execute,

```
tsc -p ./src
node ./dist/test.js
```

Outputs

```
Cat is walking
```

If you inspect the compiled JavaScript in `./dist/test.js` you will see that it is also very similar to the `./src/test.ts`.

```
'use strict'
class Cat {
    constructor() {}
    walk() {
        console.log('Cat is walking')
    }
}
```

```
const CAT = new Cat()
CAT.walk()
```

Classes are a JavaScript concept, but TypeScript allows us to add type safety to them.

Note

Note that in the above "Re compile and execute" commands I have written them as two steps. You may prefer to keep `tsc` running in watch mode as described in the TSC Watch section so that you don't need to keep running `tsc -p ./src` for every new edit.

3.3.2 Class Example 2

Below is a more complicated class including more specific functionality.

```
class Cat {
    name: string

    constructor(name: string) {
        this.name = name
    }

    walk(steps: number): void {
        console.log(
            this.name + ' the cat has walked ' + steps + ' steps.'
        )
    }
}

const CAT = new Cat('Cosmo')
CAT.walk(20)
```

Re compile and execute,

```
tsc -p ./src
node ./dist/test.js
```

Outputs

```
Cosmo the cat, has walked 20 steps.
```

If you inspect the compiled JavaScript in `./dist/test.js` once again, you will see that it is also very similar to the TypeScript source except that the main difference is that all the type annotations have once again been removed.

Looking at the second example more closely, I added a local property called `name`. This is required to be a string. When the Cat is instantiated using the `new` keyword, I am also passing in a string to be used as the name. The `constructor` will assign the `name` that was passed in, to the classes' property also called `name`, but it refers to that internal class property as `this.name`.

Further down in the walk `method`, I also use `this.name` in the outputted string, plus another attribute value `steps` which was passed into the `walk` method. Note `steps` isn't referred to as `this.steps` since `steps` is declared in the method scope, and not the class scope.

3.3.3 Class Example 3

In this third example I will expand on the return types of the class methods.

Replace `./src/test.ts` with this script below.

```typescript
class Cat {
    name: string
    stepsWalked: number = 0

    constructor(name: string) {
        this.name = name
    }

    walk(steps: number): void {
        console.log(
            this.name + ' the cat has walked ' + steps + ' steps.'
        )
        this.stepsWalked += steps
    }

    totalStepCount(): number {
        return this.stepsWalked
    }
}

const CAT = new Cat('Cosmo')
CAT.walk(20)
CAT.walk(20)
console.log(
    CAT.name +
        ' the cat, has walked a total of ' +
        CAT.totalStepCount() +
        ' steps.'
)
```

Re compile and execute,

```
tsc -p ./src
node ./dist/test.js
```

Outputs

```
Cosmo the cat, has walked 20 steps.
Cosmo the cat, has walked 20 steps.
Cosmo the cat, has walked a total of 40 steps.
```

You will notice that the `walk` method now increments a value used to keep track of the total steps walked, and the `totalStepCount()` method returns a value of type `number`.

Also note that I've initialized `stepsWalked` with the value `0`, rather than setting it to `0` in the constructor. This is your choice. In `strict` mode, you can either initialize any variables as they are declared in the class, or within the classes' constructor.

3.4 Interfaces

SBCODE Video ID #5efabc

Interfaces in TypeScript are a useful tool that you can use for your classes to ensure that they conform to any specific rules that you want them to. This is especially useful if there are many people working on the same code base, and any classes need to follow any specific rules.

To make sure that a class definition fully complies with the rules in your chosen Interface, we use the `implements` keyword.

In the first example below, we try to create a class that must implement a particular interface. The interface can describe any types that you wish, but for example may have been decided by some business rules or any other important reason. When creating the class below, the IDE and TSC have detected that the class does not fully comply.

Implementing TypeScript interfaces is an optional safety net that can be used to ensure consistency and correctness throughout your code base.

3.4.1 Interface Example 1

```
interface IAnimal {
    name: string
    age: number
}

class Cat implements IAnimal {
    name: string

    constructor(name: string) {
        this.name = name
    }
}
```

If you were to copy this above code into `./src/test.ts`, both TSC and the VSCode IDE would indicate an error

```
Class 'Cat' incorrectly implements interface 'IAnimal'.
Property 'age' is missing in type 'Cat' but required in type 'IAnimal'
```

Since the `Cat` class implements `IAnimal`, it also needs to declare the `age` property as indicated in the `IAnimal` interface.

3.4.2 Interface Example 2

Note that interface rules can also be applied to class methods.

```
interface IAnimal {
    name: string
    age: number

    feed(food: string, amount: number): void
}

class Cat implements IAnimal {
    name: string
    age: number

    constructor(name: string, age: number) {
        this.name = name
        this.age = age
    }
}
```

If you were to replace the code in `./src/test.ts` with the above code. The error would now indicate that the `feed` method was not implemented in the `Cat` class.

Note that in the `interface` declaration, the `feed` method does not have a method body. Interface methods are kept empty, and the implementation is instead written in the class that will implement the interface.

An interface is essentially a `public` contract that all classes that implement it must follow. See Access Modifiers for more information about `public`.

3.4.3 Interface Example 3

Below is a working example of the code where there are two classes named `Cat` and `Dog` that both correctly fully implement the `IAnimal` interface. I.e., they both implement the `name` and `age` properties, and also implement the `feed` method accepting attributes with the correct types.

```
interface IAnimal {
    name: string
    age: number

    feed(food: string, amount: number): void
}

class Cat implements IAnimal {
    name: string
```

```typescript
        age: number

        constructor(name: string, age: number) {
            this.name = name
            this.age = age
        }

        feed(food: string, amount: number): void {
            console.log(
                'Feeding ' +
                    this.name +
                    ' the Cat ' +
                    amount +
                    ' kg of ' +
                    food
            )
        }
    }

    class Dog implements IAnimal {
        name: string
        age: number

        constructor(name: string, age: number) {
            this.name = name
            this.age = age
        }

        feed(food: string, amount: number): void {
            console.log(
                'Feeding ' +
                    this.name +
                    ' the Dog ' +
                    amount +
                    ' kg of ' +
                    food
            )
        }
    }

    const CAT = new Cat('Cosmo', 8)
    const DOG = new Dog('Rusty', 12)
    CAT.feed('Fish', 0.1)
    DOG.feed('Beef', 0.25)
```

Re compile and execute,

```
tsc -p ./src
node ./dist/test.js
```

Outputs

```
Feeding Cosmo the Cat, 0.1kg of Fish
Feeding Rusty the Dog, 0.25kg of Beef
```

Now let's inspect the compiled JavaScript in `./dist/test.js`.

```
'use strict'
class Cat {
    constructor(name, age) {
        this.name = name
        this.age = age
    }
    feed(food, amount) {
        console.log(
            'Feeding ' +
                this.name +
                ' the Cat ' +
                amount +
                ' kg of ' +
                food
        )
    }
}
class Dog {
    constructor(name, age) {
        this.name = name
        this.age = age
    }
    feed(food, amount) {
        console.log(
            'Feeding ' +
                this.name +
                ' the Dog ' +
                amount +
                ' kg of ' +
                food
        )
    }
}
const CAT = new Cat('Cosmo', 8)
const DOG = new Dog('Rusty', 12)
CAT.feed('Fish', 0.1)
DOG.feed('Beef', 0.25)
```

Note that there is no indication of any interfaces in the compiled code. Interfaces are a TypeScript concept and are not used or enforced in JavaScript. They are useful for ensuring that code complies to chosen rules when developing a project.

3.5 Extending Classes

SBCODE Video ID #2cdbcb

You can extend any existing class templates by using the `extends` keyword. The new class definition will be made up of the original class, but can optionally include its own new bespoke constructor, properties and/or methods. The new class definition is known as the derived class or subclass.

Extending a class is a different concept than implementing an interface. An interface describes the property types and method signature rules that the class implementing it should comply with. Extending a class copies the base class template and allows you to refine or specialize it further.

With the derived class, the original class being extended is called the base or super class. It is a class that may have methods and properties that are common, but another class can be created from it that `extends` from this base/super class and has the option to override the constructor, methods and properties. The derived class also has the option to create additional methods and properties specific for its own needs. If the base class is using an interface, then any derived class will already comply provided that the base class was already correctly complying with its chosen interface.

3.5.1 Extended Class Example 1

In example 1, the `Cat` and `Dog` classes are derived from the `Animal` base/super class.

```
class Animal {
    name: string
    age: number

    constructor(name: string, age: number) {
        this.name = name
        this.age = age
    }

    feed(food: string, amount: number): void {
        console.log(
            'Feeding ' +
                this.name +
                ' the ' +
                this.constructor.name +
                ' ' +
                amount +
                ' kg of ' +
                food
        )
    }
```

```
}

class Cat extends Animal {}

class Dog extends Animal {}

const CAT = new Cat('Cosmo', 8)
const DOG = new Dog('Rusty', 12)
CAT.feed('Fish', 0.1)
DOG.feed('Beef', 0.25)
```

Replace `./src/test.ts` with this code above, compile and execute it.

```
tsc -p ./src
node ./dist/test.js
```

Outputs

```
Feeding Cosmo the Cat, 0.1kg of Fish
Feeding Rusty the Dog, 0.25kg of Beef
```

Note that the `Cat` and `Dog` classes don't actually contain any properties, constructor or methods. They `extend` the `Animal` base class, so they contain the necessary constructor, properties and methods already.

Both `Cat` and `Dog` can call the `feed` method, by using `this.feed` which will redirect to the base/super class version of the `feed` method.

Also note that if you compiled the JavaScript code using the `ES3` target, you will see that the `extends` keywords does not exist natively in the output but specialized functions for it have been added. The JavaScript `extends` keyword was introduced to the JavaScript language in the `ES6/ES2015` updates.

As an exercise, you can change the `target` parameter in your `tsconfig.json` to `ES3`, e.g.,

```
{
    "compilerOptions": {
        "strict": true,
        "target": "ES3",
        "module": "CommonJS",
        "outDir": "../dist",
        "rootDir": "./",
        "moduleResolution": "node"
    },
    "include": ["**/*.ts"]
}
```

Stop any TSC Watch process that you have running (Use CTRL-C in your terminal window to stop it), and manually run `tsc .\src\test.ts`. You may need to use `tsc.cmd .\src\test.ts` if using PowerShell.

Now look at the compiled JavaScript in `./dist/test.js` and you will see that it is significantly different code and much harder to read. The `extends` functionality has been written as functions into the compiled JavaScript since `ES3` does not understand the `extends` keyword natively.

Once finished change the `target` back to `ES2015`. Note that you can also set it to `ES6`, since `ES6` and `ES2015` are the same. Restart your TSC process in watch mode if you prefer to use this technique. Review the `ES6` version of `./dist/test.js` and you will see it is now much easier to read. NodeJS supports `ES6` syntax, so there is no need to target `ES3`.

Also take note of the usage of `this.constructor.name` in the `feed` method in the above example. Since the `CAT` and `DOG` objects are instantiated from their own new `Cat` and `Dog` classes, rather than the `Animal` class directly, their constructor name is either `CAT` or `DOG`. For a test, you could instantiate the Dog from the `Animal` class directly and see the difference in the printed output.

```
//const DOG = new Dog('Rusty', 12)
const DOG = new Animal('Rusty', 12)
```

Outputs

```
Feeding Rusty the Animal 0.25 kg of Beef
```

3.5.2 Extended Class Example 2

In example 1 above, the `Cat` and `Dog` properties, methods and constructors were created automatically behind the scenes. It was unnecessary to override there constructor, property values and `feed` method. They simply used whatever they got when they extended the `Animal` class. If you wanted to customize the constructor/properties/methods, then you can override them.

Look at the altered `Cat` class below. While it extends the `Animal` class, it also has its own additional `isHungry` property, it overrides the constructor and also overrides the `feed` method with its own bespoke implementations. The `Dog` class remains unchanged.

```
class Animal {
    name: string
    age: number

    constructor(name: string, age: number) {
        this.name = name
        this.age = age
```

```typescript
        }

    feed(food: string, amount: number): void {
        console.log(
            'Feeding ' +
                this.name +
                ' the ' +
                this.constructor.name +
                ' ' +
                amount +
                ' kg of ' +
                food
        )
    }
}

class Cat extends Animal {
    isHungry: boolean
    constructor(name: string, age: number, isHungry: boolean) {
        super(name, age)
        this.isHungry = isHungry
    }

    feed(food: string, amount: number): void {
        if (this.isHungry) {
            super.feed(food, amount)
        } else {
            console.log(
                this.name +
                    ' the ' +
                    this.constructor.name +
                    ' is not hungry'
            )
        }
    }
}

class Dog extends Animal {}

const CAT = new Cat('Cosmo', 8, false)
const DOG = new Dog('Rusty', 12)
CAT.feed('Fish', 0.1)
DOG.feed('Beef', 0.25)
```

Replace `./src/test.ts` with this code above, compile and execute it.

```
tsc -p ./src
node ./dist/test.js
```

Outputs

```
Cosmo the Cat is not hungry
Feeding Rusty the Dog 0.25 kg of Beef
```

See how the `Cat` class has its own overridden constructor, and instantiated a new variable that it can use called `isHungry`.

Also note how the constructor also calls the `super()` method along with any attributes required by the super classes constructor. The `super()` method points to the base/super classes constructor.

In derived classes, it is compulsory to call the base classes `super()` method in the constructor otherwise you get an error,

```
Constructors for derived classes must contain a 'super' call
```

In the overridden `feed` method, I have also called the `super.feed(food, amount)` method. This is calling the base classes `feed` method directly. It is not necessary to call any methods of the base class directly in your overridden methods if you don't really want to. I did it to show that it is still possible. If the cat is not hungry, then the base classes `feed` method won't actually be called at all.

3.5.3 Extended Class Example 3

Be aware if overriding any properties in your derived classes. They will now have preference over the equivalent properties in the base class if you refer to them using the `this` keyword. If you have overridden a method or property, and you still want to reference the base classes copy of the method or property, then you can use the `super` keyword as I did in the Cats feed method in example 2.

In the below example I have declared an instance of `Cat` to default with the name of `Emmy`. So using `this.name` will now point to the Cats overridden `name` property, whereas before, it would have redirected to the base classes `name` property.

Example 3 tries to highlight the difference of when you are referring to a base classes property/method versus a subclasses copy of an overridden property/method.

See that I attempt to set a default of "Emmy" for the `Cat` classes `name` property. And then when it is instantiated I pass in the name "Cosmo". I then call the `super()` method passing in the name "Cosmo". While this does update the super classes copy of the `name` property, it does not update the subclasses overridden copy of `name`. So when I print `this.name` in the feed method, it points to the subclasses copy of `name` which is still set as "Emmy" by default.

```
class Animal {
    name: string
    age: number
```

```typescript
    constructor(name: string, age: number) {
        this.name = name
        this.age = age
    }

    feed(food: string, amount: number): void {
        console.log(
            'Feeding ' +
                this.name +
                ' the ' +
                this.constructor.name +
                ' ' +
                amount +
                ' kg of ' +
                food
        )
    }
}

class Cat extends Animal {
    isHungry: boolean
    name = 'Emmy'
    constructor(name: string, age: number, isHungry: boolean) {
        super(name, age)
        this.isHungry = isHungry
    }

    feed(food: string, amount: number): void {
        if (this.isHungry) {
            super.feed(food, amount)
        } else {
            console.log(
                this.name +
                    ' the ' +
                    this.constructor.name +
                    ' is not hungry'
            )
        }
    }
}

class Dog extends Animal {}

const CAT = new Cat('Cosmo', 8, false)
const DOG = new Dog('Rusty', 12)
CAT.feed('Fish', 0.1)
DOG.feed('Beef', 0.25)
```

Outputs

```
Emmy the Cat is not hungry
Feeding Rusty the Dog 0.25 kg of Beef
```

If I wanted to use the new name "Cosmo" to override the predefined "Emmy" in the derived class, I would need to set it explicitly somewhere in the derived class, for example as I do in the `Cat` constructor `this.name = name`. See updated code below.

```
class Animal {
    name: string
    age: number

    constructor(name: string, age: number) {
        this.name = name
        this.age = age
    }

    feed(food: string, amount: number): void {
        console.log(
            'Feeding ' +
                this.name +
                ' the ' +
                this.constructor.name +
                ' ' +
                amount +
                ' kg of ' +
                food
        )
    }
}

class Cat extends Animal {
    isHungry: boolean
    name = 'Emmy'
    constructor(name: string, age: number, isHungry: boolean) {
        super(name, age)
        this.isHungry = isHungry
        this.name = name
    }

    feed(food: string, amount: number): void {
        if (this.isHungry) {
            super.feed(food, amount)
        } else {
            console.log(
                this.name +
                    ' the ' +
```

```
                    this.constructor.name +
                    ' is not hungry'
            )
        }
    }
}

class Dog extends Animal {}

const CAT = new Cat('Cosmo', 8, false)
const DOG = new Dog('Rusty', 12)
CAT.feed('Fish', 0.1)
DOG.feed('Beef', 0.25)
```

Outputs

```
Cosmo the Cat is not hungry
Feeding Rusty the Dog 0.25 kg of Beef
```

3.6 Abstract Classes

SBCODE Video ID #12a7eb

Abstract classes are like a mixture of implementing interfaces and extending a class in one step. You can create a class with optional methods and properties, but also indicate which methods and properties must be implemented in the derived class. Note that your base class, despite enforcing abstract rules, is still able to itself implement any interfaces you desire.

Use the `abstract` keyword to indicate a class contains `abstract` methods or properties.

3.6.1 Abstract Class Example 1

In this first example, the abstract class `Animal` has an abstract property `name`. Cat and Dog must implement the property `name` themselves rather than inherit from the base class.

Note that the `abstract name` in the `Animal` class definition cannot be initialized a value in either the class attribute definition or in its constructor. It is now a rule indicating that `name` must be initialized by the derived class instead.

```
abstract class Animal {
    abstract name: string
    age: number

    constructor(age: number) {
        //this.name = name // this must now be assigned in the derived class instead
        this.age = age
    }

    feed(food: string, amount: number): void {
        console.log(
            'Feeding ' +
                this.name +
                ' the ' +
                this.constructor.name +
                ' ' +
                amount +
                ' kg of ' +
                food
        )
    }
}

class Cat extends Animal {
```

```
    name: string
    constructor(name: string, age: number) {
        super(age)
        this.name = name
    }
}

class Dog extends Animal {
    name: string
    constructor(name: string, age: number) {
        super(age)
        this.name = name
    }
}

const CAT = new Cat('Cosmo', 8)
const DOG = new Dog('Rusty', 12)
CAT.feed('Fish', 0.1)
DOG.feed('Beef', 0.25)
```

Replace `./src/test.ts` with this code above, compile and execute it.

```
tsc -p ./src
node ./dist/test.js
```

Outputs

```
Feeding Cosmo the Cat, 0.1kg of Fish
Feeding Rusty the Dog, 0.25kg of Beef
```

Also note that classes marked as abstract cannot be directly instantiated. I.e.,

```
//const CAT = new Cat('Cosmo', 8)
const CAT = new Animal('Cosmo', 8)
```

will indicate an error

```
Cannot create an instance of an abstract class
```

3.6.2 Abstract Class Example 2

If any methods are marked as abstract, then they must also be implemented in the derived class.

Methods marked as abstract in the base class, do not contain a body. The body will be implemented by the derived class instead.

Also note that in the following example, `age` has been set as a default to be `-1`. Setting a default value is optional.

So, if you want the functionality offered of an interface, i.e., the rules, but you also want your interface to potentially have default or optional properties and/or methods, then you can use an abstract class instead. Don't forget the use of `super` in the derived classes' constructor so that the default or optional properties and methods are initialized.

```
abstract class Animal {
    abstract name: string
    age = -1

    constructor() {}

    abstract feed(food: string, amount: number): void
}

class Cat extends Animal {
    name: string
    constructor(name: string, age: number) {
        super()
        this.name = name
        this.age = age
    }

    feed(food: string, amount: number): void {
        console.log(
            'Feeding ' +
                this.name +
                ' the Cat ' +
                amount +
                ' kg of ' +
                food
        )
    }
}

class Dog extends Animal {
    name: string
    constructor(name: string, age: number) {
        super()
        this.name = name
        this.age = age
    }

    feed(food: string, amount: number): void {
        console.log(
            'Feeding ' +
```

```
                this.name +
                ' the Dog ' +
                amount +
                ' kg of ' +
                food
        )
    }
}

const CAT = new Cat('Cosmo', 8)
const DOG = new Dog('Rusty', 12)
CAT.feed('Fish', 0.1)
DOG.feed('Beef', 0.25)
```

Replace `./src/test.ts` with this code above, compile and execute it.

```
tsc -p ./src
node ./dist/test.js
```

Outputs

```
Feeding Cosmo the Cat, 0.1kg of Fish
Feeding Rusty the Dog, 0.25kg of Beef
```

3.7 Access Modifiers

SBCODE Video ID #dc3ca0

TypeScript supports access modifiers for your class properties and methods.

3.7.1 Public

In JavaScript, all class properties are `public` by default, so there is no need to write the `public` keyword in your TypeScript files.

```
class Cat {
    public name: string

    constructor(name: string) {
        this.name = name
    }
}

const CAT = new Cat('Cosmo')
console.log(CAT.name)
```

The final line above is able to print `CAT.name` regardless of whether the `public` modifier was used in the `name` declaration.

3.7.2 Private

In the code below, I have made the `name` property `private`.

```
class Cat {
    private name: string

    constructor(name: string) {
        this.name = name
    }
}

const CAT = new Cat('Cosmo')
console.log(CAT.name)
```

If you copy this script into the `./src/test.ts`, the VSCode IDE and TSC will show an error.

```
Property 'name' is private and only accessible within class 'Cat'
```

But if you still compiled this using TSC anyway, it would still create a JavaScript compilation where the `name` property could still be used by the JavaScript outside the `Cat` class.

Compile and run the code,

```
tsc -p ./src
node ./dist/test.js
```

Outputs

```
Cosmo
```

The JavaScript compilation ignored the `private` access modifier for the `name` method.

If you look at the JavaScript code at `./dist/test.js` you'll see that the `private` keyword was actually ignored and not added. JavaScript does not support a `private` keyword.

Now since you are using TypeScript as a tool to help enforce some rules at design time, this is not really a major issue, since TSC and the VSCode IDE is telling you that you are using a `private` property outside a class, and you can fix your code while writing it.

But if you wanted to enforce `private` properties at the JavaScript compilation as well, rather than using the `private` keyword, you can use the `#` character in front of your property declarations and any usages of them. This will have the symptom of causing your JavaScript version of the code to syntax error which effectively makes the property `private` as a consequence.

So, copy this new code into `./src/test.ts`,

```typescript
class Cat {
    #name: string

    constructor(name: string) {
        this.#name = name
    }
}

const CAT = new Cat('Cosmo')
console.log(CAT.#name)
```

Compile and run,

```
tsc -p ./src
node ./dist/test.js
```

While that TSC and VSCode IDE are still telling you that there is a problem, but you compiled it anyway, the JavaScript version now does not run and breaks at the point where it tries to read the private property outside the class.

```
console.log(CAT.);
                ^

SyntaxError: Unexpected token ')'
```

3.7.3 Protected

A `protected` property is accessible only internally within the class or any class that extends it but not externally.

In the code below, it is ok for the `Cat` class to reference the `name` property from `Animal`, but still not outside the `Animal` or `Cat` classes.

```
class Animal {
    protected name: string
    protected age: number

    constructor(name: string, age: number) {
        this.name = name
        this.age = age
    }
}

class Cat extends Animal {
    constructor(name: string, age: number) {
        super(name, age)
        console.log(this.name)
    }
}

const CAT = new Cat('Cosmo', 8)
console.log(CAT.name)
```

While TSC and the VSCode IDE indicate the error,

```
Property 'name' is protected and only accessible within class 'Animal'
and its subclasses.
```

this code can still be compiled to JavaScript, and the JavaScript compilation will ignore the `protected` accessor and allow the `name` property to be used outside the `Animal` and `Cat` classes regardless.

Outputs

```
Cosmo
Cosmo
```

There is no quick and easy way to enforce a `protected` relationship at the JavaScript compilation level, but it can still be useful to use at the TypeScript source level when developing, and you want your code to honor a `protected` type of relationship.

3.8 Static Members

SBCODE Video ID #aaca80

All the parts of a class, such as the properties, constructor and methods are called members. When you instantiate a class, e.g,

```
const CAT = new Cat()
```

You are creating a new object in memory with its own copies of all the members of the `Cat` class.

E.g, I can create two independent objects using the `Cat` class.

```
const CAT1 = new Cat()
const CAT2 = new Cat()
```

They would then have their own copies of the members independently of each other. So, if the `Cat` class described a `name` property and/or `walk` method, then calling `CAT1`'s properties, constructor and methods would return a different result than calling `CAT2`'s properties, constructor and methods. Both objects are independent in memory but were both created from the same class template.

Now it's possible to make objects that were instantiated from classes share the same methods and properties behind the scenes, and that is using the `static` keyword.

The code below shows some examples of the `static` keyword and how the `static` properties and methods are referred to.

```
class ClassWithProperty {
    abc = 123
}

class ClassWithStaticProperty {
    static abc = 123
}

class ClassWithMethod {
    method() {
        return 123
    }
}

class ClassWithStaticMethod {
    static method() {
```

```
        return 123
    }
}

const CLASS_A = new ClassWithProperty()
console.log(CLASS_A.abc)

const CLASS_B = new ClassWithStaticProperty()
// console.log(CLASS_B.abc); // undefined. 'abc' does not
// exist on CLASS_B instance.
// You must reference it via the class name instead
console.log(ClassWithStaticProperty.abc)

const CLASS_C = new ClassWithMethod()
console.log(CLASS_C.method())

const CLASS_D = new ClassWithStaticMethod()
// console.log(CLASS_D.method()); //error. CLASS_D.method is
// not a function.
// You must reference it via the class name instead
console.log(ClassWithStaticMethod.method())
```

Outputs

```
123
123
123
123
```

In the above example, note that `CLASS_B` and `CLASS_D` were not actually needed at all to be instantiated to access their static members. They were not used, and I could have just commented them out completely. Static members are referred to directly by the classes name instead.

```
console.log(ClassWithStaticProperty.abc)
console.log(ClassWithStaticMethod.method())
```

One particular example where a static property may be useful is in the example below where the property `PI` doesn't need to be recreated across each new instance of the `Circle` class, but all instances of the `circle` can point to the same value stored at the class level instead.

```
class Circle {
    radius: number
    static PI = 3.14

    constructor(radius: number) {
        this.radius = radius
```

```
        }
}

console.log('Circle.PI = ' + Circle.PI)

const CIRCLE1 = new Circle(1)
const CIRCLE2 = new Circle(2)
const CIRCLE3 = new Circle(3)
console.log('CIRCLE1 Area = ' + Circle.PI * CIRCLE1.radius ** 2)
console.log('CIRCLE2 Area = ' + Circle.PI * CIRCLE2.radius ** 2)
console.log('CIRCLE3 Area = ' + Circle.PI * CIRCLE3.radius ** 2)
```

Outputs

```
Circle.PI = 3.14
CIRCLE1 Area = 3.14
CIRCLE2 Area = 12.56
CIRCLE3 Area = 28.26
```

In the above example, each new instance of `Circle` referred to the static property of `Circle.PI` in the calculation.

Note that if using PI in your code, it is less work to use the inbuilt JavaScript static `Math` object instead.

E.g,

```
console.log('CIRCLE1 Area = ' + Math.PI * CIRCLE1.radius ** 2)
```

Visit https://developer.mozilla.org/en-US/docs/Web/JavaScript/Reference/Global_Objects/Math for more information about the `Math` object.

3.9 ES6 Imports/Exports

SBCODE Video ID #5bb54c

On larger projects, it is common to split up your code into separate files. When doing this, you will need to tell each file which other file it needs to reference in case it is using objects, classes, types or interfaces from the other files.

Replace `./src/test.ts` with this below, and create the other two files alongside also in the `./src/` folder

3.9.1 ./src/test.ts

```
import { Cat, Dog } from './animals'

const CAT = new Cat('Cosmo', 8)
console.log(CAT.name)
const DOG = new Dog('Rusty', 12)
console.log(DOG.name)
```

3.9.2 ./src/animals.ts

```
import Animal from './animal'

export class Cat extends Animal {
    constructor(name: string, age: number) {
        super(name, age)
    }
}

export class Dog extends Animal {}
```

3.9.3 ./src/animal.ts

```
export default class Animal {
    name: string
    age: number

    constructor(name: string, age: number) {
        this.name = name
        this.age = age
```

```
        }
    }
```

Re compile and execute,

```
tsc -p ./src
node ./dist/test.js
```

Outputs

```
Cosmo
Rusty
```

When looking at the code, you can see an import/export relationship. `test.ts` imports `Animals` which exports the `Cat` and `Dog` classes. `Animals` imports `Animal` which exports `Animal`.

`test.ts` and `animals.ts` can find their chosen imports, because all the classes `Animal`, `Cat` and `Dog` have all been marked as `export` throughout the files.

Note that I have used `export default` in the `Animal` class. This allows me to import it into the class. This allows me to import it into the `./src/animals.ts` by using `import Animal from './animal'`.

Whereas, I have exported the `Cat` and `Dog` classes using just the `export` keyword by itself. Which means that I need to import them using the curly braces, such as `import { Cat, Dog } from "./animals";`.

I could have split `Cat` and `Dog` into their own files as well and used the `export default` keywords, and then imported them separately without using the curly brace notation.

Note that you can only use `export default` once in any file, even if it has multiple exports. Try it by marking both `Cat` and `Dog` as `export default` and you will see the error,

```
A module cannot have multiple default exports.ts(2528)
animals.ts(3, 22): The first export default is here.
```

This is optional how you structure your files, if you want to mark exports as default or not. Throughout the design pattern examples, I will use both techniques to import/export.

4. UML Diagrams

SBCODE Video ID #735229

Unified Modeling Language (UML) Diagrams are used throughout this book to help describe the patterns.

Below are some example self-describing UML diagrams.

The left part of the diagram shows the basic concept, and the right side shows a potential example usage.

4.1 A Basic Class

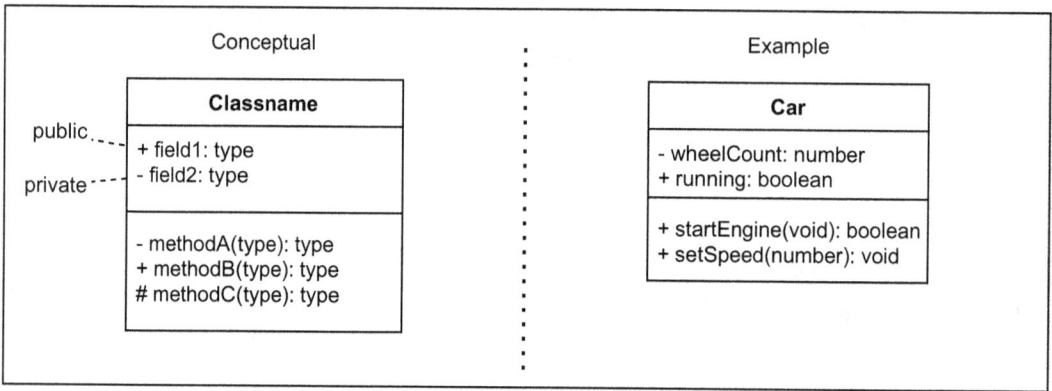

Note that I am using the word `field` as the class `properties` in the middle left square. Both terms are interchangeable. Other terms used to describe `fields` and `properties` can also be `attributes`.

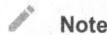 **Note**

In the bottom left square, I also have a `protected` method which is indicated by the `#` symbol. In UML, protected members are indicated using the `#` symbol which can cause confusion if indicating `private` fields/properties/variables in modern JavaScript and TypeScript.

4.2 Directed Association

A filled arrow with a line.

ClassA uses **ClassB** or an object of **ClassB**.

ClassA calls a static class method, a static abstract method or a method/property/field from an object of type ClassB. e.g., The **Person** starts the **Car** engine.

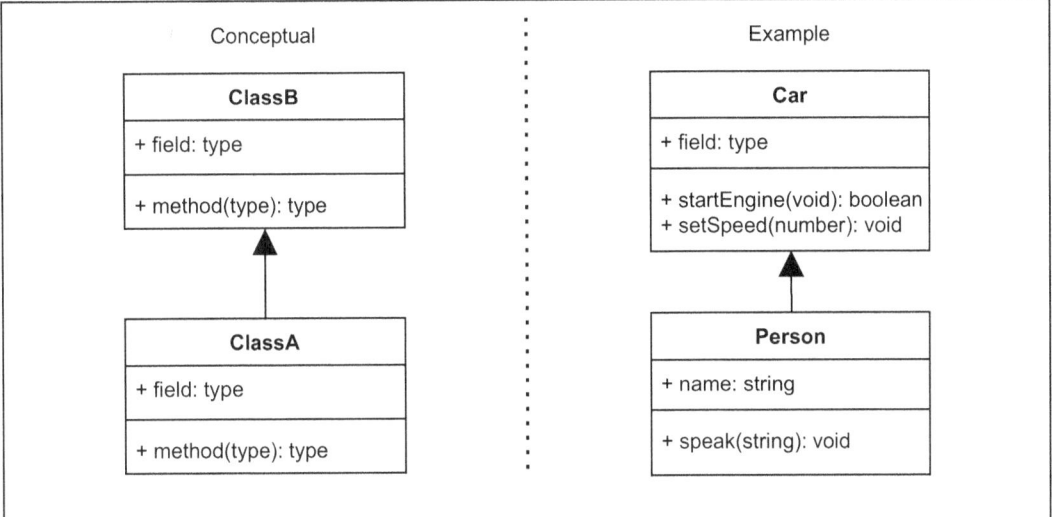

4.3 A Class That Extends/Inherits A Class

An unfilled arrow, with a line pointing to the class that is being extended/inherited.

ClassA extends **ClassB**.

The extended class contains all the attributes/fields and methods of the inherited class, including its own extra methods, attributes/fields, overrides and overloads.

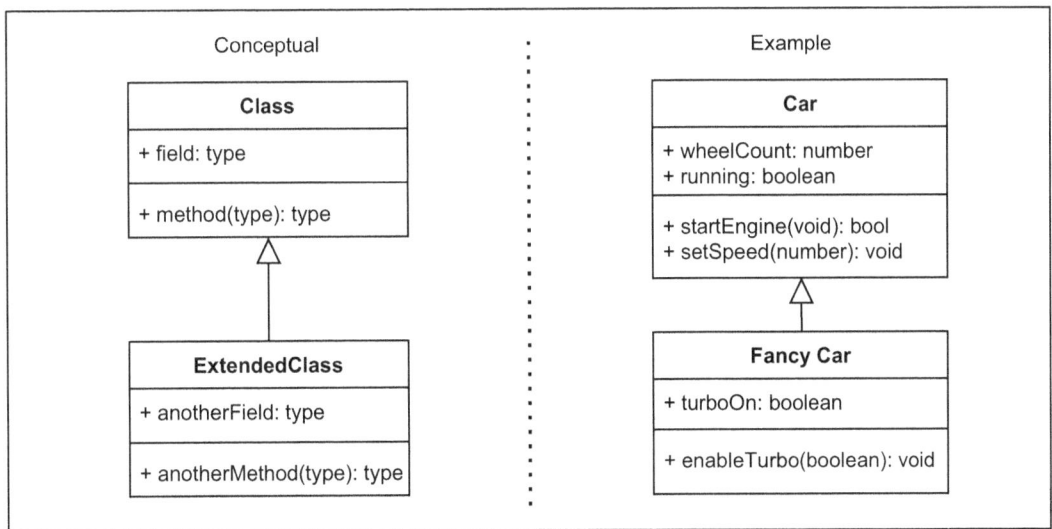

4.4 A Class That Implements an Interface

An unfilled arrow, with a dashed line pointing to the interface that is being implemented.

ClassA implements **ClassB**.

A class that implements an interface must implement all the methods declared in the interface.

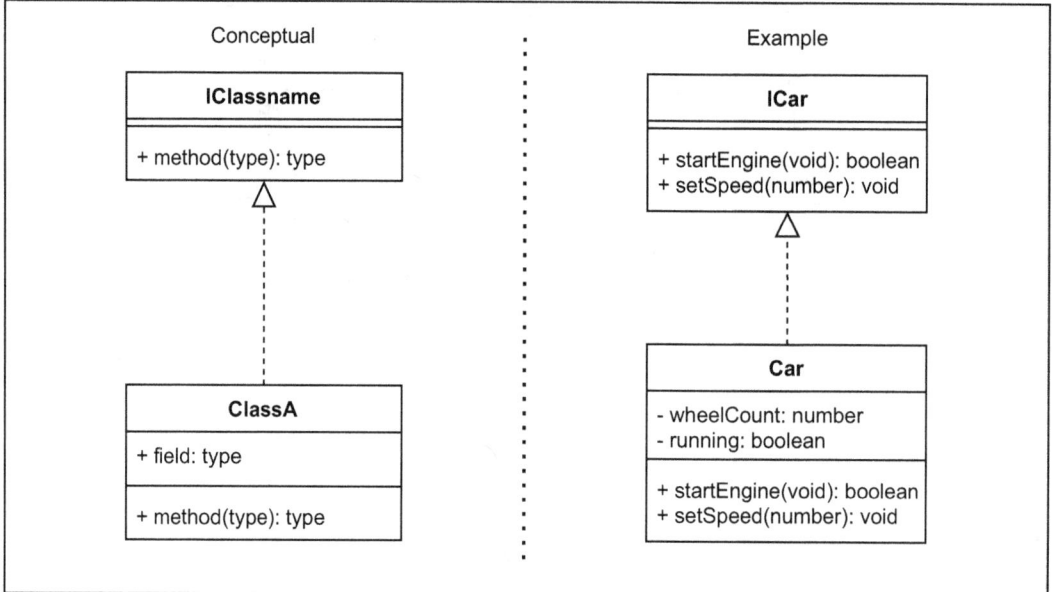

4.5 Aggregates

An unfilled diamond with a line and arrow head.

ClassA aggregates **ClassB**.

Library aggregates **Books**. Books and Library can exist independently of each other. Books can exist without the Library.

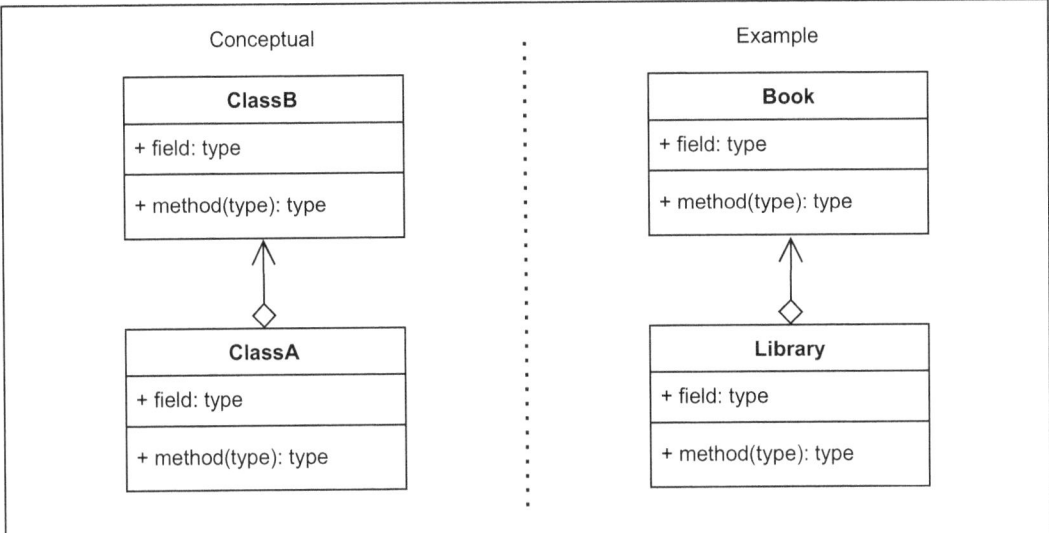

4.6 Composition

A filled diamond with a line and arrow head.

ClassA is composed of **ClassB**

Aeroplane can be composed of **Wings** and other parts. But an aero plane is no longer really an aero plane without its wings.

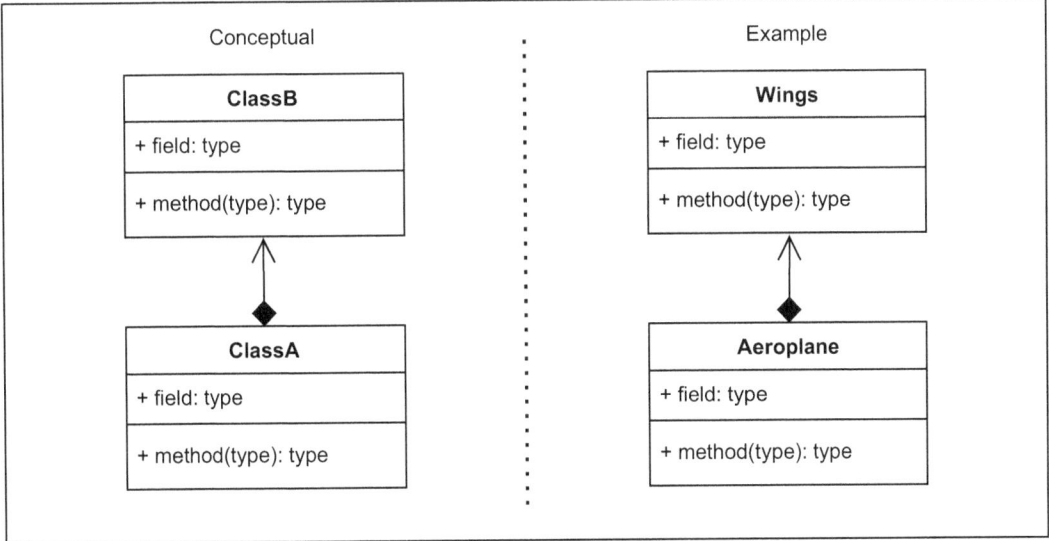

4.7 Pseudocode Annotation

A box with a dashed line and a circle placed near a class method.

4.7 Pseudocode Annotation

Pseudocode is a plain language description of the steps in an algorithm and used to portray a concept without needing to write long lines of code.

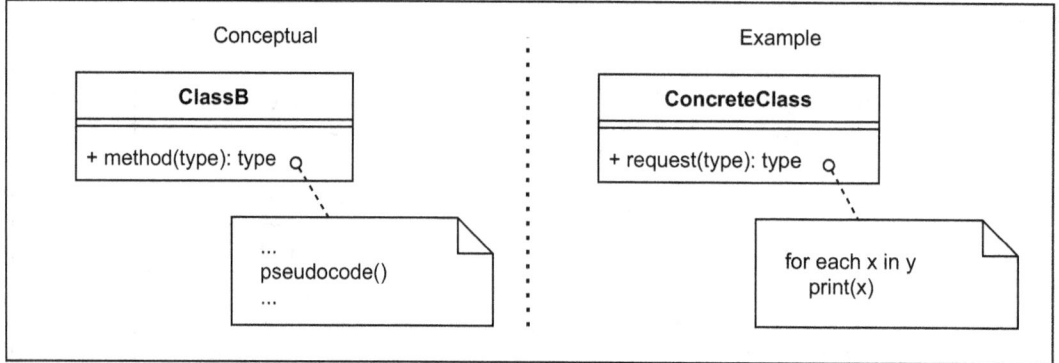

5. Creational

5.1 Factory Design Pattern

5.1.1 Overview

SBCODE Video ID #85a1c6

When developing code, you may instantiate objects directly in methods or in classes. While this is quite normal, you may want to add an extra abstraction between the creation of the object and where it is used in your project.

You can use the **Factory** pattern to add that extra abstraction. The Factory pattern is one of the easiest patterns to understand and implement.

Adding an extra abstraction will also allow you to dynamically choose classes to instantiate based on some kind of logic.

Before the abstraction, your client, class or method would directly instantiate an object of a class. After adding the factory abstraction, the concrete product (object) is now created outside the current class/method, and now in a subclass instead.

Imagine an application for designing houses and the house has a chair already added on the floor by default. By adding the factory pattern, you could give the option to the user to choose different chairs, and how many at runtime. Instead of the chair being hard coded into the project when it started, the user now has the option to choose.

Adding this extra abstraction also means that the complications of instantiating extra objects can now be hidden from the class or method that is using it.

This separation also makes your code easier to read and document.

The Factory pattern is really about adding that extra abstraction between the object creation and where it is used. This gives you extra options that you can more easily extend in the future.

5.1.2 Terminology

- **Concrete Creator**: The client application, class or method that calls the Creator (Factory method).
- **Product Interface**: The interface describing the attributes and methods that the Factory will require in order to create the final product/object.
- **Creator**: The Factory class. Declares the Factory method that will return the object requested from it.

- **Concrete Product**: The object returned from the Factory. The object implements the Product interface.

5.1.3 Factory UML Diagram

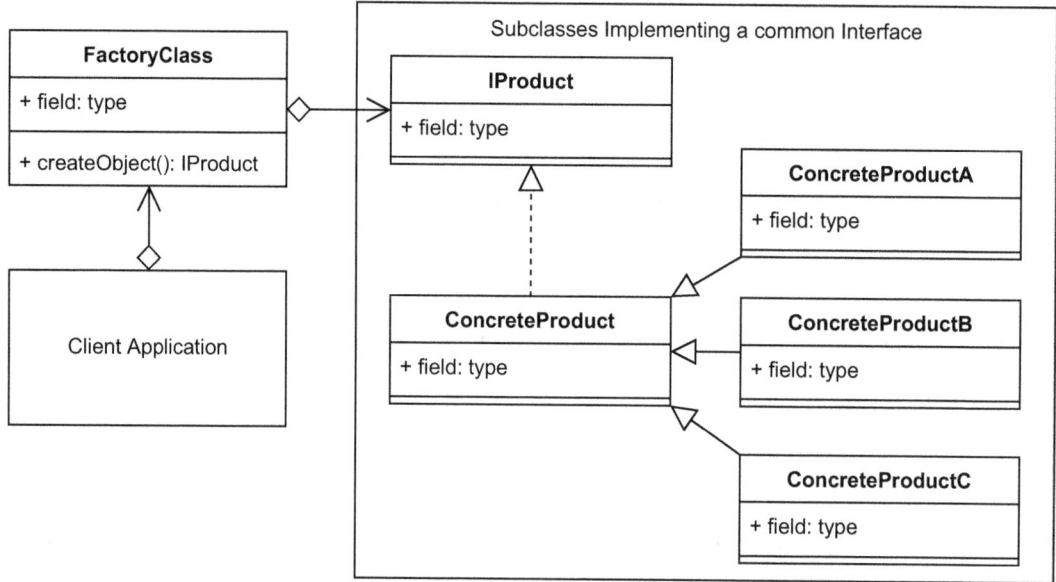

5.1.4 Source Code

In this concept example, the client wants an object named `b`

Rather than creating `b` directly in the client, it asks the creator (factory) for the object instead.

The factory finds the relevant class using some kind of logic from the attributes of the request. It then asks the subclass to instantiate the new object that it then returns as a reference back to the client asking for it.

./src/factory/factory-concept.ts

```typescript
// The Factory Concept

interface IProduct {
    name: string
}

class ConcreteProduct implements IProduct {
    name = ''
}

class ConcreteProductA extends ConcreteProduct {
```

```
        constructor() {
            super()
            this.name = 'ConcreteProductA'
        }
    }

    class ConcreteProductB extends ConcreteProduct {
        constructor() {
            super()
            this.name = 'ConcreteProductB'
        }
    }

    class ConcreteProductC extends ConcreteProduct {
        constructor() {
            super()
            this.name = 'ConcreteProductC'
        }
    }

    class Creator {
        static createObject(someProperty: string): IProduct {
            if (someProperty === 'a') {
                return new ConcreteProductA()
            } else if (someProperty === 'b') {
                return new ConcreteProductB()
            } else {
                return new ConcreteProductC()
            }
        }
    }

    // The Client
    const PRODUCT = Creator.createObject('b')
    console.log(PRODUCT.name)
```

5.1.5 Output

```
node ./dist/factory/factory-concept.js
ConcreteProductB
```

5.1.6 Factory Use Case

SBCODE Video ID #5d7340

An example use case may be a user interface where the user can select from a menu of items, such as chairs.

The user has been given a choice using some kind of navigation interface, and it is unknown what choice, or how many chairs the user will add until the application is actually running, and the user starts using it.

So, when the user selected the chair, the factory then takes some property involved with that selection, such as an ID, Type or other attribute and then decides which relevant subclass to instantiate in order to return the appropriate object.

While there are is a large amount of code in this example, and it is spread across several files, the actual factory is the `ChairFactory` class in the file `chair-factory.ts`. So, the factory is the part of your program that is creating a separation or abstraction between the instantiating of your object and where it is used.

5.1.7 Factory Example UML Diagram

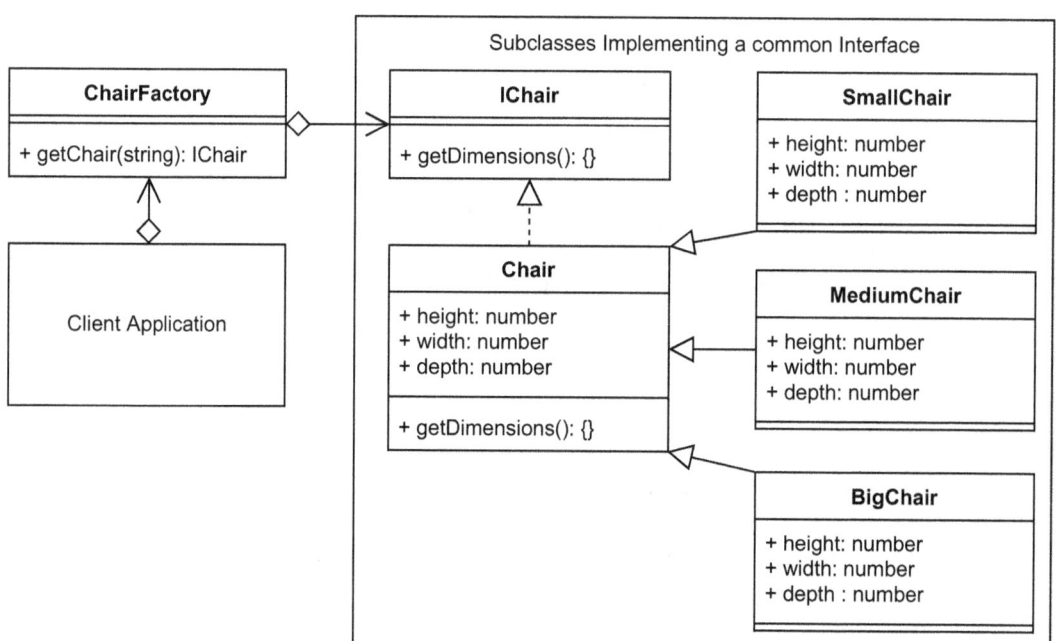

5.1.8 Source Code

./src/factory/client.ts

```
// Factory Use Case Example Code
import ChairFactory from './chair-factory'
```

```typescript
const CHAIR = ChairFactory.getChair('SmallChair')
console.log(CHAIR.getDimensions())
```

./src/factory/dimension.ts

```typescript
export type dimension = {
    height: number
    width: number
    depth: number
}
```

./src/factory/chair.ts

```typescript
import { dimension } from './dimension'

// A Chair Interface
interface IChair {
    height: number
    width: number
    depth: number
    getDimensions(): dimension
}

// The Chair Base Class
export default class Chair implements IChair {
    height = 0
    width = 0
    depth = 0

    createObject(): IChair {
        return this
    }

    getDimensions(): dimension {
        return {
            width: this.width,
            depth: this.depth,
            height: this.height,
        }
    }
}
```

./src/factory/chair-factory.ts

```typescript
import SmallChair from './small-chair'
import MediumChair from './medium-chair'
import BigChair from './big-chair'
import IChair from './chair'

export default class ChairFactory {
    static getChair(chair: string): IChair {
        if (chair == 'BigChair') {
            return new BigChair()
        } else if (chair == 'MediumChair') {
            return new MediumChair()
        } else {
            return new SmallChair()
        }
    }
}
```

./src/factory/small-chair.ts

```typescript
import Chair from './chair'

export default class SmallChair extends Chair {
    constructor() {
        super()
        this.height = 40
        this.width = 40
        this.depth = 40
    }
}
```

./src/factory/medium-chair.ts

```typescript
import Chair from './chair'

export default class MediumChair extends Chair {
    constructor() {
        super()
        this.height = 60
        this.width = 60
        this.depth = 60
    }
}
```

./src/factory/big-chair.ts

```
import Chair from './chair'

export default class BigChair extends Chair {
    constructor() {
        super()
        this.height = 80
        this.width = 80
        this.depth = 80
    }
}
```

5.1.9 Output

```
node ./dist/factory/client.js
{'width': 40, 'depth': 40, 'height': 40}
```

5.1.10 Summary

- The Factory Pattern defers the creation of the final object to a subclass.
- The Factory pattern is about inserting another layer/abstraction between instantiating an object and where in your code it is actually used.
- It is unknown what or how many objects you will need to be created until runtime.
- You want to localize knowledge of the specifics of instantiating a particular object to the subclass so that the client doesn't need to be concerned about the details.
- You want to create an external framework, that an application can import/reference, and hide the details of the specifics involved in creating the final object/product.
- The unique factor that defines the Factory pattern, is that your project now defers the creation of objects to the subclass that the factory had delegated it to.

5.2 Abstract Factory Design Pattern

5.2.1 Overview

SBCODE Video ID #62bde8

The Abstract Factory Pattern adds an abstraction layer over multiple other creational pattern implementations.

To begin with, in simple terms, think if it as a Factory that can return Factories. Although you will find examples of it also being used to return Builder, Prototypes, Singletons or other design pattern implementations.

5.2.2 Terminology

- **Client**: The client application that calls the **Abstract Factory**. It's the same process as the **Concrete Creator** in the Factory design pattern.
- **Abstract Factory**: A common interface over all the sub factories.
- **Concrete Factory**: The sub factory of the **Abstract Factory** and contains method(s) to allow creating the **Concrete Product**.
- **Abstract Product**: The interface and/or abstraction for the product that the sub factory returns.
- **Concrete Product**: The object that is finally returned.

5.2.3 Abstract Factory UML Diagram

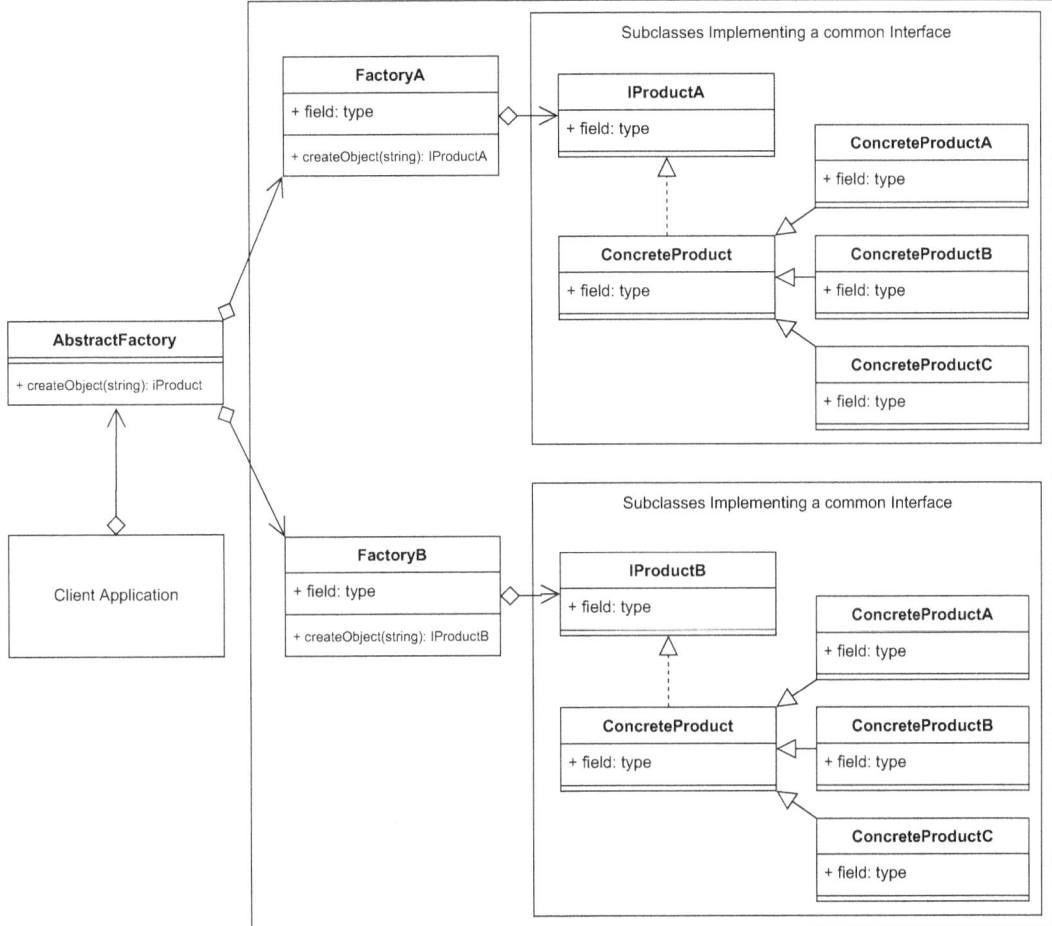

5.2.4 Source Code

./src/abstract-factory/abstract-factory-concept.ts

```
// Abstract Factory Concept Sample Code
import { FactoryA, IProductA } from './factory-a'
import { FactoryB, IProductB } from './factory-b'

interface IProduct extends IProductA, IProductB {}

class AbstractFactory {
    // The Abstract Factory Concrete Class

    static createObject(factory: string): IProduct | undefined {
        try {
            if (['aa', 'ab', 'ac'].indexOf(factory) > -1) {
                return FactoryA.getObject(factory[1])
```

```
                }
                if (['ba', 'bb', 'bc'].indexOf(factory) > -1) {
                    return FactoryB.getObject(factory[1])
                }
                throw new Error('No Factory Found')
            } catch (e) {
                console.log(e)
            }
        }
    }

    // The Client
    let PRODUCT = AbstractFactory.createObject('ab')
    console.log(PRODUCT)

    PRODUCT = AbstractFactory.createObject('bc')
    console.log(PRODUCT)
```

./src/abstract-factory/factory-a.ts

```
    // FactoryA Sample Code

    export interface IProductA {
        name: string
    }

    class ConcreteProduct implements IProductA {
        name = ''
    }

    class ConcreteProductA extends ConcreteProduct {
        constructor() {
            super()
            this.name = 'FactoryA:ConcreteProductA'
        }
    }

    class ConcreteProductB extends ConcreteProduct {
        constructor() {
            super()
            this.name = 'FactoryA:ConcreteProductB'
        }
    }

    class ConcreteProductC extends ConcreteProduct {
        constructor() {
            super()
            this.name = 'FactoryA:ConcreteProductC'
```

```typescript
        }
    }

    export class FactoryA {
        static getObject(some_property: string): IProductA {
            try {
                if (some_property === 'a') {
                    return new ConcreteProductA()
                } else if (some_property === 'b') {
                    return new ConcreteProductB()
                } else if (some_property === 'c') {
                    return new ConcreteProductC()
                } else {
                    throw new Error('Class Not Found')
                }
            } catch (e) {
                console.log(e)
            }
            return new ConcreteProduct()
        }
    }
```

./src/abstract-factory/factory-b.ts

```typescript
    // FactoryB Sample Code

    export interface IProductB {
        name: string
    }

    class ConcreteProduct implements IProductB {
        name = ''
    }

    class ConcreteProductA extends ConcreteProduct {
        constructor() {
            super()
            this.name = 'FactoryB:ConcreteProductA'
        }
    }

    class ConcreteProductB extends ConcreteProduct {
        constructor() {
            super()
            this.name = 'FactoryB:ConcreteProductB'
        }
    }
```

```
class ConcreteProductC extends ConcreteProduct {
    constructor() {
        super()
        this.name = 'FactoryB:ConcreteProductC'
    }
}

export class FactoryB {
    static getObject(some_property: string): IProductB {
        try {
            if (some_property === 'a') {
                return new ConcreteProductA()
            } else if (some_property === 'b') {
                return new ConcreteProductB()
            } else if (some_property === 'c') {
                return new ConcreteProductC()
            } else {
                throw new Error('Class Not Found')
            }
        } catch (e) {
            console.log(e)
        }
        return new ConcreteProduct()
    }
}
```

5.2.5 Output

```
node ./dist/abstract-factory/abstract-factory-concept.js
ConcreteProductB { name: 'FactoryA:ConcreteProductB' }
ConcreteProductC { name: 'FactoryB:ConcreteProductC' }
```

5.2.6 Abstract Factory Example Use Case

SBCODE Video ID #13899e

An example use case may be that you have a furniture shopfront. You sell many kinds of furniture. You sell chairs and tables. And they are manufactured at different factories using different unrelated processes that are not important for your concern. You only need the factory to deliver.

You can create an extra module called `FurnitureFactory`, to handle the chair and table factories, thus removing the implementation details from the client.

5.2.7 Abstract Factory Example UML Diagram

See this UML diagram of an Abstract Furniture Factory implementation that returns chairs and tables.

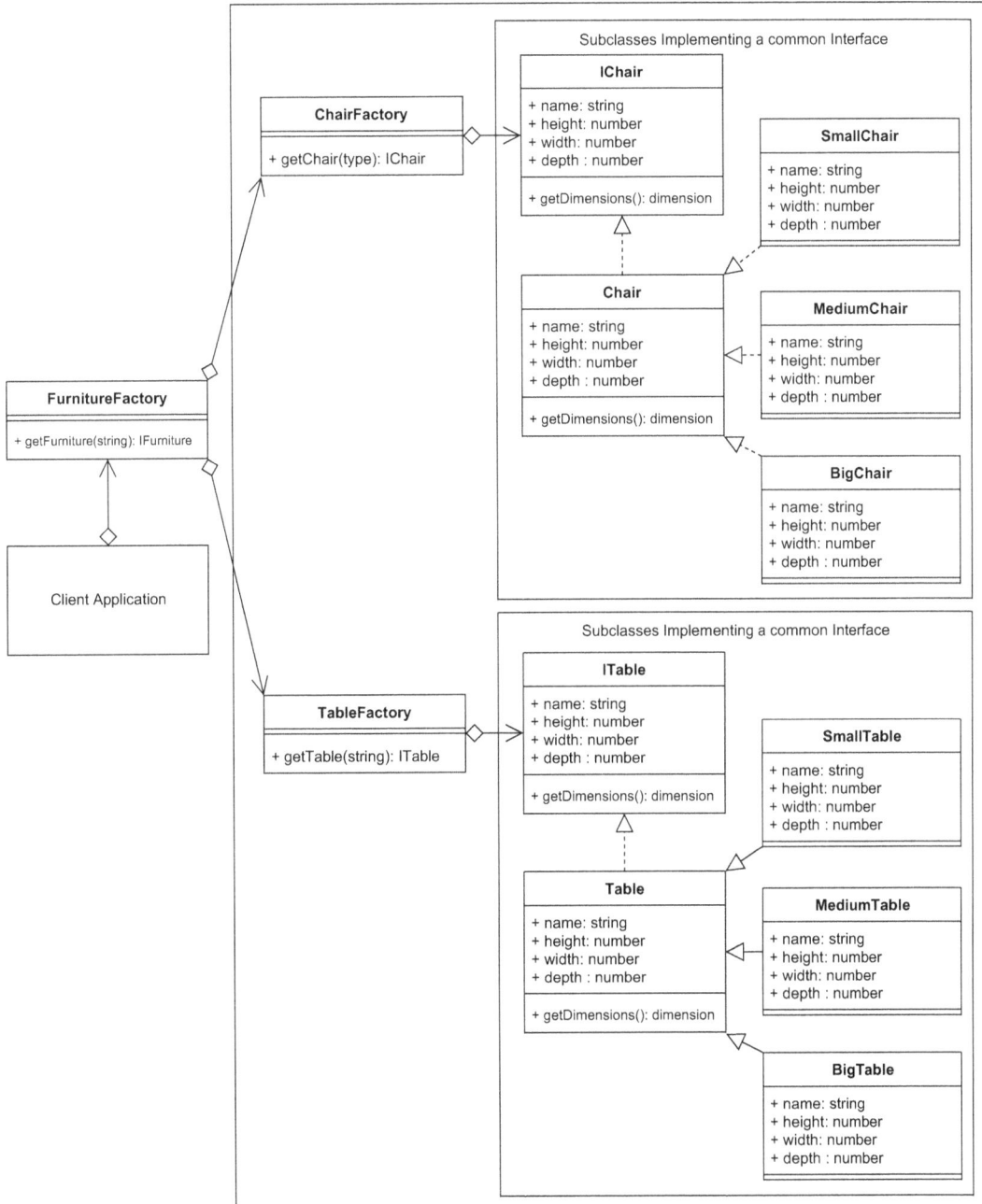

5.2.8 Source Code

./src/abstract-factory/client.ts

```typescript
// Abstract Factory Use Case Example Code
import FurnitureFactory from './furniture-factory'

let FURNITURE = FurnitureFactory.getFurniture('SmallChair')
console.log(FURNITURE?.name)
console.log(FURNITURE?.getDimensions())

FURNITURE = FurnitureFactory.getFurniture('MediumTable')
console.log(FURNITURE?.name)
console.log(FURNITURE?.getDimensions())
```

./src/abstract-factory/dimension.ts

```typescript
export type dimension = {
    height: number
    width: number
    depth: number
}
```

./src/abstract-factory/furniture-factory.ts

```typescript
// Abstract Furniture Factory

import { IChair } from './chair'
import ChairFactory from './chair-factory'
import { ITable } from './table'
import TableFactory from './table-factory'

interface IFurniture extends IChair, ITable {}

export default class FurnitureFactory {
    static getFurniture(furniture: string): IFurniture | undefined {
        try {
            if (
                ['SmallChair', 'MediumChair', 'BigChair'].indexOf(
                    furniture
                ) > -1
            ) {
                return ChairFactory.getChair(furniture)
            }
            if (
                ['SmallTable', 'MediumTable', 'BigTable'].indexOf(
                    furniture
                ) > -1
            ) {
                return TableFactory.getTable(furniture)
```

```
            }
            throw new Error('No Factory Found')
        } catch (e) {
            console.log(e)
        }
    }
}
```

./src/abstract-factory/chair-factory.ts

```
import SmallChair from './small-chair'
import MediumChair from './medium-chair'
import BigChair from './big-chair'
import { IChair } from './chair'

export default class ChairFactory {
    static getChair(chair: string): IChair {
        if (chair == 'BigChair') {
            return new BigChair()
        } else if (chair == 'MediumChair') {
            return new MediumChair()
        } else if (chair == 'SmallChair') {
            return new SmallChair()
        } else {
            throw new Error('No Chair Found')
        }
    }
}
```

./src/abstract-factory/chair.ts

```
import { dimension } from './dimension'

export interface IChair {
    name: string
    height: number
    width: number
    depth: number

    getDimensions(): dimension
}

export class Chair implements IChair {
    name = ''
    height = 0
    width = 0
```

```
        depth = 0

        getDimensions(): dimension {
            return {
                width: this.width,
                depth: this.depth,
                height: this.height,
            }
        }
    }
```

./src/abstract-factory/small-chair.ts

```
import { Chair } from './chair'

export default class SmallChair extends Chair {
    constructor() {
        super()
        this.name = 'SmallChair'
        this.height = 40
        this.width = 40
        this.depth = 40
    }
}
```

./src/abstract-factory/medium-chair.ts

```
import { Chair } from './chair'

export default class MediumChair extends Chair {
    constructor() {
        super()
        this.name = 'MediumChair'
        this.height = 60
        this.width = 60
        this.depth = 60
    }
}
```

./src/abstract-factory/big-chair.ts

```
import { Chair } from './chair'

export default class BigChair extends Chair {
    constructor() {
```

```
        super()
        this.name = 'BigChair'
        this.height = 80
        this.width = 80
        this.depth = 80
    }
}
```

./src/abstract-factory/table-factory.ts

```
import SmallTable from './small-table'
import MediumTable from './medium-table'
import BigTable from './big-table'
import { ITable } from './table'

export default class TableFactory {
    static getTable(table: string): ITable {
        if (table === 'BigTable') {
            return new BigTable()
        } else if (table === 'MediumTable') {
            return new MediumTable()
        } else if (table === 'SmallTable') {
            return new SmallTable()
        } else {
            throw new Error('No Table Found')
        }
    }
}
```

./src/abstract-factory/table.ts

```
import { dimension } from './dimension'

export interface ITable {
    name: string
    height: number
    width: number
    depth: number

    getDimensions(): dimension
}

export class Table implements ITable {
    name = ''
    height = 0
    width = 0
```

```
        depth = 0

        getDimensions(): dimension {
            return {
                width: this.width,
                depth: this.depth,
                height: this.height,
            }
        }
    }
```

./src/abstract-factory/small-table.ts

```
import { Table } from './table'

export default class SmallTable extends Table {
    constructor() {
        super()
        this.name = 'SmallTable'
        this.height = 40
        this.width = 40
        this.depth = 40
    }
}
```

./src/abstract-factory/medium-table.ts

```
import { Table } from './table'

export default class MediumTable extends Table {
    constructor() {
        super()
        this.name = 'MediumTable'
        this.height = 60
        this.width = 60
        this.depth = 60
    }
}
```

./src/abstract-factory/big-table.ts

```
import { Table } from './table'

export default class BigTable extends Table {
    constructor() {
```

```
        super()
        this.name = 'BigTable'
        this.height = 80
        this.width = 80
        this.depth = 80
    }
}
```

5.2.9 Output

```
node ./dist/abstract-factory/client.js
SmallChair
{ width: 40, depth: 40, height: 40 }
MediumTable
{ width: 60, depth: 60, height: 60 }
```

5.2.10 Summary

- Use when you want to provide a library of relatively similar products from multiple different factories.
- You want the system to be independent of how the products are created.
- It fulfills all the same use cases as the Factory method, but is a factory for creational pattern type methods.
- The client implements the abstract factory interface, rather than all the internal logic and Factories. This allows the possibility of creating a library that can be imported for using the Abstract Factory.
- The Abstract Factory defers the creation of the final products/objects to its concrete factory subclasses.
- You want to enforce consistent interfaces across products.
- You want the possibility to exchange product families.

5.3 Builder Design Pattern

5.3.1 Overview

SBCODE Video ID #6fa98c

The Builder Pattern is a creational pattern whose intent is to separate the construction of a complex object from its representation so that you can use the same construction process to create different representations.

The Builder Pattern tries to solve,

- How can a class create different representations of a complex object?
- How can a class that includes creating a complex object be simplified?

The Builder and Factory patterns are very similar in the fact they both instantiate new objects at runtime. The difference is when the process of creating the object is more complex, so rather than the Factory returning a new instance of `ObjectA`, it calls the builders' director constructor method `ObjectA.construct()` that goes through a more complex construction process involving several steps. Both return an Object/Product.

5.3.2 Terminology

- **Product**: The Product being built.
- **Builder Interface**: The Interface that the Concrete builder should implement.
- **Builder**: Provides methods to build and retrieve the concrete product. Implements the **Builder Interface**.
- **Director**: Has a `construct()` method that when called creates a customized product using the methods of the **Builder**.

5.3.3 Builder UML Diagram

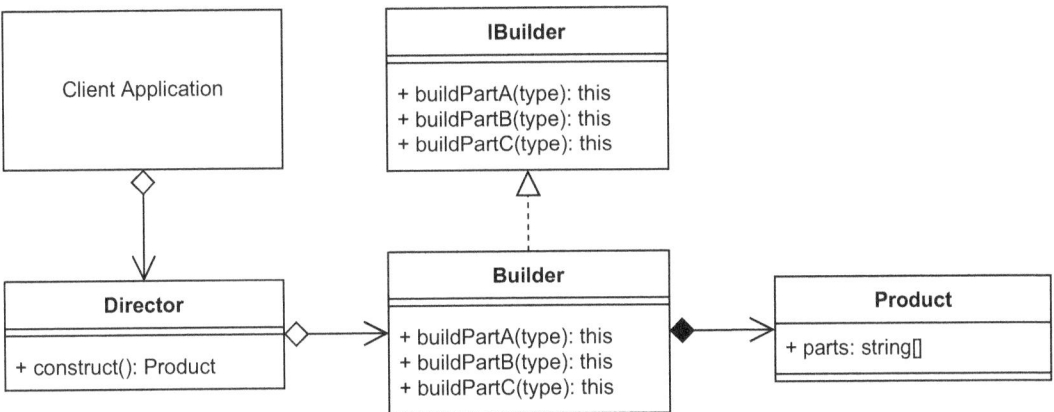

5.3.4 Source Code

1. Client creates the **Director**.
2. The Client calls the Directors `construct()` method that manages each step of the build process.
3. The Director returns the product to the client or alternatively could also provide a method for the client to retrieve it later.

./src/builder/builder-concept.ts

```typescript
// Builder Concept Sample Code
class Product {
    parts: string[] = []
}

interface IBuilder {
    buildPartA(): this
    buildPartB(): this
    buildPartC(): this
    getResult(): Product
}

class Builder implements IBuilder {
    // The Concrete Builder
    product: Product

    constructor() {
        this.product = new Product()
    }

    buildPartA() {
        this.product.parts.push('a')
```

```js
            return this
        }

        buildPartB() {
            this.product.parts.push('b')
            return this
        }

        buildPartC() {
            this.product.parts.push('c')
            return this
        }

        getResult() {
            return this.product
        }
    }

    class Director {
        // The Director, building a complex representation

        static construct() {
            // Constructs and returns the final product
            return new Builder()
                .buildPartA()
                .buildPartB()
                .buildPartC()
                .getResult()
        }
    }

    // The Client
    const PRODUCT1 = Director.construct()
    console.log(PRODUCT1.parts)
```

5.3.5 Output

```
node ./dist/builder/builder-concept.js
[ 'a', 'b', 'c' ]
```

5.3.6 Builder Use Case

SBCODE Video ID #81867f

Using the Builder Pattern in the context of a House Builder.

There are multiple directors that can create their own complex objects.

Note that in the `IglooDirector` class, not all the methods of the `HouseBuilder` were called.

The builder can construct complex objects in any order and include/exclude whichever parts it likes.

5.3.7 Example UML Diagram

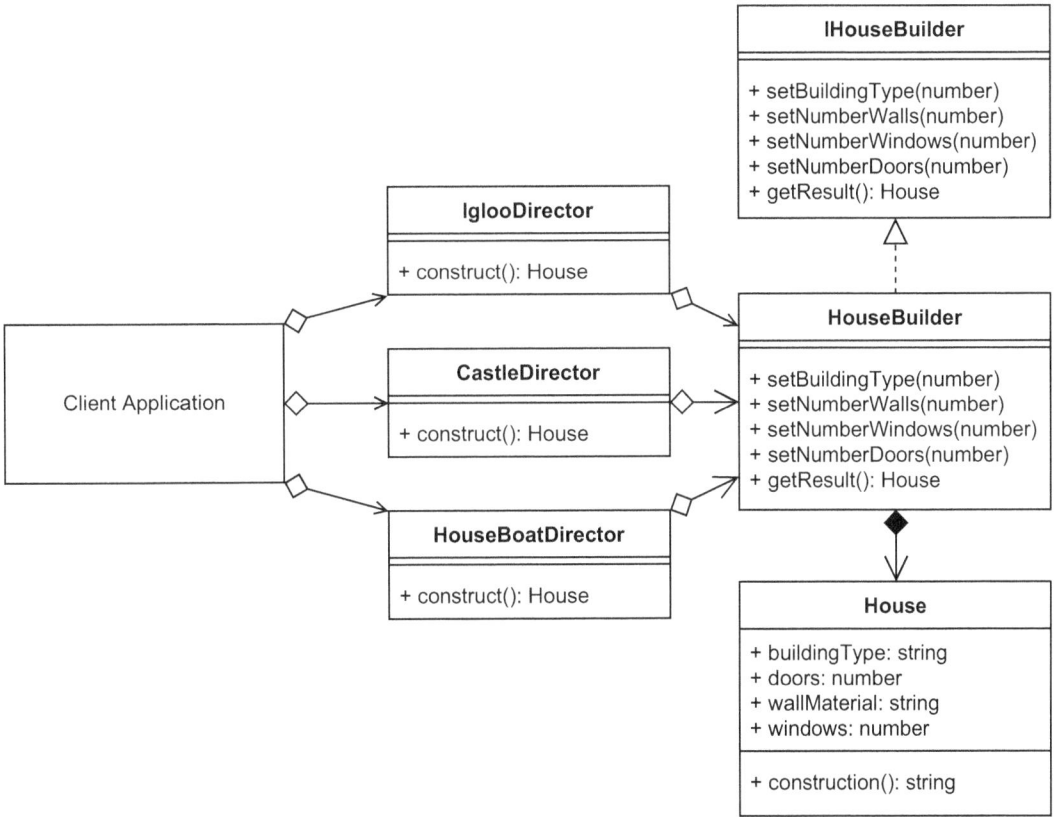

5.3.8 Source Code

./src/builder/client.ts

```
// House Builder Example Code

import IglooDirector from './igloo-director'
import CastleDirector from './castle-director'
import HouseBoatDirector from './houseboat-director'

const IGLOO = IglooDirector.construct()
const CASTLE = CastleDirector.construct()
const HOUSEBOAT = HouseBoatDirector.construct()

console.log(IGLOO.construction())
```

```
    console.log(CASTLE.construction())
    console.log(HOUSEBOAT.construction())
```

./src/builder/igloo-director.ts

```
    // A Director Class
    import House from './house'
    import HouseBuilder from './house-builder'

    export default class IglooDirector {
        static construct(): House {
            // Note that in this IglooDirector, it has omitted the
            // set_number_of windows call since this Igloo will have
            // no windows.
            return new HouseBuilder()
                .setBuildingType('Igloo')
                .setWallMaterial('Ice')
                .setNumberDoors(1)
                .getResult()
        }
    }
```

./src/builder/castle-director.ts

```
    // A Director Class
    import House from './house'
    import HouseBuilder from './house-builder'

    export default class CastleDirector {
        static construct(): House {
            return new HouseBuilder()
                .setBuildingType('Castle')
                .setWallMaterial('Sandstone')
                .setNumberDoors(100)
                .setNumberWindows(200)
                .getResult()
        }
    }
```

./src/builder/houseboat-director.ts

```
    // A Director Class
    import House from './house'
    import HouseBuilder from './house-builder'
```

```typescript
export default class HouseBoatDirector {
    static construct(): House {
        return new HouseBuilder()
            .setBuildingType('House Boat')
            .setWallMaterial('Wood')
            .setNumberDoors(6)
            .setNumberWindows(8)
            .getResult()
    }
}
```

./src/builder/house-builder.ts

```typescript
import House from './house'

interface IHouseBuilder {
    house: House
    setBuildingType(buildingType: string): this
    setWallMaterial(wallMaterial: string): this
    setNumberDoors(number: number): this
    setNumberWindows(number: number): this
    getResult(): House
}

export default class HouseBuilder implements IHouseBuilder {
    house: House

    constructor() {
        this.house = new House()
    }

    setBuildingType(buildingType: string): this {
        this.house.buildingType = buildingType
        return this
    }

    setWallMaterial(wallMaterial: string): this {
        this.house.wallMaterial = wallMaterial
        return this
    }

    setNumberDoors(number: number): this {
        this.house.doors = number
        return this
    }

    setNumberWindows(number: number): this {
        this.house.windows = number
```

```
        return this
    }

    getResult(): House {
        return this.house
    }
}
```

./src/builder/house.ts

```
// The Product

export default class House {
    doors = 0
    windows = 0
    wallMaterial = ''
    buildingType = ''

    construction(): string {
        return `This is a ${this.wallMaterial} ${this.buildingType} with ${this.doors} door(s) and ${this.windows} window(s).`
    }
}
```

5.3.9 Output

```
node ./dist/builder/client.js
This is a Ice Igloo with 1 door(s) and 0 window(s).
This is a Sandstone Castle with 100 door(s) and 200 window(s).
This is a Wood House Boat with 6 door(s) and 8 window(s).
```

5.3.10 Summary

- The Builder pattern is a creational pattern that is used to create more complex objects than you'd expect from a factory.
- The Builder pattern should be able to construct complex objects in any order and include/exclude whichever available components it likes.
- For different combinations of products than can be returned from a Builder, use a specific Director to create the bespoke combination.
- You can use an Abstract Factory to add an abstraction between the client and Director.

5.4 Prototype Design Pattern

5.4.1 Overview

SBCODE Video ID #7d8d9f

The **Prototype** design pattern is good for when creating new objects requires more resources than you want to use or have available. You can save resources by just creating a copy of any existing object that is already in memory.

E.g., A file you've downloaded from a server may be large, but since it is already in memory, you could just clone it, and work on the new copy independently of the original.

In the Prototype patterns interface, you create a `clone` method that should be implemented by all classes that use the interface. How the clone method is implemented in the concrete class is up to you. You will need to decide whether a shallow or deep copy is required.

- A shallow copy, copies and creates new references one level deep,
- A deep copy, copies and creates new references for all levels.

In JavaScript, you have mutable objects such as Arrays, Dictionaries, Sets and any custom Objects you may have created. A shallow copy, will create new copies of the objects with new references in memory, but the underlying data, e.g., the actual elements in an array, will point to the same memory location as the original array/object being copied. You will now have two arrays, but the elements within the arrays will point to the same memory location. So, changing any elements of a copied array will also affect the original array. Be sure to test your implementation that the copy method you use works as expected. Shallow copies are much faster to process than deep copies and deep copies are not always necessary if you are not going to benefit from using it.

5.4.2 Terminology

- **Prototype Interface**: The interface that describes the `clone()` method.
- **Prototype**: The Object/Product that implements the Prototype interface.
- **Client**: The client application that uses and creates the ProtoType.

5.4.3 Prototype UML Diagram

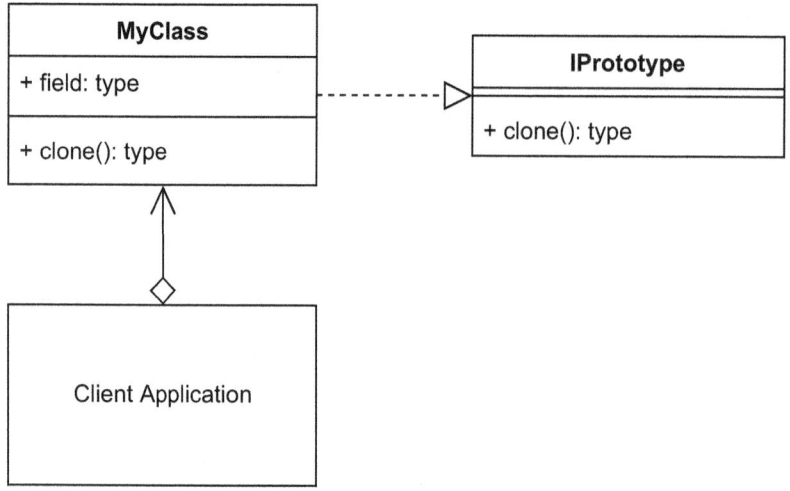

5.4.4 Source Code

Experiment with the concept code.

By default, it will shallow copy the object you've asked to be cloned.

In my example, I have created an array of numbers. At first impressions, when this array is copied, it will appear that the array was fully cloned. But the inner items of the array were not. They will point to the same memory location as the original array; however, the memory identifier of the new array is new and different from the original.

In the `MyClass.clone()` method, there is a line `return JSON.parse(JSON.stringify(this));` that is commented out. Uncomment out this line, and comment out the line before it to now be `// return Object.assign({}, this)`. Re compile and execute the file, and now the array items will be copied as well. This is a deep copy.

Remember that full deep copies can potentially be much slower for very complicated object hierarchies.

./src/prototype/prototype-concept.ts

```
interface IProtoType {
    // interface with clone method
    clone(): this
    // The clone is deep or shallow.
    // It is up to you how you want to implement
    // the details in your concrete class
}
```

```typescript
class MyClass implements IProtoType {
    // A Concrete Class
    field: number[]

    constructor(field: number[]) {
        this.field = field // any value of any type
    }

    clone() {
        return Object.assign({}, this) // shallow copy
        // return JSON.parse(JSON.stringify(this)); //deep copy
    }
}

// The Client
// Create an object containing an array
const OBJECT1 = new MyClass([1, 2, 3, 4])
console.log(`OBJECT1: ${JSON.stringify(OBJECT1)}`)

const OBJECT2 = OBJECT1.clone() // Clone
console.log(`OBJECT2: ${JSON.stringify(OBJECT2)}`)
// Change the value of one of the array elements in OBJECT2
// Depending on your clone method, either a shallow or deep copy
// was performed
OBJECT2.field[1] = 101

// Comparing OBJECT1 and OBJECT2
console.log(`OBJECT2: ${JSON.stringify(OBJECT2)}`)
console.log(`OBJECT1: ${JSON.stringify(OBJECT1)}`)
```

5.4.5 Output

When using the shallow copy approach. Changing the inner item of OBJECT2s array, also affected OBJECT1s array.

```
node ./dist/prototype/prototype-concept.js
OBJECT1: {"field":[1,2,3,4]}
OBJECT2: {"field":[1,2,3,4]}
OBJECT2: {"field":[1,101,3,4]}
OBJECT1: {"field":[1,101,3,4]}
```

When using the deep copy approach. Changing the inner item of OBJECT2s array, does not affect OBJECT1s array.

```
node ./dist/prototype/prototype-concept.js
OBJECT1: {"field":[1,2,3,4]}
OBJECT2: {"field":[1,2,3,4]}
```

```
OBJECT2: {"field":[1,101,3,4]}
OBJECT1: {"field":[1,2,3,4]}
```

5.4.6 Prototype Use Case

SBCODE Video ID #ca14c2

In this example, an object called document is cloned using shallow and deep methods.

I clone the documents instance properties and methods.

The object contains an array of two arrays. Three copies are created, and each time some part of the array is changed on the clone, and depending on the method used, it can affect the original object.

When cloning an object, it is good to understand the deep versus shallow concept of copying and whether you also want the clone to contain the classes methods.

5.4.7 Example UML Diagram

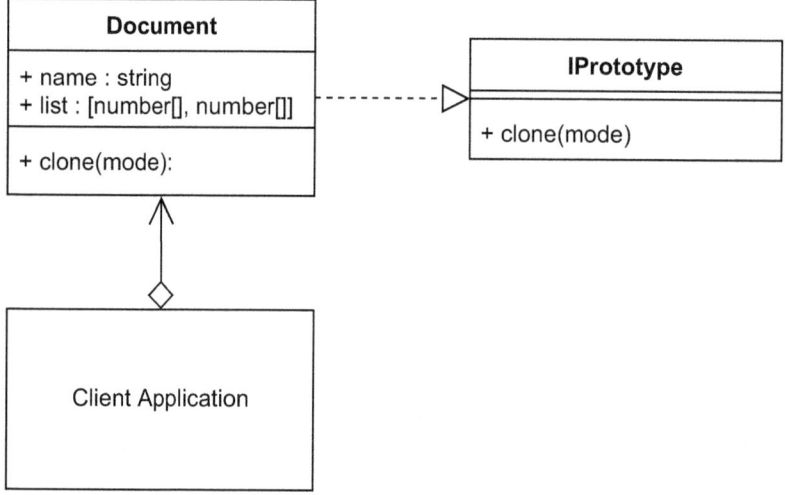

5.4.8 Source Code

./src/prototype/client.ts

```
// Prototype Use Case Example Code
import Document from './document'

// Creating a document containing an array of two arrays
const ORIGINAL_DOCUMENT = new Document('Original', [
    [1, 2, 3, 4],
    [5, 6, 7, 8],
])
```

```
console.log(ORIGINAL_DOCUMENT)
console.log()

const DOCUMENT_COPY_1 = ORIGINAL_DOCUMENT.clone(1) // shallow copy
DOCUMENT_COPY_1.name = 'Copy 1'
// This also modified ORIGINAL_DOCUMENT because of the shallow copy
// when using mode 1
DOCUMENT_COPY_1.array[1][2] = 200
console.log(DOCUMENT_COPY_1)
console.log(ORIGINAL_DOCUMENT)
console.log()

const DOCUMENT_COPY_2 = ORIGINAL_DOCUMENT.clone(1) // shallow copy
DOCUMENT_COPY_2.name = 'Copy 2'
// This does NOT modify ORIGINAL_DOCUMENT because it changes the
// complete array[1] reference that was shallow copied when using mode
1
DOCUMENT_COPY_2.array[1] = [9, 10, 11, 12]
console.log(DOCUMENT_COPY_2)
console.log(ORIGINAL_DOCUMENT)
console.log()

const DOCUMENT_COPY_3 = ORIGINAL_DOCUMENT.clone(2) // deep copy
DOCUMENT_COPY_3.name = 'Copy 3'
// This does modify ORIGINAL_DOCUMENT because it changes the element of
// array[1][0] that was deep copied recursively when using mode 2
DOCUMENT_COPY_3.array[1][0] = 1234
console.log(DOCUMENT_COPY_3)
console.log(ORIGINAL_DOCUMENT)
console.log()
```

./src/prototype/document.ts

```
// A sample document to be used in the Prototype example
import ProtoType from './iprototype'

export default class Document implements ProtoType {
    name: string
    array: [number[], number[]]

    constructor(name: string, array: [number[], number[]]) {
        this.name = name
        this.array = array
    }

    clone(mode: number): Document {
        // This clone method uses different copy techniques
        let array
```

```
            if (mode === 2) {
                // results in a deep copy of the Document
                array = JSON.parse(JSON.stringify(this.array))
            } else {
                // default, results in a shallow copy of the Document
                array = Object.assign([], this.array)
            }
            return new Document(this.name, array)
        }
    }
```

./src/prototype/iprototype.ts

```
// Prototype Concept Sample Code

import Document from './document'

export default interface IProtoType {
    // interface with clone method
    clone(mode: number): Document
    // The clone, deep or shallow.
    // It is up to you how you  want to implement
    // the details in your concrete class"""
}
```

5.4.9 Output

```
node ./dist/prototype/client.js
Document {
  name: 'Original',
  array: [ [ 1, 2, 3, 4 ], [ 5, 6, 7, 8 ] ]
}

Document {
  name: 'Copy 1',
  array: [ [ 1, 2, 3, 4 ], [ 5, 6, 200, 8 ] ]
}
Document {
  name: 'Original',
  array: [ [ 1, 2, 3, 4 ], [ 5, 6, 200, 8 ] ]
}

Document {
  name: 'Copy 2',
  array: [ [ 1, 2, 3, 4 ], [ 9, 10, 11, 12 ] ]
}
```

```
Document {
  name: 'Original',
  array: [ [ 1, 2, 3, 4 ], [ 5, 6, 200, 8 ] ]
}

Document {
  name: 'Copy 3',
  array: [ [ 1, 2, 3, 4 ], [ 1234, 6, 200, 8 ] ]
}
Document {
  name: 'Original',
  array: [ [ 1, 2, 3, 4 ], [ 5, 6, 200, 8 ] ]
}
```

5.4.10 Summary

- Just like the other creational patterns, a Prototype is used to create an object at runtime.

- A Prototype is created from an object that is already instantiated. Imagine using the existing object as the class template to create a new object, rather than calling a specific class. Note that, the clone method used in the concept video demonstrated didn't copy the class methods to the new object. The clones only contained copies of the instance properties. If you want your new clone to have the same methods of the original class, then use the classes' constructor when returning the clone as I did in the `clone(mode)` method in `document.ts`.

- The ability to create a Prototype means that you don't need to create many classes for specific combinations of objects. You can create one object, that has a specific configuration, then clone it and alter some factor of it, then create another clone from this altered configuration, and keep continuing to create many objects which are all slightly different from each other.

- New Prototypes can be created at runtime, without knowing what kind of attributes the prototype may eventually have. E.g., You have a sophisticated object that was randomly created from many factors, and you want to clone it rather than adding all those same factors over and over again until the new object matches the one that could have just been cloned.

- A prototype is also useful for when you want to create a copy of an object, but creating that copy may be very resource intensive. E.g., you can either create a new houseboat from the builder example, or clone an existing houseboat from one already in memory.

- When designing your `clone()` method, you should consider which elements will be shallow copied or deep copied.

5.5 Singleton Design Pattern

5.5.1 Overview

SBCODE Video ID #f4a24d

Sometimes you need an object in an application where there is only one instance.

You don't want there to be many versions, for example, you have a game with a score, and you want to adjust it. You may have accidentally created several instances of the class holding the score object. Or, you may be opening a database connection, there is no need to create many, when you can use the existing one that is already in memory. You may want a logging component, and you want to ensure all classes use the same instance. So, every class could declare their own logger component, but behind the scenes, they all point to the same memory address.

By creating a class and following the **Singleton** pattern, you can enforce that even if any number of instances were created, they will still refer to the original class.

The Singleton can be accessible globally, but it is not a global variable. The Singleton class can be instanced at any time, but after it is first instanced, any new instances will point to the same instance as the first.

5.5.2 Singleton UML Diagram

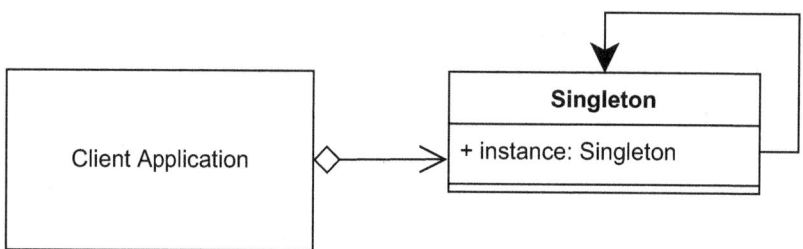

5.5.3 Source Code

In the source code below, when the Singleton constructor is called, it checks if the static `instance` property has already been set. If so, then instead of creating a new instance of a Singleton, it will return the reference to the first Singleton created.

See how when I create the two Objects (Singletons), I am also passing in a number to the constructor that I can use to act as some kind of ID. At the end of the code, I log the IDs for both Singleton objects, and they both return the number 1. This indicates that `OBJECT2` is really just `OBJECT1` behind the scenes.

A Singleton is not the same as a class containing all static properties and methods, but you could create a class of static properties and methods instead if it achieved the same purpose that you needed of controlling access to a single resource. The real difference here is in the constructor of this Singleton example in how it returns a reference to the original instance instead of creating a second, or third instance. The reason for using a Singleton would be that your Singleton can implement an interface or derive from a base class, and also the Singleton isn't actually instantiated in memory until the first time it is created when using the `new` keyword.

./src/singleton/singleton-concept.ts

```typescript
// Singleton Concept Sample Code

export class Singleton {
    // The Singleton Class
    static instance: Singleton
    id: number

    constructor(id: number) {
        this.id = id
        if (Singleton.instance) {
            return Singleton.instance
        }
        Singleton.instance = this
    }
}

// The Client
// All uses of the singleton point to the same original object

const OBJECT1 = new Singleton(1) // setting its id property to 1
const OBJECT2 = new Singleton(2) // setting its id property to 2

console.log(OBJECT1 === OBJECT2) // = true
console.log(OBJECT1.id) // returns 1
console.log(OBJECT2.id) // returns 1
```

5.5.4 Output

```
node ./dist/singleton/singleton-concept.js
true
```

5.5.5 Singleton Use Case

SBCODE Video ID #746648

In the example, there are three games created. They are all independent instances created from their own class, but they all share the same leaderboard. The leaderboard is a Singleton.

It doesn't matter how the Games where created, or how they reference the leaderboard, it is always a Singleton.

Each game independently adds a winner, and all games can read the altered leaderboard regardless of which game updated it.

5.5.6 Example UML Diagram

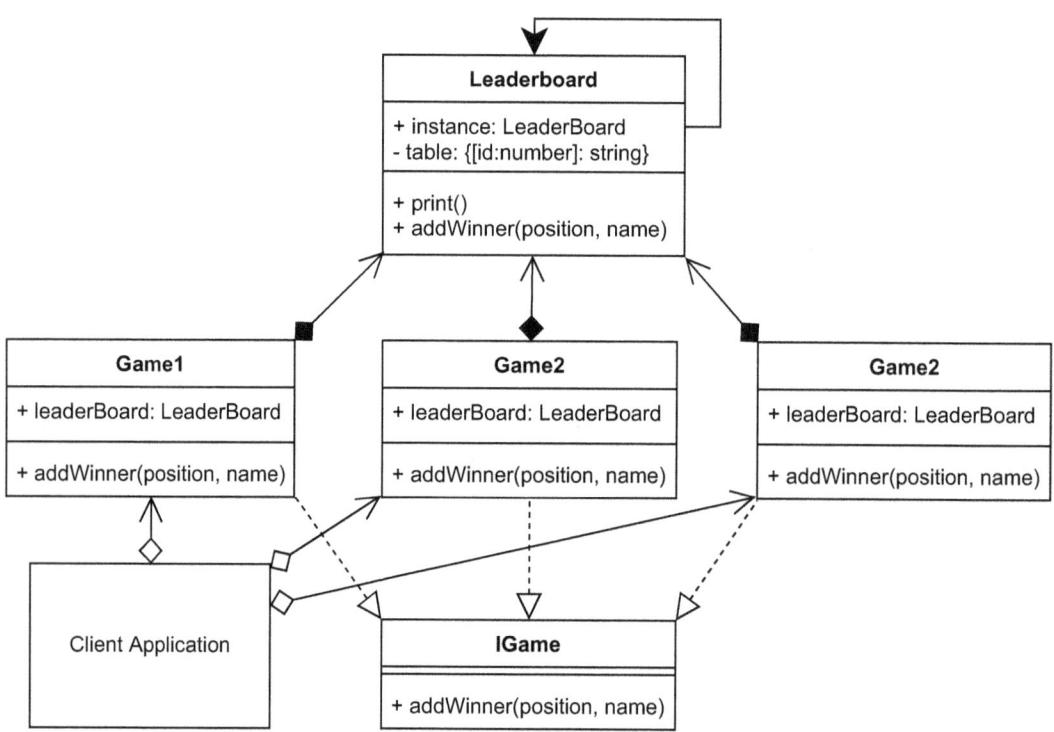

5.5.7 Source Code

./src/singleton/client.ts

```
// Singleton Use Case Example Code

import { Game1 } from './game1'
import { Game2 } from './game2'
import { Game3 } from './game3'

// The Client
// Despite all games instantiating a leaderboard, they all point
// to the same memory object since the leaderboard is a singleton.
```

```typescript
const GAME1 = new Game1()
GAME1.addWinner(2, 'Cosmo')

const GAME2 = new Game2()
GAME2.addWinner(3, 'Sean')

const GAME3 = new Game3()
GAME3.addWinner(1, 'Emmy')

GAME1.leaderboard.print()
GAME2.leaderboard.print()
GAME3.leaderboard.print()
```

./src/singleton/game1.ts

```typescript
// A Game Class that uses the Leaderboard Singleton

import Leaderboard from './leaderboard'
import Game from './igame'

export class Game1 implements Game {
    leaderboard: Leaderboard

    constructor() {
        this.leaderboard = new Leaderboard()
    }

    addWinner(position: number, name: string): void {
        this.leaderboard.addWinner(position, name)
    }
}
```

./src/singleton/game2.ts

```typescript
// A Game Class that uses the Leaderboard Singleton

import Leaderboard from './leaderboard'
import Game from './igame'

export class Game2 implements Game {
    leaderboard: Leaderboard

    constructor() {
        this.leaderboard = new Leaderboard()
    }
```

```
        addWinner(position: number, name: string): void {
            this.leaderboard.addWinner(position, name)
        }
    }
```

./src/singleton/game3.ts

```
    // A Game Class that uses the Leaderboard Singleton

    import Leaderboard from './leaderboard'
    import Game from './igame'

    export class Game3 implements Game {
        leaderboard: Leaderboard

        constructor() {
            this.leaderboard = new Leaderboard()
        }

        addWinner(position: number, name: string): void {
            this.leaderboard.addWinner(position, name)
        }
    }
```

./src/singleton/leaderboard.ts

```
    // A Leaderboard Singleton Class

    export default class Leaderboard {
        static instance: Leaderboard
        #table: { [id: number]: string } = {}

        constructor() {
            if (Leaderboard.instance) {
                return Leaderboard.instance
            }
            Leaderboard.instance = this
        }

        public addWinner(position: number, name: string): void {
            this.#table[position] = name
        }

        public print(): void {
            console.log('-----------Leaderboard-----------')
            for (const key in this.#table) {
```

```
                console.log(`|\t${key}\t|\t${this.#table[key]}\t|`)
        }
        console.log()
    }
}
```

./src/singleton/igame.ts

```
// A Game Interface

export default interface IGame {
    addWinner(position: number, name: string): void
}
```

5.5.8 Output

```
node ./dist/singleton/client
----------Leaderboard----------
|       1       |       Emmy    |
|       2       |       Cosmo   |
|       3       |       Sean    |

----------Leaderboard----------
|       1       |       Emmy    |
|       2       |       Cosmo   |
|       3       |       Sean    |

----------Leaderboard----------
|       1       |       Emmy    |
|       2       |       Cosmo   |
|       3       |       Sean    |
```

5.5.9 Summary

- To be a Singleton, there must only be one copy of the Singleton, no matter how many times, or in which class it was instantiated.
- You want the attributes or methods to be globally accessible across your application, so that other classes may be able to use the Singleton.
- You can use Singletons in other classes, as I did with the leaderboard, and they will all use the same Singleton instance regardless.
- You want controlled access to a sole instance.

- A singleton differs from a class containing just static methods and properties in the way that you can make your Singleton implement an interface and/or extend a base class. You also create an instance of a Singleton at runtime using the `new` keyword.

6. Structural

6.1 Decorator Design Pattern

6.1.1 Overview

SBCODE Video ID #ab01cd

The **decorator pattern** is a structural pattern, that allows you to attach additional responsibilities to an object at runtime.

The decorator pattern is used in both the Object-Oriented and Functional paradigms.

The decorator pattern adds extensibility without modifying the original object.

The decorator forwards requests to the enclosed object and can perform extra actions.

You can nest decorators recursively.

6.1.2 Terminology

- **Component Interface**: An interface for objects.
- **Component**: The object that may be decorated.
- **Decorator**: The class that applies the extra responsibilities to the component being decorated. It also implements the same component interface.

6.1.3 Decorator UML Diagram

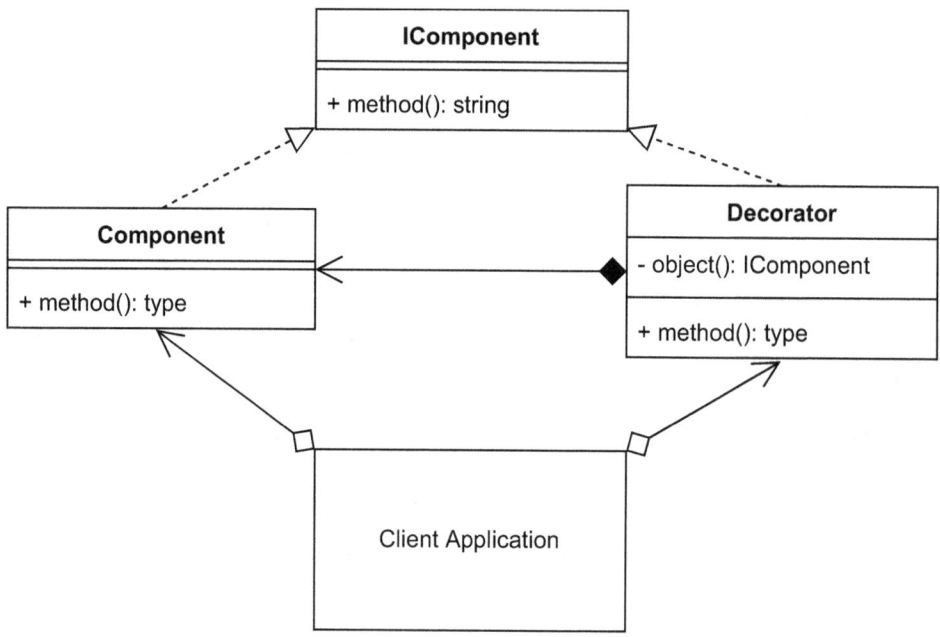

6.1.4 Source Code

./src/decorator/decorator-concept.ts

```ts
// Decorator Concept Sample Code

interface IComponent {
    method(): string
}

class Component implements IComponent {
    method(): string {
        return 'Component Method'
    }
}

class Decorator implements IComponent {
    #object: IComponent

    constructor(object: IComponent) {
        this.#object = object
    }

    method(): string {
        return `Decorator Method(${this.#object.method()})`
    }
```

```
    }

    // The Client
    const COMPONENT = new Component()
    console.log(COMPONENT.method())

    // The component can be decorated
    const Decorated = new Decorator(COMPONENT)
    console.log(Decorated.method())

    // The decorated component can be decorated again
    const Decorated2 = new Decorator(Decorated)
    console.log(Decorated2.method())
```

6.1.5 Output

```
node ./dist/decorator/decorator-concept.js
Component Method
Decorator Method(Component Method)
Decorator Method(Decorator Method(Component Method))
```

6.1.6 Decorator Use Case

SBCODE Video ID #eb9f25

Let's create a custom class called `Value` that will hold a number.

Then add decorators that allow addition (`Add`) and subtraction (`Sub`) to a number (`Value`).

The `Add` and `Sub` decorators can accept numbers directly, a custom `Value` object or other `Add` and `Sub` decorators.

`Add` , `Sub` and `Value` all implement the `IValue` interface and can be used recursively.

Note that in this example use case, I have created the `Add` , `Sub` and `Value` as functions that return new instances of classes `_Add` , `_Sub` and `_Value` . This was not necessary, but it means that I can use the `Add` , `Sub` and `Value` in a recursive manner without needing to prefix the `new` keyword in front of each usage all the time.

E.g,

```
console.log(Add(Sub(Add(C, B), A), 100).value)
```

Alternatively, I could have named my classes as `Add` , `Sub` and `Value` and then used them recursively directly as

```
console.log(new Add(new Sub(new Add(C, B), A), 100).value)
```

6.1.7 Example UML Diagram

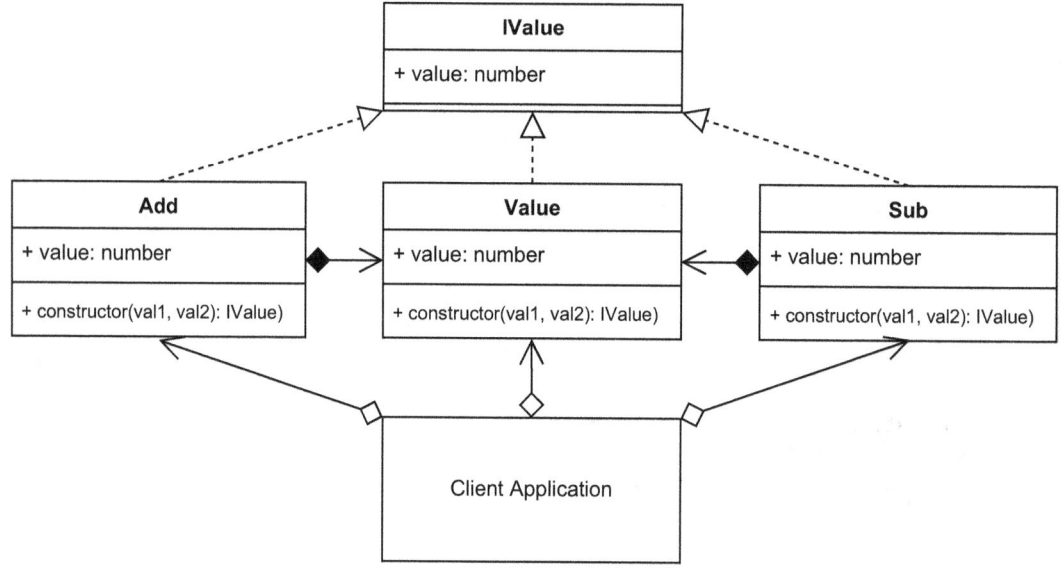

6.1.8 Source Code

./src/decorator/client.ts

```
// Decorator Use Case Example Code

import Value from './value'
import Add from './add'
import Sub from './sub'

const A = Value(1)
const B = Value(2)
const C = Value(5)

console.log(Add(A, B).value)
console.log(Add(A, 100).value)
console.log(Sub(C, A).value)
console.log(Sub(Add(C, B), A).value)
console.log(Sub(100, 101).value)
console.log(Add(Sub(Add(C, B), A), 100).value)
console.log(Sub(123, Add(C, C)).value)
console.log(Add(Sub(Add(C, 10), A), 100).value)
console.log(A.value)
```

```
    console.log(B.value)
    console.log(C.value)
```

./src/decorator/value.ts

```
    export interface IValue {
        value: number
    }

    class _Value implements IValue {
        value: number
        constructor(value: number) {
            this.value = value
        }
    }

    export default function Value(value: number): IValue {
        return new _Value(value)
    }
```

./src/decorator/add.ts

```
    import { IValue } from './value'

    class _Add implements IValue {
        value: number
        constructor(val1: IValue | number, val2: IValue | number) {
            const left = Object.prototype.hasOwnProperty.call(val1,
    'value')
                ? (val1 as IValue).value
                : (val1 as number)
            const right = Object.prototype.hasOwnProperty.call(val2,
    'value')
                ? (val2 as IValue).value
                : (val2 as number)
            this.value = left + right
        }
    }

    export default function Add(val1: IValue | number, val2: IValue |
    number): IValue {
        return new _Add(val1, val2)
    }
```

./src/decorator/sub.ts

```typescript
import { IValue } from './value'

class _Sub implements IValue {
    value: number
    constructor(val1: IValue | number, val2: IValue | number) {
        const left = Object.prototype.hasOwnProperty.call(val1,
'value')
            ? (val1 as IValue).value
            : (val1 as number)
        const right = Object.prototype.hasOwnProperty.call(val2,
'value')
            ? (val2 as IValue).value
            : (val2 as number)
        this.value = left - right
    }
}

export default function Sub(val1: IValue | number, val2: IValue |
number): IValue {
    return new _Sub(val1, val2)
}
```

6.1.9 Output

```
node ./dist/decorator/client.js
3
101
4
6
-1
106
113
114
1
2
5
```

6.1.10 Summary

- Use the decorator when you want to add responsibilities to objects dynamically without affecting the inner object.
- You want the option to later remove the decorator from an object in case you no longer need it.

- It is an alternative method to creating multiple combinations of subclasses. I.e., Instead of creating a subclass with all combinations of objects A, B, C in any order, and including/excluding objects, you could create 3 objects that can decorate each other in any order you want. E.g., (C(A(C))) or (B(C)) or (A(B(A(C))))
- The decorator, compared to extending, is more flexible since you can easily add/remove the decorators at runtime. E.g., use in a recursive function.
- A decorator supports recursive composition. E.g., halve(halve(number))
- A decorator shouldn't modify the internal objects data or references. This allows the original object to stay intact if the decorator is later removed.

6.2 Adapter Design Pattern

6.2.1 Overview

SBCODE Video ID #8b5434

Sometimes classes have been written, and you don't have the option of modifying their interface to suit your needs. This happens if the method you are calling is on a different system across a network, a library that you may import or generally something that is not viable to modify directly for your particular needs.

The **Adapter** design pattern solves these problems:

- How can a class be reused that does not have an interface that a client requires?
- How can class's that have incompatible interfaces work together?
- How can an alternative interface be provided for a class?

You may have two classes that are similar, but they have different method signatures, so you create an Adapter over top of one of the method signatures so that it is easier to implement and extend in the client.

An adapter is similar to the Decorator in the way that it also acts like a wrapper to an object. It is also used at runtime; however, it is not designed to be used recursively.

It is an alternative interface over an existing interface. Furthermore, it can also provide extra functionality that the interface being adapted may not already provide.

The adapter is similar to the Facade, but you are modifying the method signature, combining other methods and/or transforming data that is exchanged between the existing interface and the client.

The Adapter is used when you have an existing interface that doesn't directly map to an interface that the client requires. So, then you create the Adapter that has a similar functional role, but with a new compatible interface.

6.2.2 Terminology

- **Target**: The domain specific interface or class that needs to be adapted.
- **Adapter**: The concrete adapter class containing the adaption process.
- **Adapter Interface**: The interface that the adapter will need to implement in order to make the target compatible with the client.
- **Client**: The client application that will use the Adapter.

6.2.3 Adapter UML Diagram

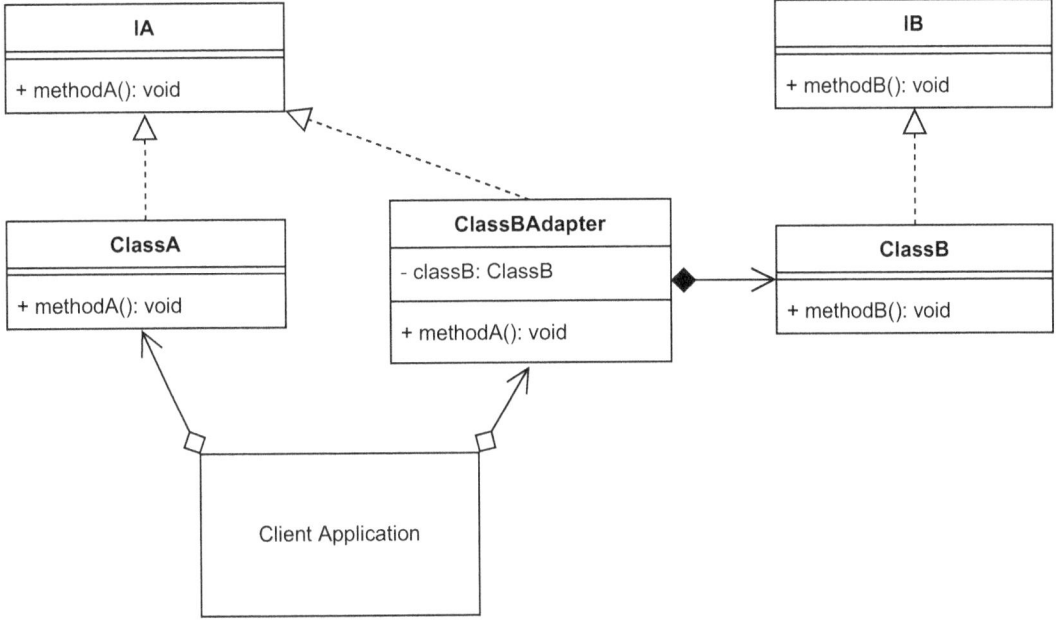

6.2.4 Source Code

In this concept source code, there are two classes, `ClassA` and `ClassB`, with different method signatures. Let's consider that `ClassA` provides the most compatible and preferred interface for the client.

I can create objects of both classes in the client, and it works. But before using each objects method, I need to do a conditional check to see which type of class it is that I am calling since the method signatures are different.

It means that the client is doing extra work. Instead, I can create an Adapter interface for the incompatible `ClassB`, that reduces the need for the extra conditional logic.

./src/adapter/adapter-concept.ts

```
// Adapter Concept Sample Code

interface IA {
    methodA(): void
}

class ClassA implements IA {
    methodA() {
        console.log('method A')
    }
```

```typescript
    }

    interface IB {
        methodB(): void
    }

    class ClassB implements IB {
        methodB() {
            console.log('method B')
        }
    }

    class ClassBAdapter implements IA {
        // ClassB does not have a methodA, so we can create an adapter

        #classB: ClassB

        constructor() {
            this.#classB = new ClassB()
        }

        methodA() {
            'calls the class b method_b instead'
            this.#classB.methodB()
        }
    }

    // The Client
    // Before the adapter I need to test the objects class to know which
    // method to call.
    const ITEMS = [new ClassA(), new ClassB()]
    ITEMS.forEach((item) => {
        if (item instanceof ClassB) {
            item.methodB()
        } else {
            item.methodA()
        }
    })

    // After creating an adapter for ClassB I can reuse the same method
    // signature as ClassA (preferred)
    const ADAPTED = [new ClassA(), new ClassBAdapter()]
    ADAPTED.forEach((item) => {
        item.methodA()
    })
```

6.2.5 Output

```
node ./dist/adapter/adapter-concept.js
method A
method B
method A
method B
```

6.2.6 Adapter Use Case

SBCODE Video ID #ae7042

The example client can manufacture a **Cube** using different tools. Each solution is invented by a different company. The client user interface manages the Cube product by indicating the **width**, **height** and **depth**. This is compatible with the company A that produces the Cube tool, but not the company B that produces their own version of the Cube tool that uses a different interface with different parameters.

In this example, the client will re-use the interface for company A's Cube and create a compatible Cube from company B.

An adapter will be needed so that the same method signature can be used by the client without the need to ask company B to modify their Cube tool for our specific domains use case.

My imaginary company needs to use both cube suppliers since there is a large demand for cubes and when one supplier is busy, I can then ask the other supplier.

6.2.7 Example UML Diagram

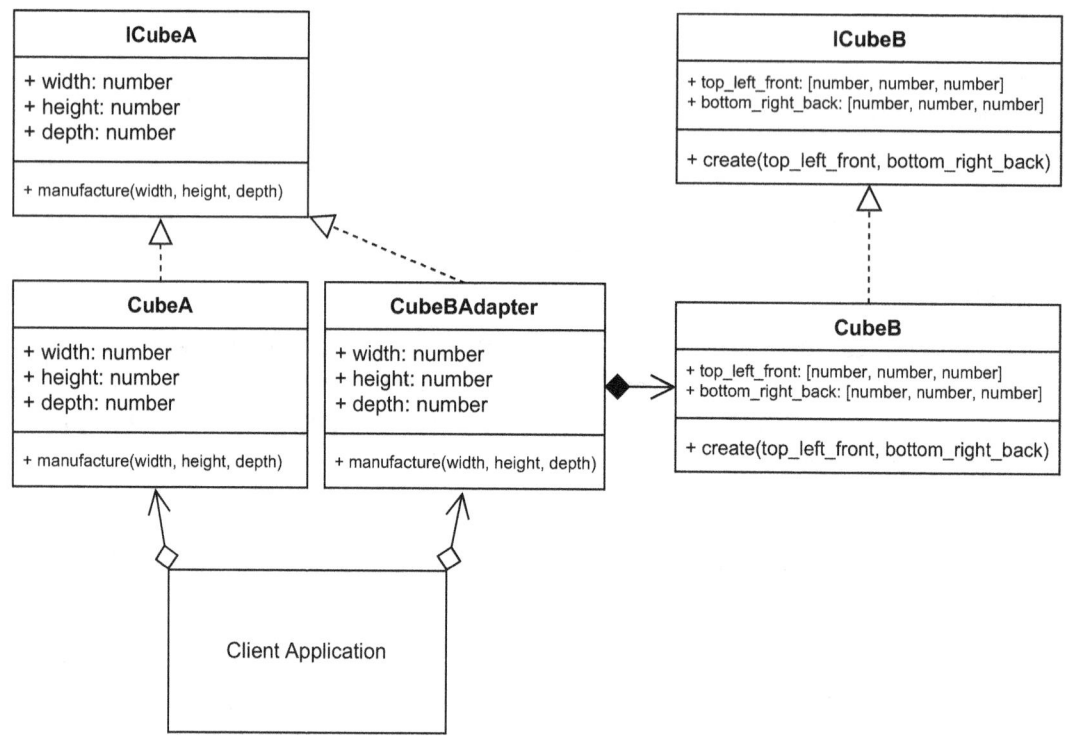

6.2.8 Source Code

./src/adapter/client.ts

```typescript
// Adapter Example Use Case
import CubeA from './cube-a'
import CubeBAdapter from './cube-b-adapter'

const totalCubes = 5
let counter = 0

const manufactureCube = () => {
    // produce 5 cubes from which ever supplier can manufacture it first
    const width = Math.floor(Math.random() * 10) + 1
    const height = Math.floor(Math.random() * 10) + 1
    const depth = Math.floor(Math.random() * 10) + 1
    let cube = new CubeA()
    let success = cube.manufacture(width, height, depth)
    if (success) {
        counter = counter + 1
    } else {
        // try other manufacturer
```

```
            console.log('Company A was busy, so trying company B')
            cube = new CubeBAdapter()
            success = cube.manufacture(width, height, depth)
            if (success) {
                counter = counter + 1
            } else {
                console.log('Company B was busy, so trying company A')
            }
        }
    }

    // wait some time between manufacturing each cube
    const interval = setInterval(() => {
        manufactureCube()
        if (counter >= totalCubes) {
            clearInterval(interval)
            console.log(`${totalCubes} cubes have been manufactured`)
        }
    }, 1000)
```

./src/adapter/cube-a.ts

```
    // A hypothetical Cube tool from Company A
    export interface ICubeA {
        manufacture(width: number, height: number, depth: number): boolean
    }

    export default class CubeA implements ICubeA {
        static last_time = Date.now()

        manufacture(width: number, height: number, depth: number): boolean
        {
            // if not busy, then manufacture a cube with dimensions
            const now = Date.now()
            if (now > CubeA.last_time + 1500) {
                console.log(
                    `Company A built Cube with dimensions ${width}x${height}x${depth}`
                )
                CubeA.last_time = now
                return true
            }
            return false // busy
        }
    }
```

./src/adapter/cube-b.ts

```typescript
// A hypothetical Cube tool from Company B
export interface ICubeB {
    create(
        top_left_front: [number, number, number],
        bottom_right_back: [number, number, number]
    ): boolean
}

export default class CubeB implements ICubeB {
    static last_time = Date.now()

    create(
        top_left_front: [number, number, number],
        bottom_right_back: [number, number, number]
    ): boolean {
        // if not busy, then manufacture a cube with coords
        const now = Date.now()
        if (now > CubeB.last_time + 3000) {
            console.log(
                `Company B built Cube with coords [${top_left_front[0]},${top_left_front[1]},${top_left_front[2]}],[${bottom_right_back[0]},${bottom_right_back[1]},${bottom_right_back[2]}]`
            )
            CubeB.last_time = now
            return true
        } else {
            return false // busy
        }
    }
}
```

./src/adapter/cube-b-adapter.ts

```typescript
// Adapter for CubeB that implements ICubeA
import { ICubeA } from './cube-a'
import CubeB from './cube-b'

export default class CubeBAdapter implements ICubeA {
    #cube: CubeB

    constructor() {
        this.#cube = new CubeB()
    }
```

```
    manufacture(width: number, height: number, depth: number): boolean
{
        const success = this.#cube.create(
            [0 - width / 2, 0 - height / 2, 0 - depth / 2],
            [0 + width / 2, 0 + height / 2, 0 + depth / 2]
        )
        return success
    }
}
```

6.2.9 Output

```
node ./dist/adapter/client.js
Company A was busy, so trying company B
Company B was busy, so trying company A
Company A built Cube with dimensions 6x5x10
Company A was busy, so trying company B
Company B built Cube with coords [-4,-3,-2.5],[4,3,2.5]
Company A built Cube with dimensions 4x5x3
Company A was busy, so trying company B
Company B was busy, so trying company A
Company A built Cube with dimensions 10x2x1
Company A was busy, so trying company B
Company B built Cube with coords [-0.5,-2,-2.5],[0.5,2,2.5]
5 cubes have been manufactured
```

6.2.10 Summary

- Use the Adapter when you want to use an existing class, but its interface does not match what you need.
- The adapter adapts to the interface of its parent class for those situations when it is not viable to modify the parent class to be domain-specific for your use case.
- Adapters will most likely provide an alternative interface over an existing object, class or interface, but it can also provide extra functionality that the object being adapted may not already provide.
- An adapter is similar to a Decorator except that it changes the interface to the object, whereas the decorator adds responsibility without changing the interface. This also allows the Decorator to be used recursively.
- An adapter is similar to the Bridge pattern and may look identical after the refactoring has been completed. However, the intent of creating the Adapter is different. The Bridge is a result of refactoring existing interfaces, whereas the Adapter is about adapting over existing interfaces that are not viable to modify due to many existing constraints. E.g., you don't have access to the

original code, or it may have dependencies that already use it and modifying it would affect those dependencies negatively.

6.3 Facade Design Pattern

6.3.1 Overview

SBCODE Video ID #46770c

Sometimes you have a system that becomes quite complex over time as more features are added or modified. It may be useful to provide a simplified API over it. This is the **Facade** pattern.

The Facade pattern essentially is an alternative, reduced or simplified interface to a set of other interfaces, abstractions and implementations within a system that may be full of complexity and/or tightly coupled.

It can also be considered as a higher-level interface that shields the consumer from the unnecessary low-level complications of integrating into many subsystems.

6.3.2 Facade UML Diagram

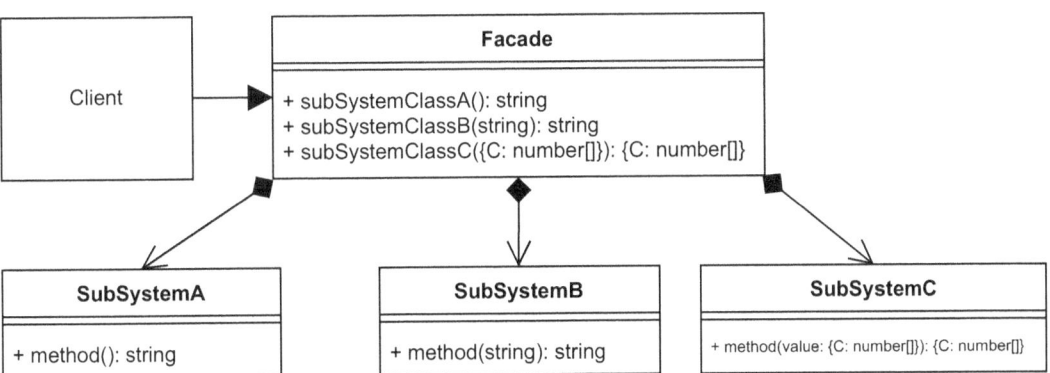

6.3.3 Source Code

./src/facade/facade-concept.ts

```
// The Facade pattern concept

class SubSystemClassA {
    // A hypothetically complicated class
    method(): string {
        return 'A'
    }
}

class SubSystemClassB {
    // A hypothetically complicated class
```

```typescript
        method(value: string): string {
            return value
        }
    }

    class SubSystemClassC {
        // A hypothetically complicated class
        method(value: { C: number[] }): { C: number[] } {
            return value
        }
    }

    class Facade {
        // A simplified facade offering the services of subsystems
        subSystemClassA(): string {
            // Uses the subsystems method
            return new SubSystemClassA().method()
        }

        subSystemClassB(value: string): string {
            // Uses the subsystems method
            return new SubSystemClassB().method(value)
        }

        subSystemClassC(value: { C: number[] }): { C: number[] } {
            // Uses the subsystems method
            return new SubSystemClassC().method(value)
        }
    }

    // The Client
    // Calling potentially complicated subsystems directly
    console.log(new SubSystemClassA().method())
    console.log(new SubSystemClassB().method('B'))
    console.log(new SubSystemClassC().method({ C: [1, 2, 3] }))

    // or using the simplified facade instead
    const FACADE = new Facade()
    console.log(FACADE.subSystemClassA())
    console.log(FACADE.subSystemClassB('B'))
    console.log(FACADE.subSystemClassC({ C: [1, 2, 3] }))
```

6.3.4 Output

```
node ./dist/facade/facade-concept.js
A
B
{ C: [ 1, 2, 3 ] }
```

```
A
B
{ C: [ 1, 2, 3 ] }
```

6.3.5 Facade Use Case

SBCODE Video ID #e86c30

This is an example of a game engine API. The facade layer is creating one streamlined interface consisting of several methods from several larger API backend systems.

The client could connect directly to each subsystem's API and implement its authentication protocols, specific methods, etc. While it is possible, it would be quite a lot of consideration for each of the development teams, so the facade API unifies the common methods that becomes much less overwhelming for each new client developer to integrate into.

6.3.6 Example UML Diagram

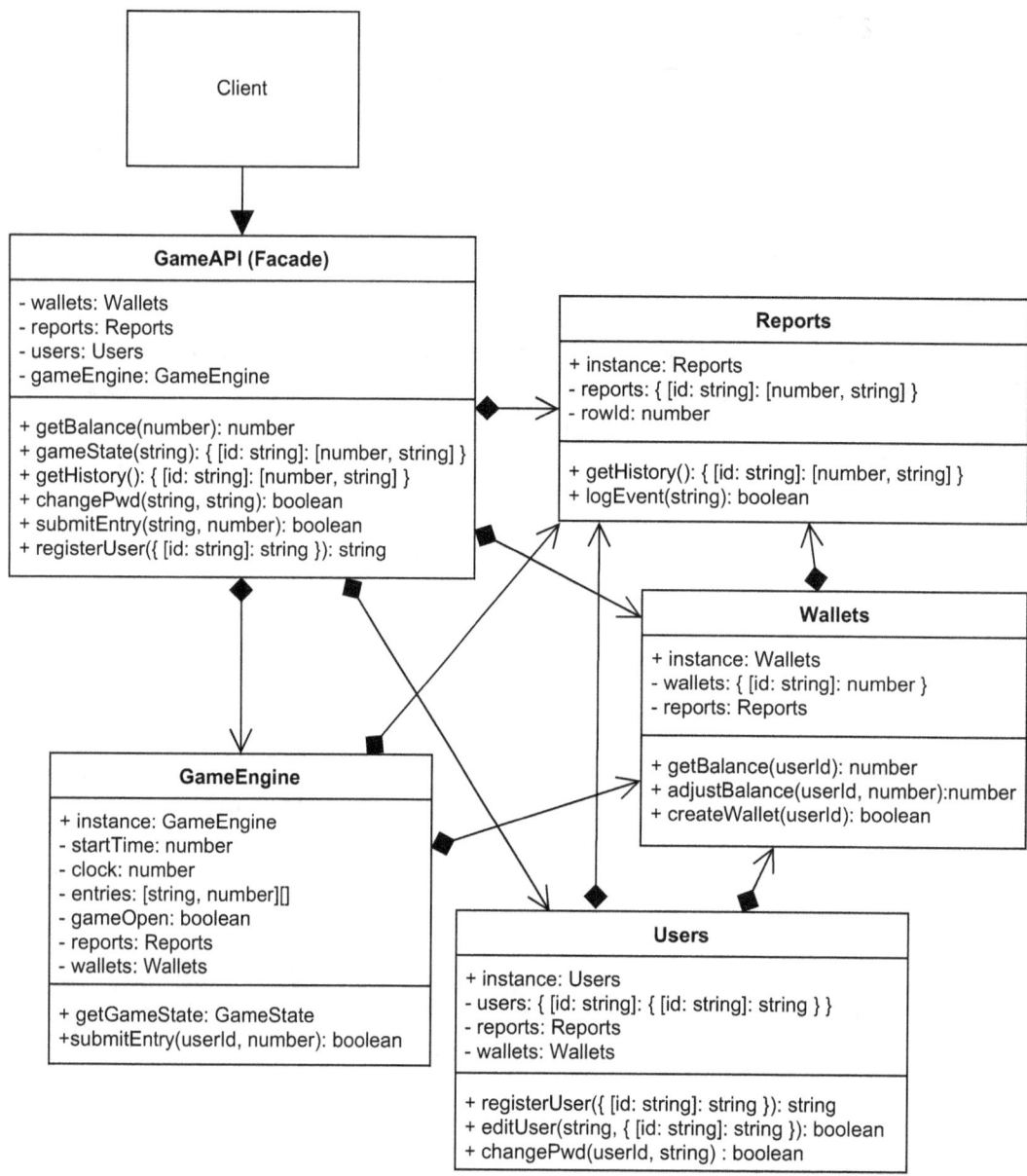

6.3.7 Source Code

./src/facade/client.ts

```
// The Facade Example Use Case

import GameAPI from './game-api'

function sleep(ms: number) {
```

```typescript
        return new Promise((resolve) => setTimeout(resolve, ms))
    }

    async function facadeExample() {
        const gameAPI = new GameAPI()

        const user = { user_name: 'sean' }
        const userId = gameAPI.registerUser(user)

        await sleep(500)

        gameAPI.submitEntry(userId, 5)

        await sleep(500)

        console.log()
        console.log('---- GameState Snapshot ----')
        console.log(gameAPI.gameState())

        await sleep(1000)

        const HISTORY = gameAPI.getHistory()

        console.log()
        console.log('---- Reports History ----')
        Object.keys(HISTORY).forEach((key) => {
            console.log(`${key} : ${HISTORY[key][0]} : ${HISTORY[key][1]}`)
        })

        await sleep(1000)

        console.log()
        console.log('---- User Balance ----')
        console.log(user.user_name + ' : ' + gameAPI.getBalance(userId))

        await sleep(1000)

        console.log()
        console.log('---- GameState Snapshot ----')
        console.log(gameAPI.gameState())
    }
    facadeExample()
```

./src/facade/game-api.ts

```typescript
    // The Game API facade

    import Reports from './reports'
```

```
import Wallets from './wallets'
import Users from './users'
import GameEngine, { GameState } from './game-engine'

export default class GameAPI {
    #wallets: Wallets
    #reports: Reports
    #users: Users
    #gameEngine: GameEngine

    constructor() {
        this.#wallets = new Wallets()
        this.#reports = new Reports()
        this.#users = new Users()
        this.#gameEngine = new GameEngine()
    }

    getBalance(userId: string): number {
        // Get a players balance
        return this.#wallets.getBalance(userId)
    }

    gameState(): GameState {
        // Get the current game state
        return this.#gameEngine.getGameState()
    }

    getHistory(): { [id: string]: [number, string] } {
        // get the game history
        return this.#reports.getHistory()
    }

    changePwd(userId: string, password: string): boolean {
        // change users password
        return this.#users.changePwd(userId, password)
    }

    submitEntry(userId: string, entry: number): boolean {
        // submit a bet
        return this.#gameEngine.submitEntry(userId, entry)
    }

    registerUser(value: { [id: string]: string }): string {
        // register a new user and returns the new id
        return this.#users.registerUser(value)
    }
}
```

./src/facade/users.ts

```typescript
// A Singleton Dictionary of Users

import Reports from './reports'
import Wallets from './wallets'

export default class Users {
    static instance: Users
    #users: { [id: string]: { [id: string]: string } } = {}
    #reports = new Reports()
    #wallets = new Wallets()

    constructor() {
        if (Users.instance) {
            return Users.instance
        }
        Users.instance = this
    }

    registerUser(newUser: { [id: string]: string }): string {
        // register a user
        if (!(newUser['user_name'] in this.#users)) {
            // generate really complicated unique user_id.
            // Using the existing user_name as the id for simplicity
            const userId = newUser['user_name']
            this.#users[userId] = newUser
            this.#reports.logEvent(`new user '${userId}' created`)
            // create a wallet for the new user
            this.#wallets.createWallet(userId)
            // give the user a sign up bonus
            this.#reports.logEvent(`Give new user '${userId}' sign up bonus of 10`)
            this.#wallets.adjustBalance(userId, 10)
            return userId
        }
        return ''
    }

    editUser(userId: string, user: { [id: string]: string }): boolean {
        // do nothing. Not implemented yet
        console.log(userId)
        console.log(user)
        return false
    }

    changePwd(userId: string, password: string): boolean {
        // do nothing. Not implemented yet
        console.log(userId)
```

```typescript
            console.log(password)
            return false
        }
    }
```

./src/facade/wallets.ts

```typescript
// A Singleton Dictionary of User Wallets

import Reports from './reports'

export default class Wallets {
    static instance: Wallets
    #wallets: { [id: string]: number } = {}
    #reports = new Reports()

    constructor() {
        if (Wallets.instance) {
            return Wallets.instance
        }
        Wallets.instance = this
    }

    createWallet(userId: string): boolean {
        // A method to initialize a users wallet
        if (!(userId in this.#wallets)) {
            this.#wallets[userId] = 0
            this.#reports.logEvent(`wallet for '${userId}' created and set to 0`)
            return true
        }
        return false
    }

    getBalance(userId: string): number {
        // A method to check a users balance
        this.#reports.logEvent(
            `Balance check for '${userId}' = ${this.#wallets[userId]}`
        )
        return this.#wallets[userId]
    }

    adjustBalance(userId: string, amount: number): number {
        // A method to adjust a user balance up or down
        this.#wallets[userId] = this.#wallets[userId] + amount
        this.#reports.logEvent(
            `Balance adjustment for '${userId}'. New balance = ${
                this.#wallets[userId]
```

```
                }`
            )
            return this.#wallets[userId]
        }
    }
```

./src/facade/reports.ts

```
    // A Singleton Dictionary of Reported Events

    export default class Reports {
        static instance: Reports
        #reports: { [id: string]: [number, string] } = {}
        #rowId = 0

        constructor() {
            if (Reports.instance) {
                return Reports.instance
            }
            Reports.instance = this
        }

        getHistory(): { [id: string]: [number, string] } {
            return this.#reports
        }

        logEvent(event: string): boolean {
            this.#reports[this.#rowId] = [Date.now(), event]
            this.#rowId = this.#rowId + 1
            return true
        }
    }
```

./src/facade/game-engine.ts

```
    // The Game Engine

    import Reports from './reports'
    import Wallets from './wallets'

    export type GameState = {
        clock: number
        gameOpen: boolean
        entries: [string, number][]
    }
```

```typescript
export default class GameEngine {
    static instance: GameEngine
    #startTime = 0
    #clock = 0
    #entries: [string, number][] = []
    #gameOpen = true
    #reports = new Reports()
    #wallets = new Wallets()

    constructor() {
        if (GameEngine.instance) {
            return GameEngine.instance
        }
        this.#startTime = Math.floor(Date.now() / 1000)
        this.#clock = 60
        GameEngine.instance = this
    }

    getGameState(): GameState {
        // Get a snapshot of the current game state
        const now = Math.floor(Date.now() / 1000)
        let timeRemaining = this.#startTime - now + this.#clock
        console.log('getGameState ' + timeRemaining)
        if (timeRemaining < 0) {
            timeRemaining = 0
        }
        this.#gameOpen = false
        return {
            clock: timeRemaining,
            gameOpen: this.#gameOpen,
            entries: this.#entries,
        } as GameState
    }

    submitEntry(userId: string, entry: number): boolean {
        // Submit a new entry for the user in this game
        const now = Math.floor(Date.now() / 1000)
        const time_remaining = this.#startTime - now + this.#clock
        if (time_remaining > 0) {
            if (this.#wallets.getBalance(userId) > 1) {
                if (this.#wallets.adjustBalance(userId, -1)) {
                    this.#entries.push([userId, entry])
                    this.#reports.logEvent(
                        `New entry '${entry}' submitted by '${userId}'`
                    )
                    return true
                }
                this.#reports.logEvent(`Problem adjusting balance for '${userId}'`)
```

```
                    return false
                }
                this.#reports.logEvent(`User Balance for '${userId}' to
low`)
                return false
            }
            this.#reports.logEvent('Game Closed')
            return false
        }
    }
```

6.3.8 Output

```
node ./dist/facade/client.js

---- GameState Snapshot ----
getGameState 59
{ clock: 59, gameOpen: false, entries: [ [ 'sean', 5 ] ] }

---- Reports History ----
0 : 1619260983800 : new user 'sean' created
1 : 1619260983800 : wallet for 'sean' created and set to 0
2 : 1619260983800 : Give new user 'sean' sign up bonus of 10
3 : 1619260983800 : Balance adjustment for 'sean'. New balance = 10
4 : 1619260984312 : Balance check for 'sean' = 10
5 : 1619260984312 : Balance adjustment for 'sean'. New balance = 9
6 : 1619260984312 : New entry '5' submitted by 'sean'

---- User Balance ----
sean : 9

---- GameState Snapshot ----
getGameState 56
{ clock: 56, gameOpen: false, entries: [ [ 'sean', 5 ] ] }
```

6.3.9 Summary

- Use when you want to provide a simple interface to a complex subsystem.
- You want to layer your subsystems into an abstraction that is easier to understand.
- Abstract Factory and Facade can be considered very similar. An Abstract Factory is about creating in interface over several creational classes of similar objects, whereas the Facade is more like an API layer over many creational, structural and/or behavioral patterns.

- The Mediator is similar to the Facade in the way that it abstracts existing classes. The Facade is not intended to modify, load balance or apply any extra logic. A subsystem does not need to consider that existence of the facade, it would still work without it.
- A Facade is a minimal interface that could also be implemented as a Singleton.
- A Facade is an optional layer that does not alter the subsystem. The subsystem does not need to know about the Facade, and could even be used by many other facades created for different audiences.

6.4 Bridge Design Pattern

6.4.1 Overview

SBCODE Video ID #83202d

The **Bridge pattern** is similar to the Adapter except in the intent that you developed it.

The Bridge is an approach to refactor already existing code, whereas the Adapter creates an interface on top of existing code through existing available means without refactoring any existing code or interfaces.

The motivation for converting your code to the Bridge pattern is that it may be tightly coupled. There is logic and abstraction close together that is limiting your choices in how you can extend your solution in the way that you need.

E.g., you may have one Car class, that produces a very nice car.

```
const CAR = new Car()
> Car has wheels and engine and windows and everything else.
```

But you would like to delegate the engine dynamically from a separate set of classes or solutions.

```
const ENGINE = new EngineA()
const CAR = new Car(ENGINE)
```

The Bridge pattern is a process about separating abstraction and implementation, so this will allow you more ways of using your classes.

A Bridge didn't exist before, but since after the separation of interface and logic, each side can be extended independently of each other.

The Bridge pattern should use composition instead of inheritance. This means that you assign the relationship when the object is created at runtime rather than hard coded in the class definition.

I.e., `CAR = new Car(EngineA)` rather than `class Car extends EngineA`

A Bridge implementation will generally be cleaner than an Adapter solution that was bolted on. Since it involved refactoring existing code, rather than layering on top of legacy or third-party solutions that may not have been intended for your particular use case.

6.4.2 Terminology

- **Abstraction Interface**: An interface implemented by the refined abstraction describing the common methods to implement.
- **Refined Abstraction**: A refinement of an idea into another class or two. The classes should implement the Abstraction Interface and assign which concrete implementer.
- **Implementer Interface**: The implementer interface that concrete implementers implement.
- **Concrete Implementer**: The implementation logic that the refined abstraction will use.

6.4.3 Bridge UML Diagram

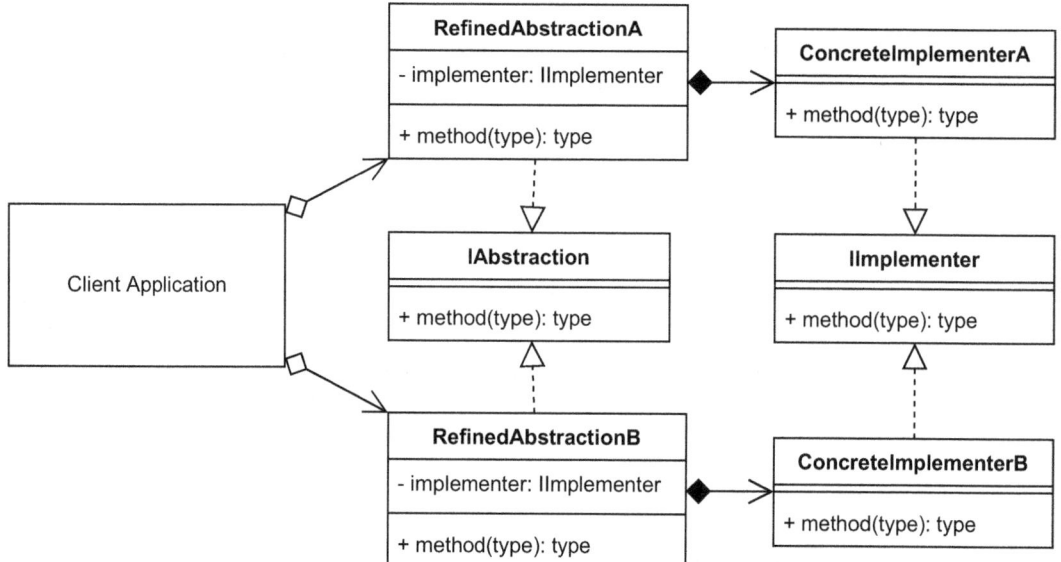

6.4.4 Source Code

In the concept demonstration code, imagine that the classes were tightly coupled. The concrete class would print out some text to the console.

After abstracting the class along a common ground, it is now more versatile. The implementation has been separated from the abstraction, and now it can print out the same text in two different ways.

The benefit now is that each refined abstraction and implementer can now be worked on independently without affecting the other implementations.

./src/bridge/bridge-concept.ts

```
// Bridge Pattern Concept Sample Code
```

```
interface IAbstraction {
    method(value: string[]): void
}

class RefinedAbstractionA implements IAbstraction {
    #implementer: IImplementer

    constructor(implementer: IImplementer) {
        this.#implementer = implementer
    }

    method(value: string[]) {
        this.#implementer.method(value)
    }
}

class RefinedAbstractionB implements IAbstraction {
    #implementer: IImplementer

    constructor(implementer: IImplementer) {
        this.#implementer = implementer
    }

    method(value: string[]) {
        this.#implementer.method(value)
    }
}

interface IImplementer {
    method(value: string[]): void
}

class ConcreteImplementerA implements IImplementer {
    method(value: string[]) {
        console.log(value)
    }
}

class ConcreteImplementerB implements IImplementer {
    method(value: string[]) {
        value.forEach((v) => console.log(v))
    }
}

// The Client
const VALUES = ['a', 'b', 'c']

const REFINED_ABSTRACTION_A = new RefinedAbstractionA(new
ConcreteImplementerA())
```

```
REFINED_ABSTRACTION_A.method(VALUES)

const REFINED_ABSTRACTION_B = new RefinedAbstractionB(new
ConcreteImplementerB())
REFINED_ABSTRACTION_B.method(VALUES)
```

6.4.5 Output

```
node ./dist/bridge/bridge-concept.js
[ 'a', 'b', 'c' ]
a
b
c
```

6.4.6 Bridge Use Case

SBCODE Video ID #96a335

In this example, I draw a square and a circle. Both of these can be categorized as shapes.

The shape is set up as the abstraction interface. The refined abstractions, `Square` and `Circle`, implement the `IShape` interface.

When the Square and Circle objects are created, they are also assigned their appropriate implementers being `SquareImplementer` and `CircleImplementer`.

When each shape's `draw` method is called, the equivalent method within their implementer is called.

The Square and Circle are bridged and each implementer and abstraction can be worked on independently.

6.4.7 Example UML Diagram

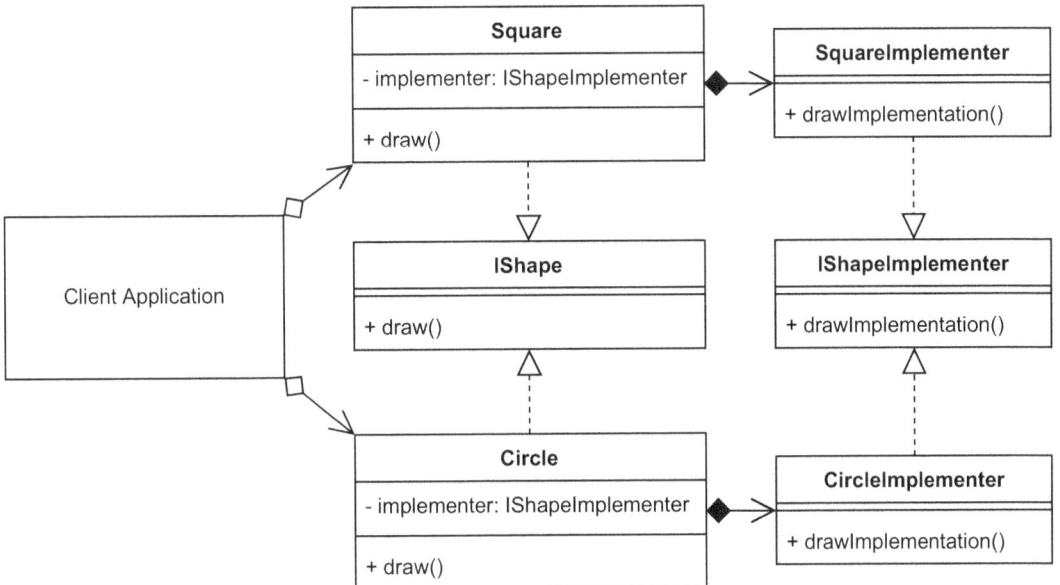

6.4.8 Source Code

./src/bridge/client.ts

```ts
// Bridge Pattern Concept Sample Code

import CircleImplementer from './circle-implementer'
import SquareImplementer from './square-implementer'
import Circle from './circle'
import Square from './square'

const CIRCLE = new Circle(new CircleImplementer())
CIRCLE.draw()

const SQUARE = new Square(new SquareImplementer())
SQUARE.draw()
```

./src/bridge/circle-implementer.ts

```ts
import IShapeImplementor from './ishape-implementer'

export default class CircleImplementer implements IShapeImplementor {
    drawImplementation(): void {
        console.log('    ******')
        console.log('   **    **')
        console.log('  *        *')
```

```
            console.log('*              *')
            console.log('*              *')
            console.log(' *            *')
            console.log('  **        **')
            console.log('    ******')
    }
}
```

./src/bridge/square-implementer.ts

```typescript
import IShapeImplementer from './ishape-implementer'

export default class SquareImplementer implements IShapeImplementer {
    drawImplementation(): void {
        console.log('**************')
        console.log('*            *')
        console.log('*            *')
        console.log('*            *')
        console.log('*            *')
        console.log('*            *')
        console.log('*            *')
        console.log('**************')
    }
}
```

./src/bridge/circle.ts

```typescript
// A Circle Abstraction

import IShape from './ishape'
import IShapeImplementor from './ishape-implementer'

export default class Circle implements IShape {
    #implementer: IShapeImplementor

    constructor(implementer: IShapeImplementor) {
        this.#implementer = implementer
    }

    draw(): void {
        this.#implementer.drawImplementation()
    }
}
```

./src/bridge/square.ts

```typescript
// A Square Abstraction

import IShape from './ishape'
import IShapeImplementor from './ishape-implementer'

export default class Square implements IShape {
    #implementer: IShapeImplementor

    constructor(implementer: IShapeImplementor) {
        this.#implementer = implementer
    }

    draw(): void {
        this.#implementer.drawImplementation()
    }
}
```

./src/bridge/ishape-implementer.ts

```typescript
// The Shape Implementor Interface

export default interface IShapeImplementor {
    drawImplementation(): void
}
```

./src/bridge/ishape.ts

```typescript
// The Shape Abstraction Interface

export default interface IShape {
    draw(): void
}
```

6.4.9 Output

```
node ./dist/bridge/client.js
    ******
  **      **
 *          *
*            *
*            *
 *          *
```

6.4.10 Summary

- Use when you want to separate a solution where the abstraction and implementation may be tightly coupled, and you want to break it up into smaller conceptual parts.

- Once you have added the bridge abstraction, you should be able to extend each side of it separately without breaking the other.

- Also, once the bridge abstraction exists, you can more easily create extra concrete implementations for other similar products that may also happen to be split across similar conceptual lines.

- The Bridge pattern is similar to the adapter pattern except in the intent that you developed it. The bridge is an approach to refactor already existing code, whereas the adapter adapts to the existing code through its existing interfaces and methods without changing the internals.

6.5 Composite Design Pattern

6.5.1 Overview

SBCODE Video ID #a8068a

The **Composite** design pattern is a structural pattern useful for hierarchical management.

The Composite design pattern,

- Allows you to represent individual entities(leaves) and groups of leaves as the same.
- Is a structural design pattern that lets you compose objects into a changeable tree structure.
- Is great if you need the option of swapping hierarchical relationships around.
- Allows you to add/remove components to the hierarchy.
- Provides flexibility of structure

Examples of using the Composite Design Pattern can be seen in a file system directory structure where you can swap the hierarchy of files and folders, and also in a drawing program where you can group, ungroup, transform objects and change multiple objects at the same time.

6.5.2 Terminology

- **Component Interface**: The interface that all leaves and composites should implement.
- **Leaf**: A single object that can exist inside or outside a composite.
- **Composite**: A collection of leaves and/or other composites.

6.5.3 Composite UML Diagram

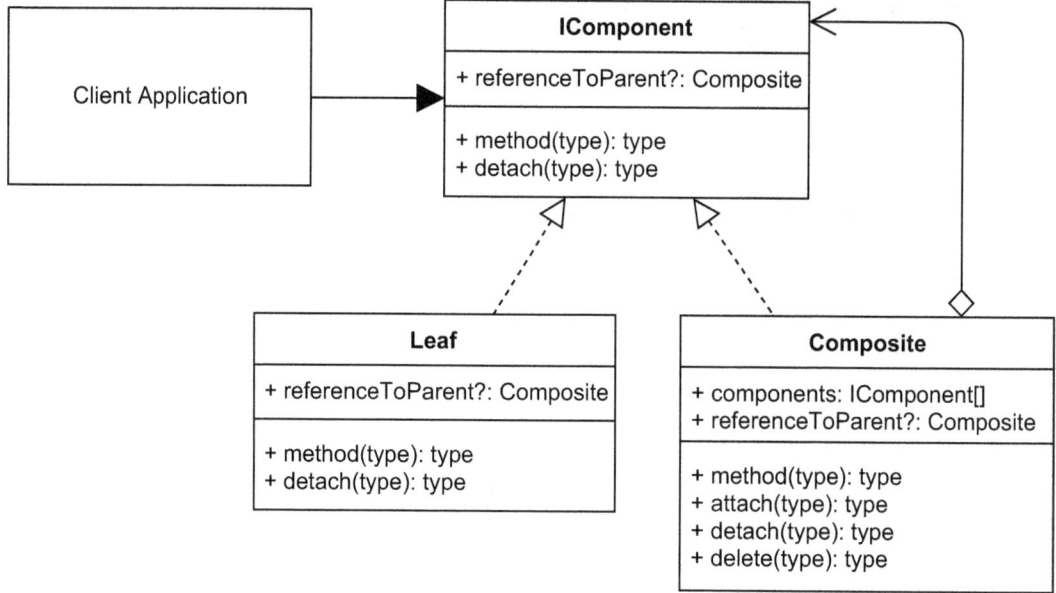

6.5.4 Source Code

In this concept code, two leaves are created, `LEAF_A` and `LEAF_B`, and two composites are created, `COMPOSITE_1` and `COMPOSITE_2`.

`LEAF_A` is attached to `COMPOSITE_1`.

Then I change my mind and attach `LEAF_A` to `COMPOSITE_2`.

I then attach `COMPOSITE_1` to `COMPOSITE_2`.

`LEAF_B` is not attached to composites.

./src/composite/composite-concept.ts

```typescript
// The Composite pattern concept

interface ICompositeComponent {
    // A component interface describing the common
    // fields and methods of leaves and composites
    name: string // A name for this component
    referenceToParent?: Composite // Parents are composites, and not leaves
    method():
void // A method each Leaf and composite container should implement
    detach(): void // Called before a leaf is attached to a composite
```

```typescript
}

class Leaf implements ICompositeComponent {
    // A Leaf can be added to a composite, but not a leaf
    referenceToParent?: Composite = undefined
    name: string
    constructor(name: string) {
        this.name = name
    }

    method(): void {
        const parent = this.referenceToParent ? 
this.referenceToParent.name : 'none'
        console.log(`<Leaf>\t\tname:${this.name}\tParent:\t${parent}`)
    }

    detach(): void {
        // Detaching this leaf from its parent composite
        if (this.referenceToParent) {
            this.referenceToParent.delete(this)
        }
    }
}

class Composite implements ICompositeComponent {
    // A composite can contain leaves and composites

    referenceToParent?: Composite
    components: ICompositeComponent[]
    name: string

    constructor(name: string) {
        this.name = name
        this.components = []
    }

    method(): void {
        const parent = this.referenceToParent ? 
this.referenceToParent.name : 'none'
        console.log(
            `<Composite>\tname:${this.name}\tParent:\t${parent}\tComponents:${this.components.length}`
        )
        this.components.forEach((component) => {
            component.method()
        })
    }

    attach(component: ICompositeComponent): void {
```

```typescript
            // Detach leaf/composite from any current parent reference and
            // then set the parent reference to this composite
            component.detach()
            component.referenceToParent = this
            this.components.push(component)
    }

    delete(component: ICompositeComponent): void {
        // Removes leaf/composite from this composite this.components
        const index = this.components.indexOf(component)
        if (index > -1) {
            this.components.splice(index, 1)
        }
    }

    detach(): void {
        // Detaching this composite from its parent composite
        if (this.referenceToParent) {
            this.referenceToParent.delete(this)
            this.referenceToParent = undefined
        }
    }
}

// The Client
const LEAF_A = new Leaf('leaf-a')
const LEAF_B = new Leaf('leaf-b')
const COMPOSITE_1 = new Composite('comp-1')
const COMPOSITE_2 = new Composite('comp-2')

// Attach LEAF_A to COMPOSITE_1
COMPOSITE_1.attach(LEAF_A)

// Instead, attach LEAF_A to COMPOSITE_2
COMPOSITE_2.attach(LEAF_A)

// Attach COMPOSITE1 to COMPOSITE_2
COMPOSITE_2.attach(COMPOSITE_1)

// Run the methods that
LEAF_B.method() // not in any composites
COMPOSITE_2.method() // COMPOSITE_2 contains both COMPOSITE_1 and
LEAF_A
```

6.5.5 Output

```
node ./dist/composite/composite-concept.js
<Leaf>          name:leaf-b      Parent: none
```

```
<Composite>      name:comp-2    Parent: none    Components:2
<Leaf>           name:leaf-a    Parent: comp-2
<Composite>      name:comp-1    Parent: comp-2  Components:0
```

6.5.6 Composite Use Case

SBCODE Video ID #a0767c

Demonstration of a simple in memory hierarchical file system.

A root object is created that is a composite.

Several files (leaves) are created and added to the root folder.

More folders (composites) are created, and more files are added, and then the hierarchy is reordered.

6.5.7 Composite Example UML Diagram

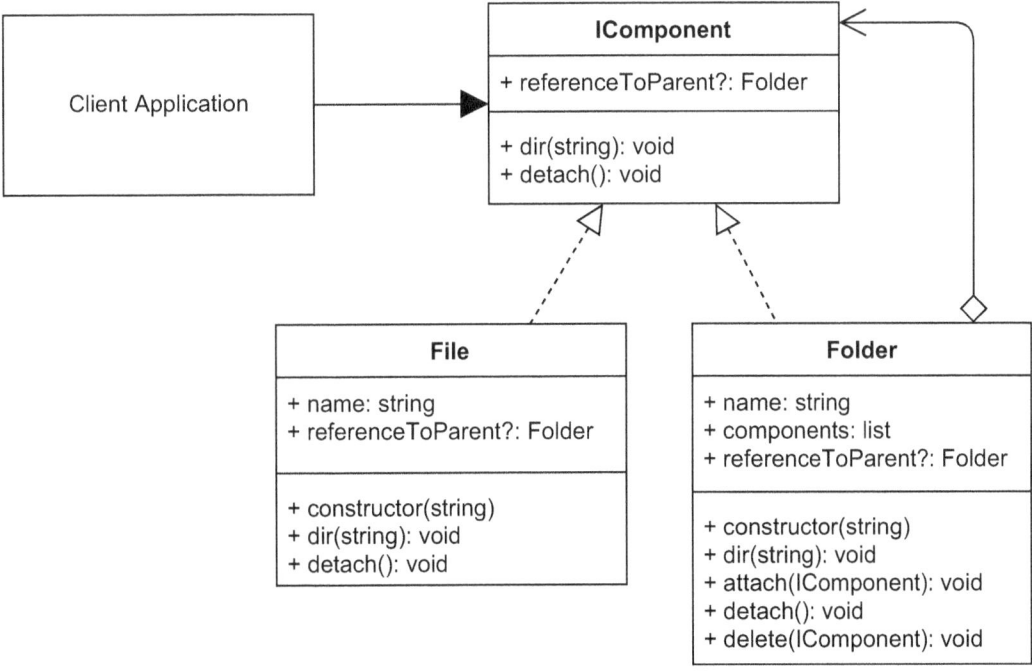

6.5.8 Source Code

./src/composite/client.ts

```
// A use case of the composite pattern.

import File from './file'
import Folder from './folder'
```

```
const FILESYSTEM = new Folder('root')
const FILE_1 = new File('abc.txt')
const FILE_2 = new File('123.txt')
FILESYSTEM.attach(FILE_1)
FILESYSTEM.attach(FILE_2)
const FOLDER_A = new Folder('folder_a')
FILESYSTEM.attach(FOLDER_A)
const FILE_3 = new File('xyz.txt')
FOLDER_A.attach(FILE_3)
const FOLDER_B = new Folder('folder_b')
const FILE_4 = new File('456.txt')
FOLDER_B.attach(FILE_4)
FILESYSTEM.attach(FOLDER_B)
FILESYSTEM.dir('')

// now move FOLDER_A and its contents to FOLDER_B
console.log()
FOLDER_B.attach(FOLDER_A)
FILESYSTEM.dir('')
```

./src/composite/file.ts

```
import IComponent from './icomponent'
import Folder from './folder'

export default class File implements IComponent {
    // The File Class. The files are the leaves

    name: string
    referenceToParent?: Folder = undefined

    constructor(name: string) {
        this.name = name
    }

    dir(indent: string): void {
        console.log(`${indent}<FILE> ${this.name}`)
    }

    detach(): void {
        // Detaching this leaf from its parent composite
        if (this.referenceToParent) {
            this.referenceToParent.delete(this)
        }
    }
}
```

./src/composite/folder.ts

```typescript
import IComponent from './icomponent'

export default class Folder implements IComponent {
    // A composite can contain leaves and composites

    referenceToParent?: Folder
    name: string
    components: IComponent[]

    constructor(name: string) {
        this.name = name
        this.components = []
    }

    dir(indent: string): void {
        console.log(`${indent}<DIR>  ${this.name}`)

        this.components.forEach((component) => {
            component.dir(indent + '..')
        })
    }

    attach(component: IComponent): void {
        // Detach leaf / composite from any current parent reference and
        // then set the parent reference to this composite
        component.detach()
        component.referenceToParent = this
        this.components.push(component)
    }

    delete(component: IComponent): void {
        // Removes leaf/composite from this composite this.components
        const index = this.components.indexOf(component)
        if (index > -1) {
            this.components.splice(index, 1)
        }
    }

    detach(): void {
        // Detaching this composite from its parent composite
        if (this.referenceToParent) {
            this.referenceToParent.delete(this)
            this.referenceToParent = undefined
        }
```

        }
    }

./src/composite/icomponent.ts

```
import Folder from './folder'

export default interface IComponent {
    // A component interface describing the common
    // fields and methods of leaves and composites

    referenceToParent?: Folder // Parents are composites, and not leaves

    dir(indent: string): void
    // A method each Leaf and composite container should implement

    detach(): void
    // Called before a leaf is attached to a composite
}
```

6.5.9 Output

```
node ./dist/composite/client.js
<DIR>   root
..<FILE> abc.txt
..<FILE> 123.txt
..<DIR>  folder_a
....<FILE> xyz.txt
..<DIR>  folder_b
....<FILE> 456.txt

<DIR>   root
..<FILE> abc.txt
..<FILE> 123.txt
..<DIR>  folder_b
....<FILE> 456.txt
....<DIR>  folder_a
......<FILE> xyz.txt
```

6.5.10 Summary

- The Composite design pattern allows you to structure components in a manageable hierarchical order.

- It provides flexibility of structure since you can add/remove and reorder components.
- File explorer on Windows is a very good example of the composite design pattern in use.
- Any system where you need to offer at runtime the ability to group, ungroup, modify multiple objects at the same time, would benefit from the composite design pattern structure. Programs that allow you to draw shapes and graphics will often also use this structure as well.

6.6 Flyweight Design Pattern

6.6.1 Overview

SBCODE Video ID #98a1c6

Fly in the term **Flyweight** means light/not heavy.

Instead of creating thousands of objects that share common attributes, and result in a situation where a large amount of memory or other resources are used, you can modify your classes to share multiple instances simultaneously by using some kind of reference to the shared object instead.

The best example to describe this is a document containing many words and sentences and made up of many letters. Rather than storing a new object for each individual letter describing its font, position, color, padding and many other potential things. You can store just a lookup ID of a character in a collection of some sort and then dynamically create the object with its proper formatting etc., only as you need to.

This approach saves a lot of memory at the expense of using some extra CPU instead to create the object at presentation time.

The Flyweight pattern, describes how you can share objects rather than creating thousands of almost repeated objects unnecessarily.

A Flyweight acts as an independent object in any number of contexts. A context can be a cell in a table, or a div on an HTML page. A context is using the Flyweight.

You can have many contexts, and when they ask for a Flyweight, they will get an object that may already be shared amongst other contexts, or already within itself somewhere else.

When describing flyweights, it is useful to describe it in terms of intrinsic and extrinsic attributes.

Intrinsic (in or including) are the attributes of a flyweight that are internal and unique from the other flyweights. E.g., a new flyweight for every letter of the alphabet. Each letter is intrinsic to the flyweight.

Extrinsic (outside or external) are the attributes that are used to present the flyweight in terms of the context where it will be used. E.g., many letters in a string can be right aligned with each other. The extrinsic property of each letter is the new positioning of its X and Y on a grid.

6.6.2 Terminology

- **Flyweight Interface**: An interface that describes the intrinsic properties of the flyweight.
- **Concrete Flyweight**: The actual flyweight object that stores the intrinsic attributes and is instantiated when needed by the factory.

- **Flyweight Factory**: Creates and manages the flyweights at runtime. It reuses flyweights or creates a new one on demand.
- **Context**: Any object(s) within your application that will use the Flyweight Factory.
- **Client**: The client application that contains contexts.

6.6.3 Flyweight UML Diagram

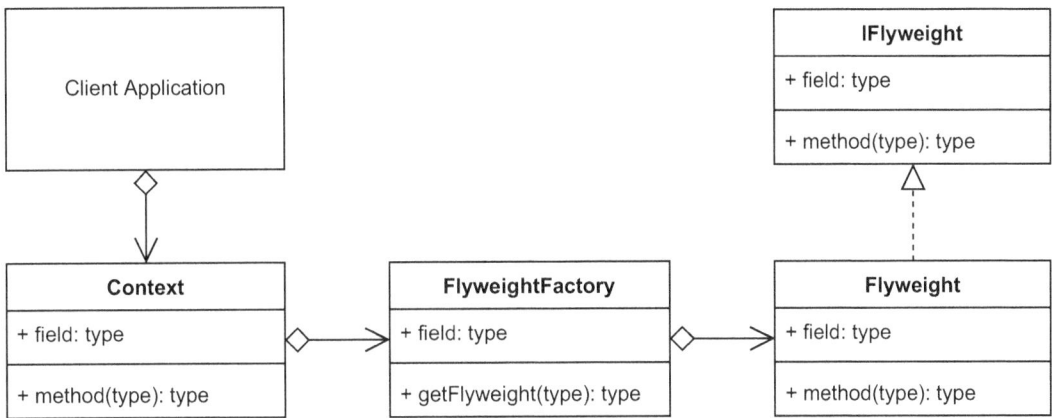

6.6.4 Source Code

A context is created using the string `abracadabra`.

As it is output, it asks the Flyweight factory for the next character. The Flyweight factory will either return an existing Flyweight, or create a new one before returning it.

`abracadabra` has many re-used characters, so only 5 flyweights needed to be created.

./src/flyweight/flyweight-concept.ts

```
// The Flyweight Concept

interface IFlyweight {
    code: number
}

class Flyweight implements IFlyweight {
    // The Concrete Flyweight
    code: number
    constructor(code: number) {
        this.code = code
    }
}
```

```typescript
class FlyweightFactory {
    // Creating the FlyweightFactory as a static class

    static flyweights: { [id: number]: Flyweight } = {}

    static getFlyweight(code: number): Flyweight {
        // A static method to get a flyweight based on a code
        if (!(code in FlyweightFactory.flyweights)) {
            FlyweightFactory.flyweights[code] = new Flyweight(code)
        }
        return FlyweightFactory.flyweights[code]
    }

    static getCount(): number {
        // Return the number of flyweights in the cache
        return Object.keys(FlyweightFactory.flyweights).length
    }
}

class AppContext {
    // An example context that holds references to the flyweights in a
    // particular order and converts the code to an ascii letter
    private codes: number[] = []

    constructor(codes: string) {
        for (let i = 0; i < codes.length; i++) {
            this.codes.push(codes.charCodeAt(i))
        }
    }

    output() {
        // The context specific output that uses flyweights
        let ret = ''
        this.codes.forEach((c) => {
            ret = ret +
String.fromCharCode(FlyweightFactory.getFlyweight(c).code)
        })

        return ret
    }
}

// The Client
const APP_CONTEXT = new AppContext('abracadabra')

// use flyweights in a context
console.log(APP_CONTEXT.output())

console.log(`abracadabra has ${'abracadabra'.length} letters`)
```

```
console.log(`FlyweightFactory has ${FlyweightFactory.getCount()}
flyweights`)
```

6.6.5 Output

```
node ./dist/flyweight/flyweight-concept.js
abracadabra
abracadabra has 11 letters
FlyweightFactory has 5 flyweights
```

6.6.6 Flyweight Use Case

SBCODE Video ID #d9ffbd

In this example, I create a dynamic table with 3 rows and 3 columns each. The columns are then filled with some kind of text, and also chosen to be left, right or center aligned.

The letters are the flyweights and only a code indicating the letter is stored. The letters and numbers are shared many times.

The column cells are the contexts, and they pass the extrinsic vales describing the combination of letters, the justification left, right or center, and the width of the table column that is then used for the space padding.

6.6.7 Example UML Diagram

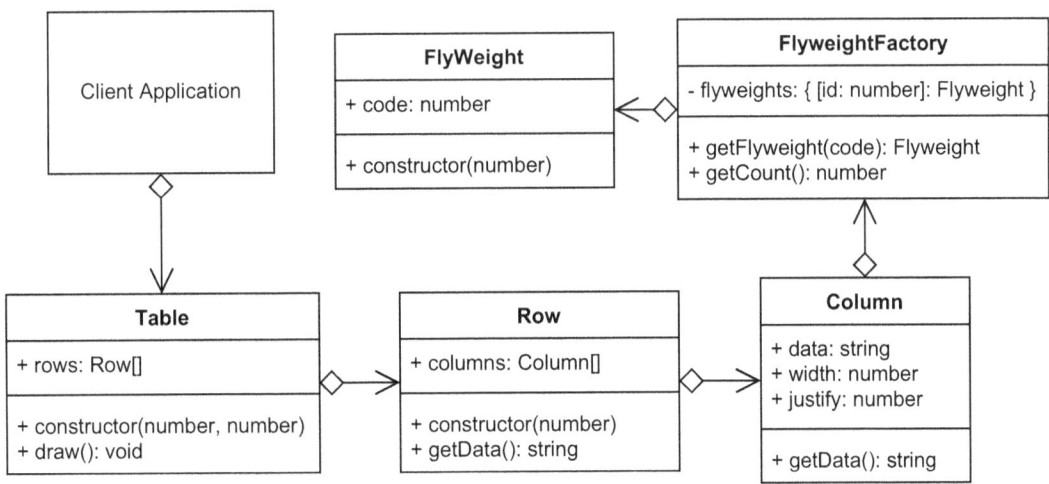

6.6.8 Source Code

./src/flyweight/client.ts

```ts
// The Flyweight Use Case Example

import Table from './table'
import FlyweightFactory from './flyweight-factory'

const TABLE = new Table(3, 3)
TABLE.rows[0].columns[0].data = 'abra'
TABLE.rows[0].columns[1].data = '112233'
TABLE.rows[0].columns[2].data = 'cadabra'
TABLE.rows[1].columns[0].data = 'racadab'
TABLE.rows[1].columns[1].data = '12345'
TABLE.rows[1].columns[2].data = '332211'
TABLE.rows[2].columns[0].data = 'cadabra'
TABLE.rows[2].columns[1].data = '445566'
TABLE.rows[2].columns[2].data = 'aa 22 bb'

TABLE.rows[0].columns[0].justify = 1
TABLE.rows[1].columns[0].justify = 1
TABLE.rows[2].columns[0].justify = 1
TABLE.rows[0].columns[2].justify = 2
TABLE.rows[1].columns[2].justify = 2
TABLE.rows[2].columns[2].justify = 2
TABLE.rows[0].columns[1].width = 15
TABLE.rows[1].columns[1].width = 15
TABLE.rows[2].columns[1].width = 15

TABLE.draw()

console.log(`FlyweightFactory has ${FlyweightFactory.getCount()} flyweights`)
```

./src/flyweight/flyweight.ts

```ts
export default class Flyweight {
    // The Concrete Flyweight
    code: number
    constructor(code: number) {
        this.code = code
    }
}
```

./src/flyweight/flyweight-factory.ts

```ts
import Flyweight from './flyweight'

export default class FlyweightFactory {
```

```typescript
    // Creating the FlyweightFactory as a static class

    static flyweights: { [id: number]: Flyweight } = {}

    static getFlyweight(code: number): Flyweight {
        // A static method to get a flyweight based on a code
        if (!(code in FlyweightFactory.flyweights)) {
            FlyweightFactory.flyweights[code] = new Flyweight(code)
        }
        return FlyweightFactory.flyweights[code]
    }

    static getCount(): number {
        // Return the number of flyweights in the cache
        return Object.keys(FlyweightFactory.flyweights).length
    }
}
```

./src/flyweight/column.ts

```typescript
// A Column that is used in a Row

import FlyweightFactory from './flyweight-factory'

export default class Column {
    // The columns are the contexts.
    // They will share the Flyweights via the FlyweightsFactory.
    // `data`, `width` and `justify` are extrinsic values. They are outside
    // of the flyweights.
    data = ''
    width = 10
    justify = 0

    getData(): string {
        // Get the flyweight value from the factory, and apply the extrinsic values
        const codes = []
        for (let i = 0; i < this.data.length; i++) {
            codes.push(this.data.charCodeAt(i))
        }
        let ret = ''
        Array.from(codes).forEach((c) => {
            ret = ret + String.fromCharCode(FlyweightFactory.getFlyweight(c).code)
        })

        switch (this.justify) {
```

```
                case 1:
                    ret = this.leftAlign(this.width, ret, ' ')
                    break
                case 2:
                    ret = this.rightAlign(this.width, ret, ' ')
                    break
                default:
                    ret = this.center(this.width, ret, ' ')
            }

            return ret
        }

        center(width: number, string: string, padding: string): string {
            return width <= string.length
                ? string
                : this.centerAlternate(width, padding + string, padding)
        }
        centerAlternate(width: number, string: string, padding: string):
    string {
            return width <= string.length
                ? string
                : this.center(width, string + padding, padding)
        }
        leftAlign(width: number, string: string, padding: string): string {
            return width <= string.length
                ? string
                : this.leftAlign(width, string + padding, padding)
        }
        rightAlign(width: number, string: string, padding: string): string
    {
            return width <= string.length
                ? string
                : this.rightAlign(width, padding + string, padding)
        }
    }
```

./src/flyweight/row.ts

```
// A Row in the Table

import Column from './column'

export default class Row {
    columns: Column[]

    constructor(column_count: number) {
        this.columns = []
```

```
        for (let i = 0; i < column_count; i++) {
            this.columns.push(new Column())
        }
    }
    getData(): string {
        // Format the row before returning it to the table
        let ret = ''
        this.columns.forEach((column) => {
            ret = `${ret}${column.getData()}|`
        })
        return ret
    }
}
```

./src/flyweight/table.ts

```
// A Formatted Table

import Row from './row'

export default class Table {
    rows: Row[]

    constructor(row_count: number, column_count: number) {
        this.rows = []
        for (let i = 0; i < row_count; i++) {
            this.rows.push(new Row(column_count))
        }
    }

    draw(): void {
        // Draws the table formatted in the console
        let maxRowLength = 0
        const rows: string[] = []
        this.rows.forEach((row) => {
            const rowData = row.getData()
            rows.push(`|${rowData}`)
            const rowLength = rowData.length + 1
            if (maxRowLength < rowLength) {
                maxRowLength = rowLength
            }
        })
        console.log('-'.repeat(maxRowLength))
        rows.forEach((row) => {
            console.log(row)
        })
        console.log('-'.repeat(maxRowLength))
```

    }
}
```

## 6.6.9 Output

```
node ./dist/flyweight/client.js
---------------------------------------
|abra      |     112233    |   cadabra|
|racadab   |     12345     |    332211|
|cadabra   |     445566    |  aa 22 bb|
---------------------------------------
FlyweightFactory has 12 flyweights
```

6.6.10 Summary

- Clients should access Flyweight objects only the through a `FlyweightFactory` object to ensure that they are shared.

- Intrinsic values are stored internally in the Flyweight.

- Extrinsic values are passed to the Flyweight and customize it depending on the context.

- Implementing the flyweight is a balance between storing all objects in memory, versus storing small unique parts in memory, and potentially calculating extrinsic values in the context objects.

- Use the flyweight to save memory when it is beneficial. The offset is that extra CPU may be required during calculating and passing extrinsic values to the flyweights.

- The flyweight reduces memory footprint because it shares objects and allows the possibility of dynamically creating extrinsic attributes.

- The contexts will generally calculate the extrinsic values used by the flyweights, but it is not necessary. Values can be stored or referenced from other objects if necessary.

- When architecting the flyweight, start with considering which parts of a common object may be able to be split and applied using extrinsic attributes.
```

6.7 Proxy Design Pattern

6.7.1 Overview

SBCODE Video ID #c0f2d0

The **Proxy** design pattern is a class functioning as an interface to another class or object.

A Proxy could be for anything, such as a network connection, an object in memory, a file, or anything else you need to provide an abstraction between.

Types of proxies,

- **Virtual Proxy**: An object that can cache parts of the real object, and then complete loading the full object when necessary.
- **Remote Proxy**: Can relay messages to a real object that exists in a different address space.
- **Protection Proxy**: Apply an authentication layer in front of the real object.
- **Smart Reference**: An object whose internal attributes can be overridden or replaced.

Additional functionality can be provided at the proxy abstraction if required. E.g., caching, authorization, validation, lazy initialization, logging.

The proxy should implement the subject interface as much as possible so that the proxy and subject appear identical to the client.

The Proxy Pattern can also be called **Monkey Patching** or **Object Augmentation**

6.7.2 Terminology

- **Proxy**: An object with an interface identical to the real subject. Can act as a placeholder until the real subject is loaded or as gatekeeper applying extra functionality.
- **Subject Interface**: An interface implemented by both the Proxy and Real Subject.
- **Real Subject**: The actual real object that the proxy is representing.
- **Client**: The client application that uses and creates the Proxy.

6.7.3 Proxy UML Diagram

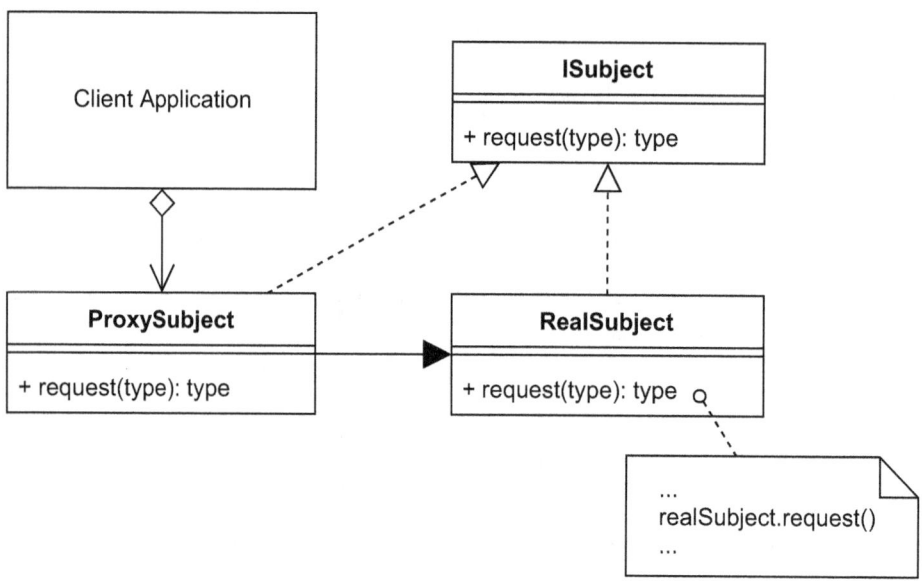

6.7.4 Source Code

This concept example will simulate a virtual proxy. The real subject will be called via the proxy. The first time the request is made, the proxy will retrieve the data from the real subject. The second time it is called, it will return the data from the proxies own cache which it created from the first request.

./src/proxy/proxy-concept.ts

```typescript
// A Proxy Concept Example

interface ISubject {
    // An interface implemented by both the Proxy and Real Subject
    request(): void
    // A method to implement
}

class RealSubject implements ISubject {
    // The actual real object that the proxy is representing

    enormousData: number[]

    constructor() {
        // hypothetically enormous amounts of data
        this.enormousData = [1, 2, 3]
    }

    request() {
```

```typescript
            return this.enormousData
    }
}

class ProxySubject implements ISubject {
    // In this case the proxy will act as a cache for
    // `enormous_data` and only populate the enormous_data when it
    // is actually necessary

    enormousData: number[]
    realSubject: RealSubject

    constructor() {
        this.enormousData = []
        this.realSubject = new RealSubject()
    }
    request() {
        // Using the proxy as a cache, and loading data into it only if
        // it is needed
        if (this.enormousData.length === 0) {
            console.log('pulling data from RealSubject')
            this.enormousData = this.realSubject.request()
            return this.enormousData
        }
        console.log('pulling data from Proxy cache')
        return this.enormousData
    }
}

// The Client
const PROXY_SUBJECT = new ProxySubject()
// Use the Subject. First time it will load the enormous amounts of
data
console.log(PROXY_SUBJECT.request())
// Use the Subject again, but this time it retrieves it from the local
cache
console.log(PROXY_SUBJECT.request())
```

6.7.5 Output

```
node ./dist/proxy/proxy-concept.js
pulling data from RealSubject
[ 1, 2, 3 ]
pulling data from Proxy cache
[ 1, 2, 3 ]
```

6.7.6 Proxy Use Case

SBCODE Video ID #883f9a

In this example, I dynamically change the class of an object. So, I am essentially using an object as a proxy to other classes.

Every time the `tell_me_the_future()` method is called; it will randomly change the object to use a different class.

The object `PROTEUS` will then use the same static attributes and class methods of the new class instead.

6.7.7 Example UML Diagram

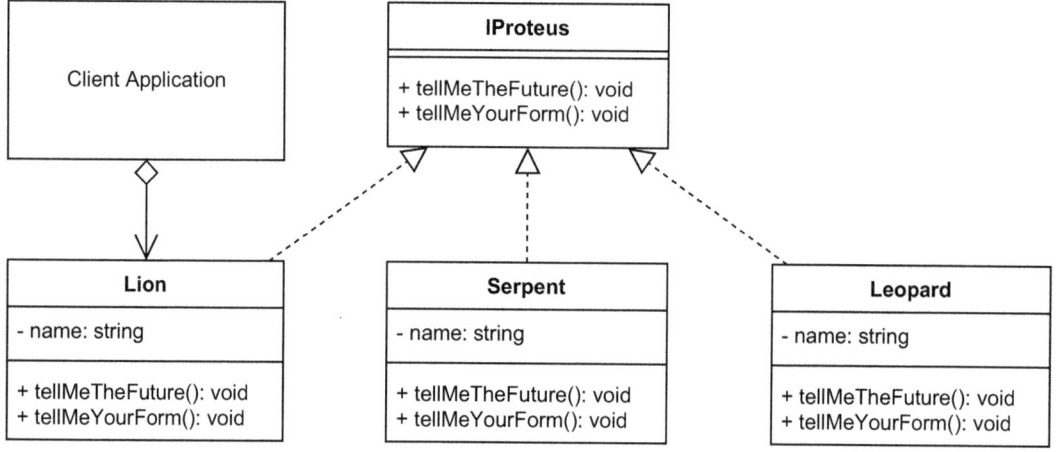

6.7.8 Source Code

./src/proxy/client.ts

```
import Lion from './lion'

const PROTEUS = new Lion()
PROTEUS.tellMeYourForm()
PROTEUS.tellMeTheFuture()
PROTEUS.tellMeYourForm()
PROTEUS.tellMeTheFuture()
PROTEUS.tellMeYourForm()
PROTEUS.tellMeTheFuture()
PROTEUS.tellMeYourForm()
PROTEUS.tellMeTheFuture()
PROTEUS.tellMeYourForm()
PROTEUS.tellMeTheFuture()
PROTEUS.tellMeYourForm()
```

```
PROTEUS.tellMeTheFuture()
PROTEUS.tellMeYourForm()
```

./src/proxy/iproteus.ts

```typescript
// The Proteus Interface
export default interface IProteus {
    // A Greek mythological character that can change to many forms

    tellMeTheFuture(): void
    // Proteus will change form rather than tell you the future

    tellMeYourForm(): void
    // The form of Proteus is elusive like the sea
}
```

./src/proxy/lion.ts

```typescript
import IProteus from './iproteus'
import Leopard from './leopard'
import Serpent from './serpent'

export default class Lion implements IProteus {
    // Proteus in the form of a Lion

    name = 'Lion'

    tellMeTheFuture(): void {
        // Proteus will change to something random
        if (Math.floor(Math.random() * 2)) {
            Object.assign(this, new Serpent())
            this.tellMeTheFuture = Serpent.prototype.tellMeTheFuture
            this.tellMeYourForm = Serpent.prototype.tellMeYourForm
        } else {
            Object.assign(this, new Leopard())
            this.tellMeTheFuture = Leopard.prototype.tellMeTheFuture
            this.tellMeYourForm = Leopard.prototype.tellMeYourForm
        }
    }

    tellMeYourForm(): void {
        console.log(`I am the form of ${this.name}`)
    }
}
```

./src/proxy/serpent.ts

```typescript
import IProteus from './iproteus'
import Leopard from './leopard'
import Lion from './lion'

export default class Serpent implements IProteus {
    // Proteus in the form of a Serpent

    name = 'Serpent'

    tellMeTheFuture(): void {
        // Proteus will change to something random
        if (Math.floor(Math.random() * 2)) {
            Object.assign(this, new Leopard())
            this.tellMeTheFuture = Leopard.prototype.tellMeTheFuture
            this.tellMeYourForm = Leopard.prototype.tellMeYourForm
        } else {
            Object.assign(this, new Lion())
            this.tellMeTheFuture = Lion.prototype.tellMeTheFuture
            this.tellMeYourForm = Lion.prototype.tellMeYourForm
        }
    }

    tellMeYourForm(): void {
        console.log(`I am the form of ${this.name}`)
    }
}
```

./src/proxy/leopard.ts

```typescript
import IProteus from './iproteus'
import Lion from './lion'
import Serpent from './serpent'

export default class Leopard implements IProteus {
    // Proteus in the form of a Leopard

    name = 'Leopard'

    tellMeTheFuture(): void {
        // Proteus will change to something random
        if (Math.floor(Math.random() * 2)) {
            Object.assign(this, new Lion())
            this.tellMeTheFuture = Lion.prototype.tellMeTheFuture
            this.tellMeYourForm = Lion.prototype.tellMeYourForm
        } else {
```

```
            Object.assign(this, new Serpent())
            this.tellMeTheFuture = Serpent.prototype.tellMeTheFuture
            this.tellMeYourForm = Serpent.prototype.tellMeYourForm
        }
    }

    tellMeYourForm(): void {
        console.log(`I am the form of ${this.name}`)
    }
}
```

6.7.9 Output

```
node ./dist/proxy/client.js
I am the form of Lion
I am the form of Serpent
I am the form of Lion
I am the form of Serpent
I am the form of Leopard
I am the form of Lion
I am the form of Leopard
```

6.7.10 Summary

- Proxy forwards requests onto the Real Subject when applicable, depending on the kind of proxy.
- A virtual proxy can cache elements of a real subject before loading the full object into memory.
- A protection proxy can provide an authentication layer. For example, an NGINX proxy can add Basic Authentication restriction to an HTTP request.
- A proxy can perform multiple tasks if necessary.
- A proxy is different from an Adapter. The Adapter will try to adapt two existing interfaces together. The Proxy will use the same interface as the subject.
- It is also very similar to the Facade, except you can add extra responsibilities, just like the Decorator. The Decorator however can be used recursively.
- The intent of the Proxy is to provide a stand in for when it is inconvenient to access a real subject directly.
- The Proxy design pattern may also be called the Surrogate design pattern.

7. Behavioral

7.1 Command Design Pattern

7.1.1 Overview

SBCODE Video ID #8c8ea3

The **Command** pattern is a behavioral design pattern, in which an abstraction exists between an object that invokes a command, and the object that performs it.

E.g., a button will call the **Invoker**, that will call a pre-registered **Command**, that the **Receiver** will perform.

A Concrete Class will delegate a request to a command object, instead of implementing the request directly.

The command pattern is a good solution for implementing UNDO/REDO functionality into your application.

Uses:

- GUI Buttons, menus
- Macro recording
- Multi-level undo/redo
- Networking - send whole command objects across a network, even as a batch
- Parallel processing or thread pools
- Transactional behavior
- Wizards

7.1.2 Terminology

- **Receiver**: The object that will receive and execute the command.
- **Invoker**: The object that sends the command to the receiver. E.g., A button.
- **Command Object**: Itself, an object, that implements an `execute()`, or other action method, and contains all required information to execute it.
- **Client**: The application or component that is aware of the Receiver, Invoker and Commands.

7.1.3 Command Pattern UML Diagram

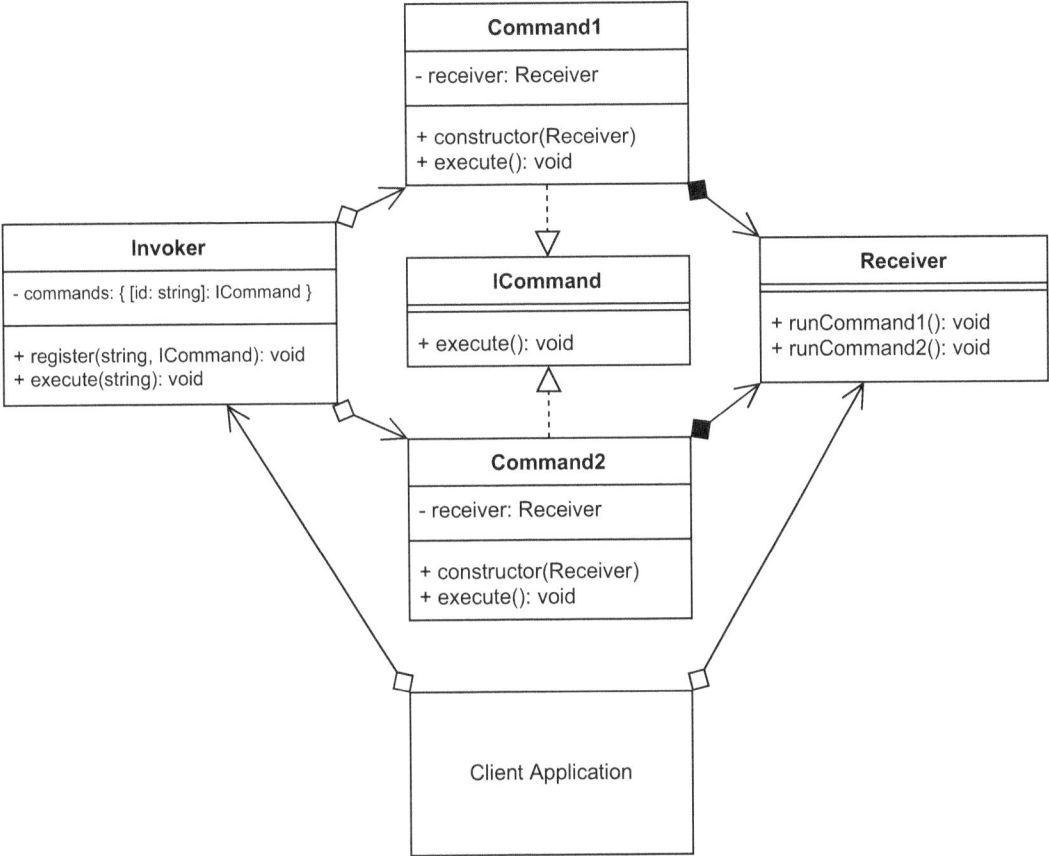

7.1.4 Source Code

The Client instantiates a Receiver that accepts certain commands that do things.

The Client then creates two Command objects that will call one of the specific commands on the Receiver.

The Client then creates an Invoker, E.g., a user interface with buttons, and registers both Commands into the Invokers' dictionary of commands.

The Client doesn't call the receivers commands directly, but the via the Invoker, that then calls the registered Command objects `execute()` method.

This abstraction between the invoker, command and receiver, allows the Invoker to add extra functionality such as history, replay, UNDO/REDO, logging, alerting and any other useful things that may be required.

./src/command/command-concept.ts

7.1.4 Source Code

```
// The Command Pattern Concept

interface ICommand {
    execute(): void
}

class Invoker {
    // The Invoker Class
    #commands: { [id: string]: ICommand }

    constructor() {
        this.#commands = {}
    }

    register(commandName: string, command: ICommand) {
        // Register commands in the Invoker
        this.#commands[commandName] = command
    }

    execute(commandName: string) {
        // Execute any registered commands
        if (commandName in this.#commands) {
            this.#commands[commandName].execute()
        } else {
            console.log(`Command [${commandName}] not recognised`)
        }
    }
}

class Receiver {
    // The Receiver

    runCommand1() {
        // A set of instructions to run
        console.log('Executing Command 1')
    }

    runCommand2() {
        // A set of instructions to run
        console.log('Executing Command 2')
    }
}

class Command1 implements ICommand {
    // A Command object, that implements the ICommand interface and
    // runs the command on the designated receiver

    #receiver: Receiver
```

```
    constructor(receiver: Receiver) {
        this.#receiver = receiver
    }

    execute() {
        this.#receiver.runCommand1()
    }
}

class Command2 implements ICommand {
    // A Command object, that implements the ICommand interface and
    // runs the command on the designated receiver

    #receiver: Receiver

    constructor(receiver: Receiver) {
        this.#receiver = receiver
    }

    execute() {
        this.#receiver.runCommand2()
    }
}

// The Client
// Create a receiver
const RECEIVER = new Receiver()

// Create Commands
const COMMAND1 = new Command1(RECEIVER)
const COMMAND2 = new Command2(RECEIVER)

// Register the commands with the invoker
const INVOKER = new Invoker()
INVOKER.register('1', COMMAND1)
INVOKER.register('2', COMMAND2)

// Execute the commands that are registered on the Invoker
INVOKER.execute('1')
INVOKER.execute('2')
INVOKER.execute('1')
INVOKER.execute('2')
```

7.1.5 Output

```
node ./dist/command/command-concept.js
Executing Command 1
Executing Command 2
```

```
Executing Command 1
Executing Command 2
```

7.1.6 Command Use Case

SBCODE Video ID #30566d

This will be a smart light switch.

This light switch will keep a history of each time one of its commands was called.

And it can replay its commands.

A smart light switch could be extended in the future to be called remotely or automated depending on sensors.

7.1.7 Example UML Diagram

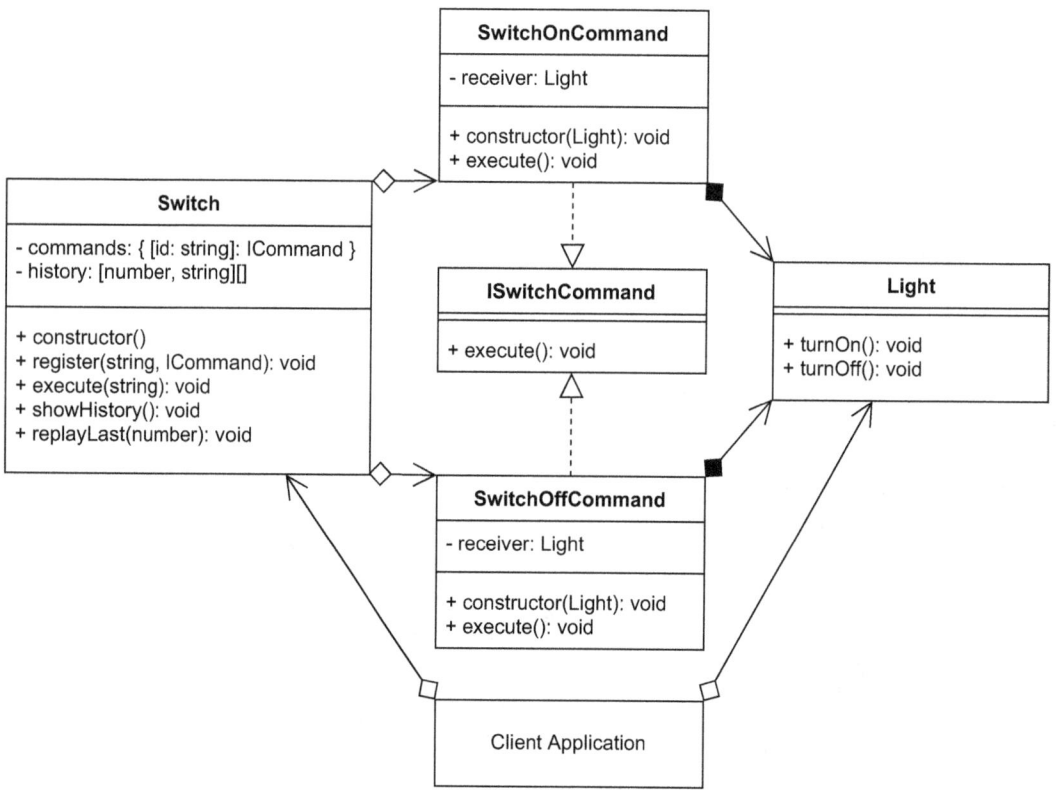

7.1.8 Source Code

./src/command/client.ts

```typescript
// The Command Pattern Use Case Example. A smart light Switch

import Light from './light'
import Switch from './switch'
import SwitchOnCommand from './switch-on-command'
import SwitchOffCommand from './switch-off-command'

// Create a receiver
const LIGHT = new Light()

// Create Commands
const SWITCH_ON = new SwitchOnCommand(LIGHT)
const SWITCH_OFF = new SwitchOffCommand(LIGHT)

// Register the commands with the invoker
const SWITCH = new Switch()
SWITCH.register('ON', SWITCH_ON)
SWITCH.register('OFF', SWITCH_OFF)

// Execute the commands that are registered on the Invoker
SWITCH.execute('ON')
SWITCH.execute('OFF')
SWITCH.execute('ON')
SWITCH.execute('OFF')

// show history
SWITCH.showHistory()

// replay last two executed commands
SWITCH.replayLast(2)
```

./src/command/light.ts

```typescript
// The Light. The Receiver

export default class Light {
    turnOn(): void {
        // A set of instructions to run
        console.log('Light turned ON')
    }

    turnOff(): void {
        // A set of instructions to run
        console.log('Light turned OFF')
    }
}
```

./src/command/switch.ts

```typescript
// The Switch (Invoker) Class.

import ICommand from './icommand'

export default class Switch {
    #commands: { [id: string]: ICommand }
    #history: [number, string][]

    constructor() {
        this.#commands = {}
        this.#history = []
    }

    showHistory(): void {
        // Print the history of each time a command was invoked"
        this.#history.forEach((row) => {
            console.log(`${row[0]} : ${row[1]}`)
        })
    }

    register(commandName: string, command: ICommand): void {
        // Register commands in the Invoker
        this.#commands[commandName] = command
    }

    execute(commandName: string): void {
        // Execute any registered commands
        if (commandName in this.#commands) {
            this.#commands[commandName].execute()
            this.#history.push([Date.now(), commandName])
        } else {
            console.log(`Command [${commandName}] not recognised`)
        }
    }

    replayLast(numberOfCommands: number): void {
        // Replay the last N commands
        const commands = this.#history.slice(
            this.#history.length - numberOfCommands,
            this.#history.length
        )
        commands.forEach((command) => {
            this.#commands[command[1]].execute()
            // or if you wanted to also record this replay in history
            // this.execute(command[1])
        })
```

```
        }
    }
```

./src/command/icommand.ts

```
    export default interface ICommand {
        execute(): void
    }
```

./src/command/iswitch-command.ts

```
    export default interface ISwitchCommand {
        execute(commandName: string): void
    }
```

./src/command/switch-on-command.ts

```
    import ISwitchCommand from './iswitch-command'
    import Light from './light'

    export default class SwitchOnCommand implements ISwitchCommand {
        #light: Light

        constructor(light: Light) {
            this.#light = light
        }

        execute(): void {
            this.#light.turnOn()
        }
    }
```

./src/command/switch-off-command.ts

```
    import ISwitchCommand from './iswitch-command'
    import Light from './light'

    export default class SwitchOffCommand implements ISwitchCommand {
        #light: Light

        constructor(light: Light) {
            this.#light = light
        }
```

```
    execute(): void {
        this.#light.turnOff()
    }
}
```

7.1.9 Output

```
node ./dist/command/client.js
Light turned ON
Light turned OFF
Light turned ON
Light turned OFF
1619288201312 : ON
1619288201313 : OFF
1619288201313 : ON
1619288201313 : OFF
Light turned ON
Light turned OFF
```

7.1.10 Summary

- State should not be managed in the Command object itself.
- There can be one or more Invokers that can execute the Command at a later time.
- The Command object is especially useful if you want to UNDO/REDO commands at later time.
- The Command pattern is similar to the Memento pattern in the way that it can also be used for UNDO/REDO purposes. However, the Memento pattern is about recording and replacing the state of an object, whereas the Command pattern executes a predefined command. E.g., Draw, Turn, Resize, Save, etc.

7.2 Chain of Responsibility Design Pattern

7.2.1 Overview

SBCODE Video ID #e4659e

Chain of Responsibility pattern is a behavioral pattern used to achieve loose coupling in software design.

In this pattern, an object is passed to a **Successor**, and depending on some kind of logic, will or won't be passed onto another successor and processed. There can be any number of different successors and successors can be re-processed recursively.

This process of passing objects through multiple successors is called a chain.

The object that is passed between each successor does not know about which successor will handle it. It is an independent object that may or may not be processed by a particular successor before being passed onto the next.

The chain that the object will pass through is normally dynamic at runtime, although you can hard code the order or start of the chain, so each successor will need to comply with a common interface that allows the object to be received and passed onto the next successor.

7.2.2 Terminology

- **Handler Interface**: A common interface for handling and passing objects through each successor.
- **Concrete Handler**: The class acting as the **Successor** handling the requests and passing onto the next.
- **Client**: The application or class that initiates the call to the first concrete handler (successor) in the chain.

7.2.3 Chain of Responsibility UML Diagram

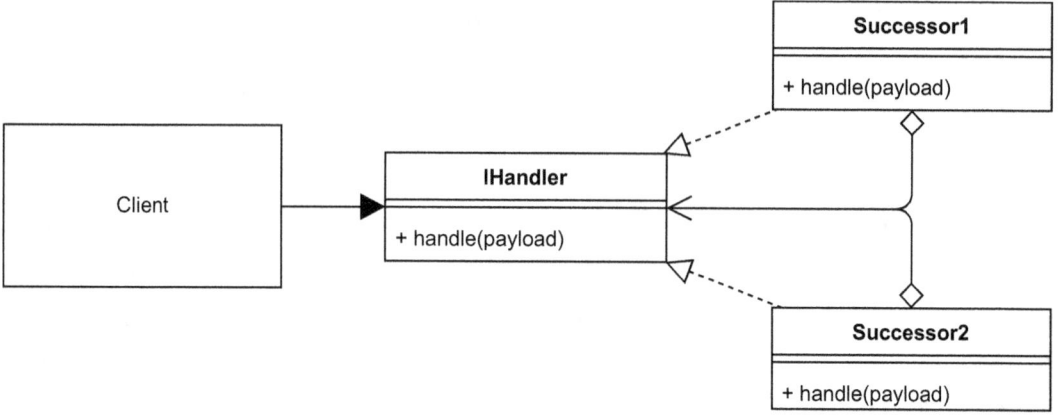

7.2.4 Source Code

In this concept code, a chain is created with a default first successor. A number is passed to a successor, that then does a random test, and depending on the result will modify the number and then pass it onto the next successor. The process is randomized and will end at some point when there are no more successors designated.

./src/chain-of-responsibility/chain-of-responsibility-concept.ts

```typescript
// The Chain Of Responsibility Pattern Concept

interface IHandler {
    // The Handler Interface that the Successors should implement
    handle(payload: number): number
}

class Successor1 implements IHandler {
    // A Concrete Handler
    handle(payload: number) {
        console.log(`Successor1 payload = ${payload}`)
        const test = Math.floor(Math.random() * 2) + 1
        if (test === 1) {
            payload += 1
            payload = new Successor1().handle(payload)
        } else {
            payload -= 1
            payload = new Successor2().handle(payload)
        }
        return payload
    }
}
```

```
class Successor2 implements IHandler {
    // A Concrete Handler
    handle(payload: number) {
        console.log(`Successor2 payload = ${payload}`)
        const test = Math.floor(Math.random() * 3) + 1
        if (test === 1) {
            payload = payload * 2
            payload = new Successor1().handle(payload)
        } else if (test === 2) {
            payload = payload / 2
            payload = new Successor2().handle(payload)
        } // if test = 3 then assign no further successors
        return payload
    }
}

class Chain {
    // A chain with a default first successor
    start(payload: number) {
        // Setting the first successor that will modify the payload
        return new Successor1().handle(payload)
    }
}

// The Client
const CHAIN = new Chain()
const PAYLOAD = 1
const OUT = CHAIN.start(PAYLOAD)
console.log(`Finished result = ${OUT}`)
```

7.2.5 Output

```
node ./dist/chain-of-responsibility/chain-of-responsibility-concept.js
Successor1 payload = 1
Successor2 payload = -1
Successor2 payload = -0.5
Successor2 payload = -0.25
Successor1 payload = -0.5
Successor1 payload = 0.5
Successor2 payload = -1.5
Finished result = -1.5
```

7.2.6 Chain of Responsibility Use Case

SBCODE Video ID #d89543

In the ATM example below, the chain is hard coded in the client first to dispense amounts of £50s, then £20s and then £10s in order.

This default chain order helps to ensure that the minimum number of notes will be dispensed. Otherwise, it might dispense 5 x £10 when it would have been better to dispense 1 x £50.

7.2.7 Example UML Diagram

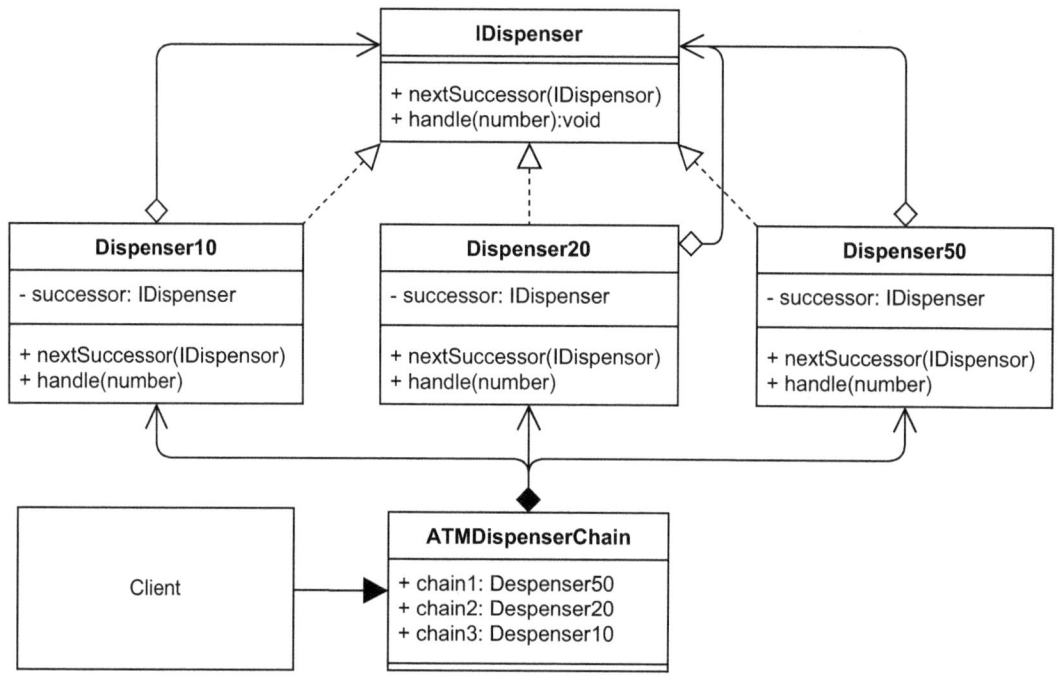

7.2.8 Source Code

./src/chain-of-responsibility/client.ts

```
// An ATM Dispenser that dispenses denominations of notes

import ATMDispenserChain from './atm-dispenser-chain'

const ATM = new ATMDispenserChain()
console.log('Enter amount to withdrawal : ')
process.stdin.on('data', (data: string) => {
    if (parseInt(data)) {
        const amount = parseInt(data)
        if (amount < 10 || amount % 10 != 0) {
            console.log(
                'Amount should be positive and in multiple of 10s.'
            )
        } else {
```

```
            // process the request
            ATM.chain1.handle(amount)
            console.log('Now go spoil yourself')
            process.exit()
        }
    } else {
        console.log('Please enter a number.')
    }
})
```

./src/chain-of-responsibility/atm-dispenser-chain.ts

```
// The ATM Dispenser Chain

import Dispenser10 from './dispenser10'
import Dispenser20 from './dispenser20'
import Dispenser50 from './dispenser50'

export default class ATMDispenserChain {
    chain1: Dispenser50
    chain2: Dispenser20
    chain3: Dispenser10

    constructor() {
        // initializing the successors chain
        this.chain1 = new Dispenser50()
        this.chain2 = new Dispenser20()
        this.chain3 = new Dispenser10()
        // Setting a default successor chain that will process the 50s first,
        // the 20s second and the 10s last. The successor chain will be
        // recalculated dynamically at runtime.
        this.chain1.nextSuccessor(this.chain2)
        this.chain2.nextSuccessor(this.chain3)
    }
}
```

./src/chain-of-responsibility/idispenser.ts

```
interface IDispenser {
    nextSuccessor(successor: IDispenser): void
    handle(amount: number): void
}
```

./src/chain-of-responsibility/dispenser10.ts

```typescript
// A dispenser of £10 notes

export default class Dispenser10 implements IDispenser {
    // Dispenses £10s if applicable, otherwise continues to next successor
    #successor: IDispenser | undefined

    nextSuccessor(successor: IDispenser): void {
        // Set the next successor
        this.#successor = successor
    }

    handle(amount: number): void {
        // Handle the dispensing of notes"
        if (amount >= 10) {
            const num = Math.floor(amount / 10)
            const remainder = amount % 10
            console.log(`Dispensing ${num} £10 note`)
            if (remainder !== 0) {
                ;(this.#successor as IDispenser).handle(remainder)
            }
        } else {
            ;(this.#successor as IDispenser).handle(amount)
        }
    }
}
```

./src/chain-of-responsibility/dispenser20.ts

```typescript
// A dispenser of £20 notes

export default class Dispenser20 implements IDispenser {
    // Dispenses £10s if applicable, otherwise continues to next successor
    #successor: IDispenser | undefined

    nextSuccessor(successor: IDispenser): void {
        // Set the next successor
        this.#successor = successor
    }

    handle(amount: number): void {
        // Handle the dispensing of notes"
        if (amount >= 20) {
            const num = Math.floor(amount / 20)
```

```
            const remainder = amount % 20
            console.log(`Dispensing ${num} £20 note`)
            if (remainder !== 0) {
                ;(this.#successor as IDispenser).handle(remainder)
            }
        } else {
            ;(this.#successor as IDispenser).handle(amount)
        }
    }
}
```

./src/chain-of-responsibility/dispenser50.ts

```
// A dispenser of £50 notes

export default class Dispenser50 implements IDispenser {
    // Dispenses £10s if applicable, otherwise continues to next successor
    #successor: IDispenser | undefined

    nextSuccessor(successor: IDispenser): void {
        // Set the next successor
        this.#successor = successor
    }

    handle(amount: number): void {
        // Handle the dispensing of notes"
        if (amount >= 50) {
            const num = Math.floor(amount / 50)
            const remainder = amount % 50
            console.log(`Dispensing ${num} £50 note`)
            if (remainder !== 0) {
                ;(this.#successor as IDispenser).handle(remainder)
            }
        } else {
            ;(this.#successor as IDispenser).handle(amount)
        }
    }
}
```

7.2.9 Output

```
node ./dist/chain-of-responsibility/client.js
Enter amount to withdrawal :
180
Dispensing 3 £50 note
```

```
Dispensing 1 £20 note
Dispensing 1 £10 note
Now go spoil yourself
```

7.2.10 Summary

In the Chain of Responsibility,

- The object/payload will propagate through the chain until fully processed.
- The object does not know which successor or how many will process it.
- The next successor in the chain can either be chosen dynamically at runtime depending on logic from within the current successor, or hard coded if it is more beneficial.
- Successors implement a common interface that makes them work independently of each other, so that they can be used recursively or possibly in a different order.
- A user wizard, or dynamic questionnaire are other common use cases for the chain of responsibility pattern.
- Consider the Chain of Responsibility pattern like the Composite pattern (structural) but with logic applied (behavioral).

7.3 Observer Pattern

7.3.1 Overview

SBCODE Video ID #f5a0d3

The **Observer** pattern is a software design pattern in which an object, called the **Subject** (**Observable**), manages a list of dependents, called **Observers**, and notifies them automatically of any internal state changes by calling one of their methods.

The Observer pattern follows the publisher/subscribe concept. A subscriber, subscribes to a publisher. The publisher then notifies the subscribers when necessary.

The observer stores state that should be consistent with the subject. The observer only needs to store what is necessary for its own purposes.

A typical place to use the observer pattern is between your application and presentation layers. Your application is the manager of the data and is the single source of truth, and when the data changes, it can update all the subscribers, that could be part of multiple presentation layers. For example, the score was changed in a televised cricket game, so all the web browser clients, mobile phone applications, leaderboard display on the ground and television graphics overlay, can all now have the updated information synchronized.

The Observer pattern allows you to vary subjects and observers independently. You can reuse subjects without reusing their observers, and vice versa. It lets you add observers without modifying the subject or any of the other observers.

The observer pattern is commonly described as a push model, where the subject pushes the update to all observers. But observers can pull for updates and also only if it decides it is necessary.

Whether you decide to use a push or pull concept to move data, then there are pros and cons to each. You may decide to use a combination of both to manage reliability.

E.g., When sending messages across a network, the receiving client, can be slow to receive the full message that was sent, or even timeout. This pushing from the sender's side can increase the amount of network hooks or threads if there are many messages still waiting to be fully delivered. The subject is taking responsibility for the delivery.

On the other hand, if the observer requests for an update from the subscriber, then the subject (observable) can return the information as part of the requests' response. The observer could also indicate as part of the request, to only return data applicable to X, that would then make the response message smaller to transfer at the expense of making the observable more coupled to the observer.

Use a push mechanism from the subject when updates are absolutely required in as close to real time from the perspective of the observer, noting that you may need to manage the potential of extra unresolved resources queuing up at the sender.

If updates on the observer end are allowed to suffer from some delay, then a pull mechanism is most reliable and easiest to manage since it is then the observers responsibly to synchronize its own state.

7.3.2 Terminology

- **Subject Interface**: (Observable Interface) The interface that the subject should implement.
- **Concrete Subject**: (Observable) The object that is the subject.
- **Observer Interface**: The interface that the observer should implement.
- **Concrete Observer**: The object that is the observer. There can be a variable number of observers that can subscribe/unsubscribe during runtime.

7.3.3 Observer UML Diagram

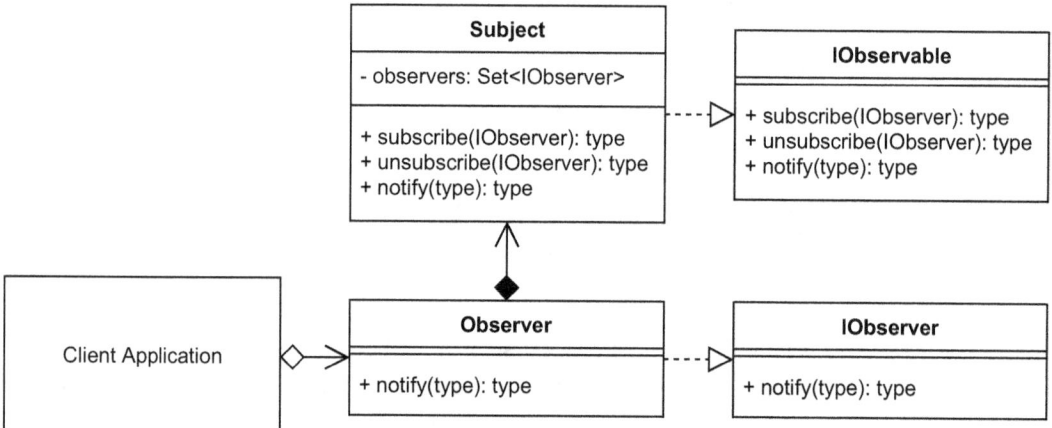

7.3.4 Source Code

A Subject (Observable) is created.

Two Observers are created. They could be across a network, but for demonstration purposes are within the same client.

The Subject notifies the Observers.

One of the Observers unsubscribes,

The Subject notifies the remaining Observer again.

./src/observer/observer-concept.ts

```typescript
// Observer Design Pattern Concept

interface IObservable {
    // The Subject Interface

    subscribe(observer: IObserver): void
    // The subscribe method

    unsubscribe(observer: IObserver): void
    // The unsubscribe method

    notify(...args: unknown[]): void
    // The notify method
}

class Subject implements IObservable {
    // The Subject (a.k.a Observable)
    #observers: Set<IObserver>
    constructor() {
        this.#observers = new Set()
    }

    subscribe(observer: IObserver) {
        this.#observers.add(observer)
    }

    unsubscribe(observer: IObserver) {
        this.#observers.delete(observer)
    }

    notify(...args: unknown[]) {
        this.#observers.forEach((observer) => {
            observer.notify(...args)
        })
    }
}

interface IObserver {
    // A method for the Observer to implement

    notify(...args: unknown[]): void
    // Receive notifications"
}

class Observer implements IObserver {
    // The concrete observer
    #id: number
```

```
    constructor(observable: IObservable) {
        this.#id = COUNTER++
        observable.subscribe(this)
    }

    notify(...args: unknown[]) {
        console.log(`OBSERVER_${this.#id} received $
{JSON.stringify(args)}`)
    }
}

// The Client
let COUNTER = 1 // An ID to help distinguish between objects

const SUBJECT = new Subject()
const OBSERVER_1 = new Observer(SUBJECT)
const OBSERVER_2 = new Observer(SUBJECT)

SUBJECT.notify('First Notification', [1, 2, 3])

// Unsubscribe OBSERVER_2
SUBJECT.unsubscribe(OBSERVER_2)

SUBJECT.notify('Second Notification', { A: 1, B: 2, C: 3 })
```

7.3.5 Output

```
node ./dist/observer/observer-concept.js
OBSERVER_1 received ["First Notification",[1,2,3]]
OBSERVER_2 received ["First Notification",[1,2,3]]
OBSERVER_1 received ["Second Notification",{"A":1,"B":2,"C":3}]
```

7.3.6 Observer Use Case

SBCODE Video ID #0f7fc5

Most applications that involve a separation of data into a presentation layer can be broken further down into the Model-View-Controller (MVC) concept.

- **Controller** : The single source of truth.
- **Model** : The link or relay between a controller and a view. It may use any of the structural patterns (adapter, bridge, facade, proxy, etc.) at some point.
- **View** : The presentation layer of the data from the model.

The observer pattern can be used to manage the transfer of data across any layer and even internally to itself to add an abstraction. In the MVC structure, the View can be a subscriber to the Model, that in turn can also be a subscriber to the controller. It can also happen the other way around if the use case warrants.

This example mimics the **MVC** approach.

There is an external process called a `DataController`, and a client process that holds a `DataModel` and multiple `DataViews` that are a Pie graph, Bar graph and Table view.

Note that this example runs in a single process, but imagine that the `DataController` is actually an external process running on a different server.

The `DataModel` subscribes to the `DataController` and the `DataViews` subscribe to the `DataModel`.

The client sets up the various views with a subscription to the `DataModel`.

The hypothetical external `DataController` then updates the external data, and the data then propagates through the layers to the views.

Note that in reality this example would be much more complex if multiple servers are involved. I am keeping it brief to demonstrate one possible use case of the observer pattern.

Also note that in the `DataController`, the references to the observers are contained in a Set, while in the `DataModel` I have used a Dictionary instead, so that you can see an alternate approach.

7.3.7 Example UML Diagram

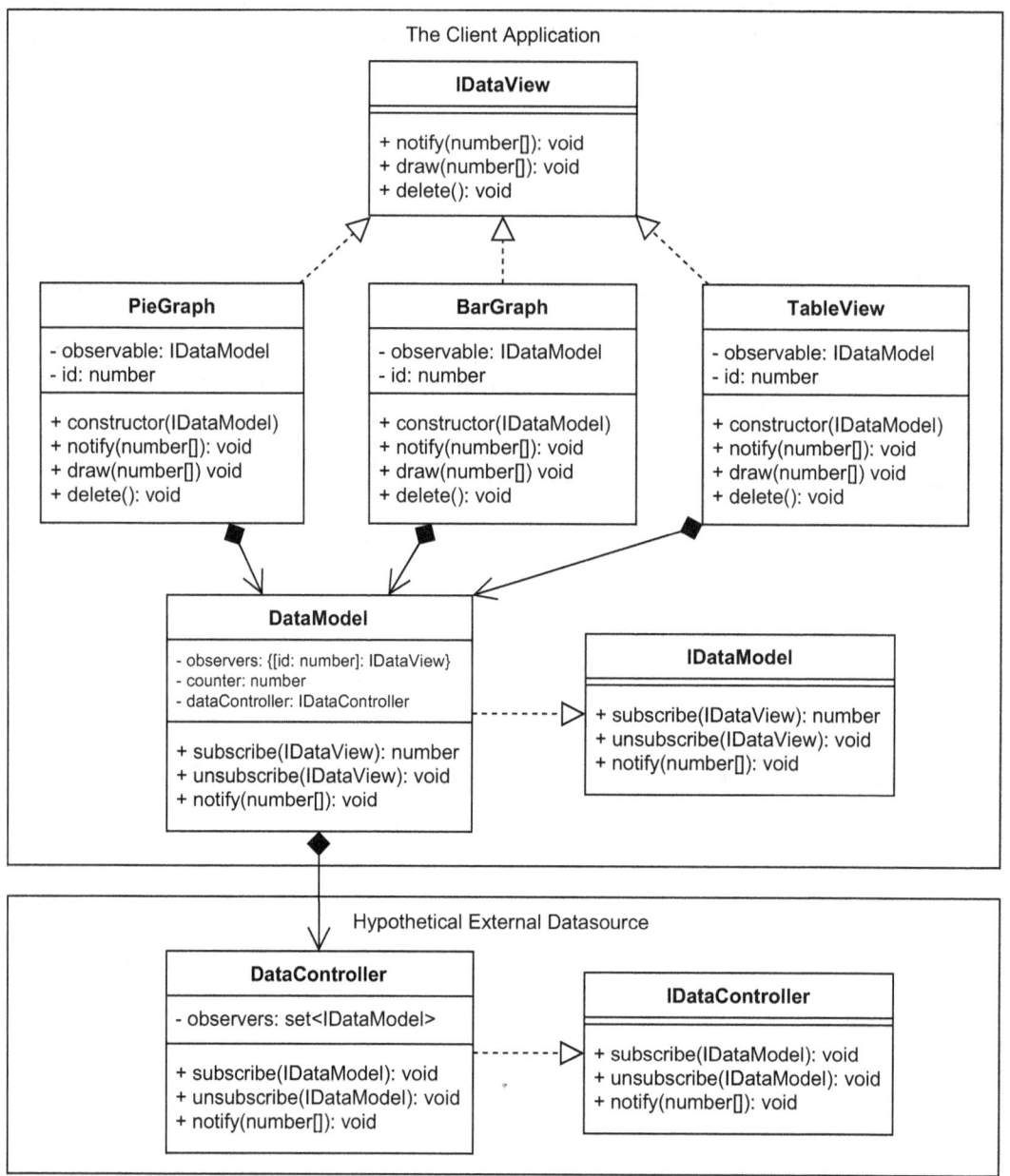

7.3.8 Source Code

./src/observer/client.ts

```
// Observer Design Pattern Concept

import { DataController } from './data-controller'
import { DataModel } from './data-model'
```

```typescript
import { BarGraphView, PieGraphView, TableView } from './data-view'

// A local data view that the hypothetical external controller updates
const DATA_MODEL = new DataModel()

// Add some visualisation that use the dataview
const PIE_GRAPH_VIEW = new PieGraphView(DATA_MODEL)
const BAR_GRAPH_VIEW = new BarGraphView(DATA_MODEL)
const TABLE_VIEW = new TableView(DATA_MODEL)

// A hypothetical data controller running in a different process
const DATA_CONTROLLER = new DataController() // (Singleton)

// The hypothetical external data controller updates some data
DATA_CONTROLLER.notify([1, 2, 3])

// Client now removes a local BAR_GRAPH
BAR_GRAPH_VIEW.delete()

// The hypothetical external data controller updates the data again
DATA_CONTROLLER.notify([4, 5, 6])
```

./src/observer/data-view.ts

```typescript
import { IDataModel } from './data-model'

export interface IDataView {
    // A Subject Interface
    notify(data: number[]): void
    draw(data: number[]): void
    delete(): void
}

export class BarGraphView implements IDataView {
    // A concrete observer
    #observable: IDataModel
    #id: number

    constructor(observable: IDataModel) {
        this.#observable = observable
        this.#id = this.#observable.subscribe(this)
    }

    notify(data: number[]): void {
        console.log(`BarGraph, id:${this.#id}`)
        this.draw(data)
    }
```

```typescript
    draw(data: number[]): void {
        console.log(`Drawing a Bar graph using data:$
{JSON.stringify(data)}`)
    }

    delete(): void {
        this.#observable.unsubscribe(this.#id)
    }
}

export class PieGraphView implements IDataView {
    // A concrete observer
    #observable: IDataModel
    #id: number

    constructor(observable: IDataModel) {
        this.#observable = observable
        this.#id = this.#observable.subscribe(this)
    }

    notify(data: number[]): void {
        console.log(`PieGraph, id:${this.#id}`)
        this.draw(data)
    }

    draw(data: number[]): void {
        console.log(`Drawing a Pie graph using data:${data}`)
    }

    delete(): void {
        this.#observable.unsubscribe(this.#id)
    }
}

export class TableView implements IDataView {
    // A concrete observer
    #observable: IDataModel
    #id: number

    constructor(observable: IDataModel) {
        this.#observable = observable
        this.#id = this.#observable.subscribe(this)
    }

    notify(data: number[]): void {
        console.log(`TableView, id:${this.#id}`)
        this.draw(data)
    }
```

```
    draw(data: number[]): void {
        console.log(`Drawing a Table using data:${JSON.stringify(data)}
`)
    }

    delete(): void {
        this.#observable.unsubscribe(this.#id)
    }
}
```

./src/observer/data-model.ts

```
import { IDataController, DataController } from './data-controller'
import { IDataView } from './data-view'

export interface IDataModel {
    // A Subject Interface
    subscribe(observer: IDataView): number
    unsubscribe(observerId: number): void
    notify(data: number[]): void
}

export class DataModel implements IDataModel {
    // A Subject (a.k.a Observable)

    #observers: { [id: number]: IDataView } = {}
    #dataController: IDataController
    #counter: number

    constructor() {
        this.#counter = 0
        this.#dataController = new DataController()
        this.#dataController.subscribe(this)
    }

    subscribe(observer: IDataView): number {
        this.#counter++
        this.#observers[this.#counter] = observer
        return this.#counter
    }

    unsubscribe(observerId: number): void {
        delete this.#observers[observerId]
    }

    notify(data: number[]): void {
        Object.keys(this.#observers).forEach((observer) => {
            this.#observers[parseInt(observer)].notify(data)
```

```
            })
        }
    }
```

./src/observer/data-controller.ts

```
    import { IDataModel } from './data-model'

    // A Data Controller Interface
    export interface IDataController {
        // A Subject Interface
        subscribe(observer: IDataModel): void
        unsubscribe(observer: IDataModel): void
        notify(data: number[]): void
    }

    export class DataController implements IDataController {
        // A Subject (a.k.a Observable)

        static instance: DataController
        #observers: Set<IDataModel> = new Set()

        constructor() {
            if (DataController.instance) {
                return DataController.instance
            }
            DataController.instance = this
        }

        subscribe(observer: IDataModel): void {
            this.#observers.add(observer)
        }

        unsubscribe(observer: IDataModel): void {
            this.#observers.delete(observer)
        }

        notify(data: number[]): void {
            this.#observers.forEach((observer) => {
                observer.notify(data)
            })
        }
    }
```

7.3.9 Output

```
node ./dist/observer/client.js
PieGraph, id:1
Drawing a Pie graph using data:1,2,3
BarGraph, id:2
Drawing a Bar graph using data:[1,2,3]
TableView, id:3
Drawing a Table using data:[1,2,3]
PieGraph, id:1
Drawing a Pie graph using data:4,5,6
TableView, id:3
Drawing a Table using data:[4,5,6]
```

7.3.10 Summary

- Use when a change to one object requires changing others, and you don't know how many other objects need to be changed.

- A subject has a list of observers, each conforming to the observer interface. The subject doesn't need to know about the concrete class of any observer. It will notify the observer using the method described in the interface.

- Subjects and Observers can belong to any layer of a system whether extremely large or small.

- Using a Push or Pull mechanism for the Observer will depend on how you want your system to manage redundancy for particular data transfers. These things become more of a consideration when the Observer is separated further away from a subject and the message needs to traverse many layers, processes and systems.

7.4 Interpreter Design Pattern

7.4.1 Overview

SBCODE Video ID #5b415b

The **Interpreter** pattern helps to convert information from one language into another.

The language can be anything such as words in a sentence, numerical formulas or even software code.

The process is to convert the source information, into an **Abstract Syntax Tree (AST)** of **Terminal** and **Non-Terminal** expressions that all implement an `interpret()` method.

A Non-Terminal expression is a combination of other Non-Terminal and/or Terminal expressions.

Terminal means terminated, i.e., there is no further processing involved.

An AST root starts with a Non-Terminal expression and then resolves down each branch until all expressions terminate.

An example expression is `A + B`.

The `A` and `B` are Terminal expressions and the `+` is Non-Terminal because it depends on the two other Terminal expressions.

The Image below, is an AST for the expression `5 + 4 - 3 + 7 - 2`

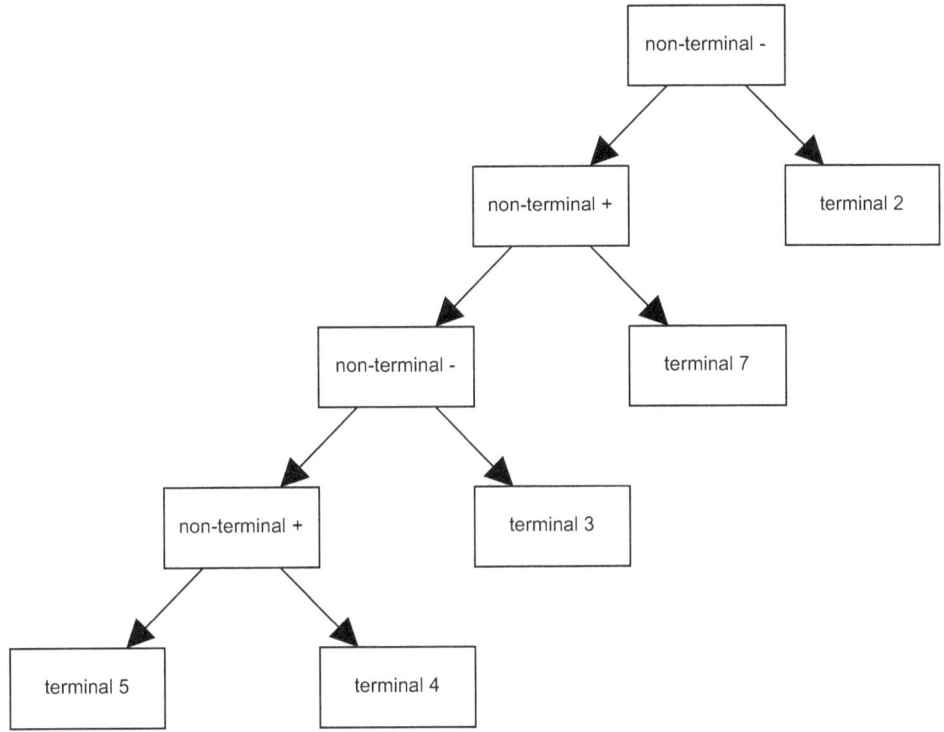

The official Interpreter pattern described in the original GoF Design Patterns book does not state how to construct an Abstract Syntax Tree. How your tree is constructed will depend on the grammatical constructs of your sentence that you want to interpret.

Abstract Syntax Trees can be created manually or dynamically from a custom parser script. In the first example code below, I construct the AST manually.

Once the AST is created, you can then choose the root node and then run the Interpret operation on that, and it should interpret the whole tree recursively.

7.4.2 Terminology

- **Abstract Expression**: Describe the method(s) that Terminal and Non-Terminal expressions should implement.
- **Non-Terminal Expression**: A composite of Terminal and/or Non-Terminal expressions.
- **Terminal Expression**: A leaf node Expression.
- **Context**: Context is state that can be passed through interpret operations if necessary.
- **Client**: Builds or is given an Abstract Syntax Tree to interpret.

7.4.3 Interpreter UML Diagram

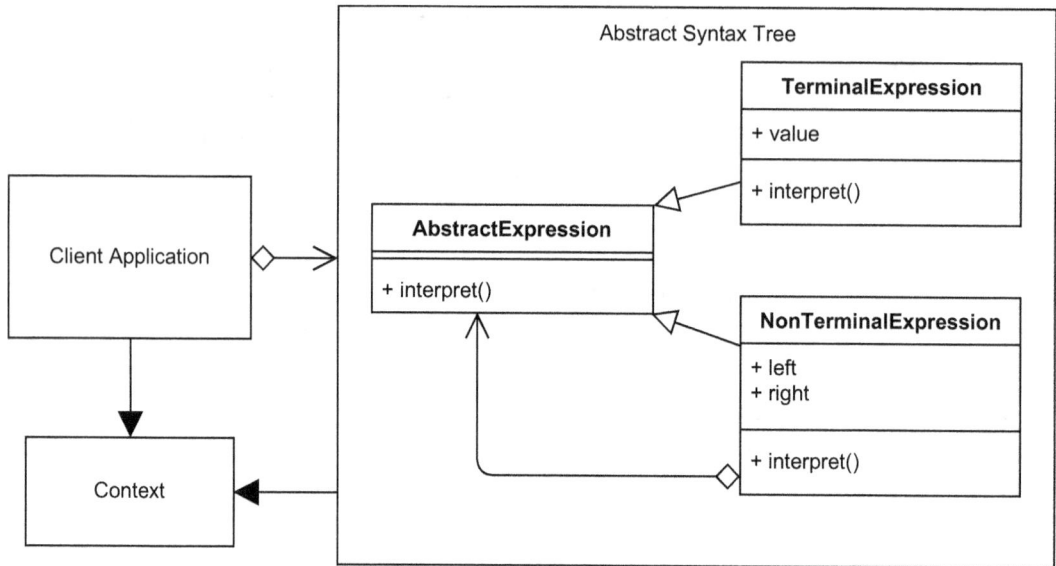

7.4.4 Source Code

In this example, I interpret the string `5 + 4 - 3 + 7 - 2` and then calculate the result.

The grammar of the string follows a pattern of Number → Operator → Number → etc.

I convert the string into a list of tokens that I can refer to by index in the array.

I then construct the AST manually, by adding a

1. Non-Terminal `Add` row containing two Terminals for the `5` and `4`,
2. Non-Terminal `Subtract` row containing the previous Non-Terminal row and the `3`
3. Non-Terminal `Add` row containing the previous Non-Terminal row and the `7`
4. Non-Terminal `Subtract` row containing the previous Non-Terminal row and the `2`

The AST root becomes the final row that was added, and then I can run the `interpret()` method on that, which will interpret the full AST recursively because each AST row references the row above it.

./src/interpreter/interpreter-concept.ts

```
// The Interpreter Pattern Concept

interface IAbstractExpression {
    // All Terminal and Non-Terminal expressions will implement
    // an `interpret` method
```

```typescript
    interpret(): number
}

class Numeral implements IAbstractExpression {
    // Terminal Expression

    value: number

    constructor(value: string) {
        this.value = parseInt(value)
    }

    interpret(): number {
        return this.value
    }
}

class Add implements IAbstractExpression {
    // Non-Terminal Expression.
    left: IAbstractExpression
    right: IAbstractExpression

    constructor(left: IAbstractExpression, right: IAbstractExpression)
    {
        this.left = left
        this.right = right
    }

    interpret() {
        return this.left.interpret() + this.right.interpret()
    }
}

class Subtract implements IAbstractExpression {
    // Non-Terminal Expression.
    left: IAbstractExpression
    right: IAbstractExpression

    constructor(left: IAbstractExpression, right: IAbstractExpression)
    {
        this.left = left
        this.right = right
    }

    interpret() {
        return this.left.interpret() - this.right.interpret()
    }
}
```

```typescript
// The Client
// The sentence complies with a simple grammar of
// Number -> Operator -> Number -> etc,
const SENTENCE = '5 + 4 - 3 + 7 - 2'
console.log(SENTENCE)

// Split the sentence into individual expressions that will be added to
// an Abstract Syntax Tree(AST) as Terminal and Non - Terminal
expressions
const TOKENS = SENTENCE.split(' ')
console.log(JSON.stringify(TOKENS))

// Manually Creating an Abstract Syntax Tree from the tokens
const AST: IAbstractExpression[] = [] // An array of
AbstractExpressions
AST.push(new Add(new Numeral(TOKENS[0]), new Numeral(TOKENS[2]))) // 5
+ 4
AST.push(new Subtract(AST[0], new Numeral(TOKENS[4]))) // ^ - 3
AST.push(new Add(AST[1], new Numeral(TOKENS[6]))) // ^ + 7
AST.push(new Subtract(AST[2], new Numeral(TOKENS[8]))) // ^ - 2

// Use the final AST row as the root node.
const AST_ROOT = AST.pop()

// Interpret recursively through the full AST starting from the root.
console.log((AST_ROOT as IAbstractExpression).interpret())

// Print out a representation of the AST_ROOT
console.dir(AST_ROOT, { depth: null })
```

7.4.5 Output

```
node ./dist/interpreter/interpreter-concept.js
5 + 4 - 3 + 7 - 2
["5","+","4","-","3","+","7","-","2"]
11
Subtract {
  left: Add {
    left: Subtract {
      left: Add { left: Numeral { value: 5 }, right: Numeral { value:
4 } },
      right: Numeral { value: 3 }
    },
    right: Numeral { value: 7 }
  },
  right: Numeral { value: 2 }
}
```

7.4.6 Interpreter Use Case

SBCODE Video ID #eb7859

The example use case will expand on the concept example by dynamically creating the AST and converting Roman numerals to integers as well as calculating the final result.

The Image below, is an AST for the expression `5 + IV - 3 + VII - 2`

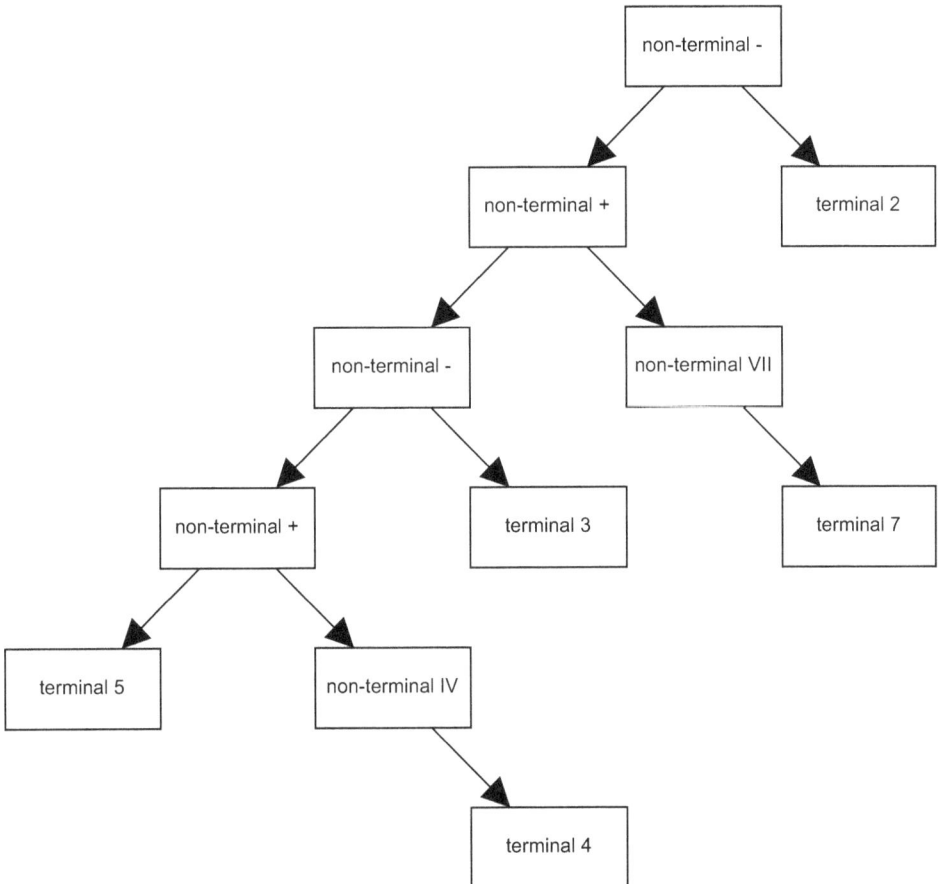

7.4.7 Example UML Diagram

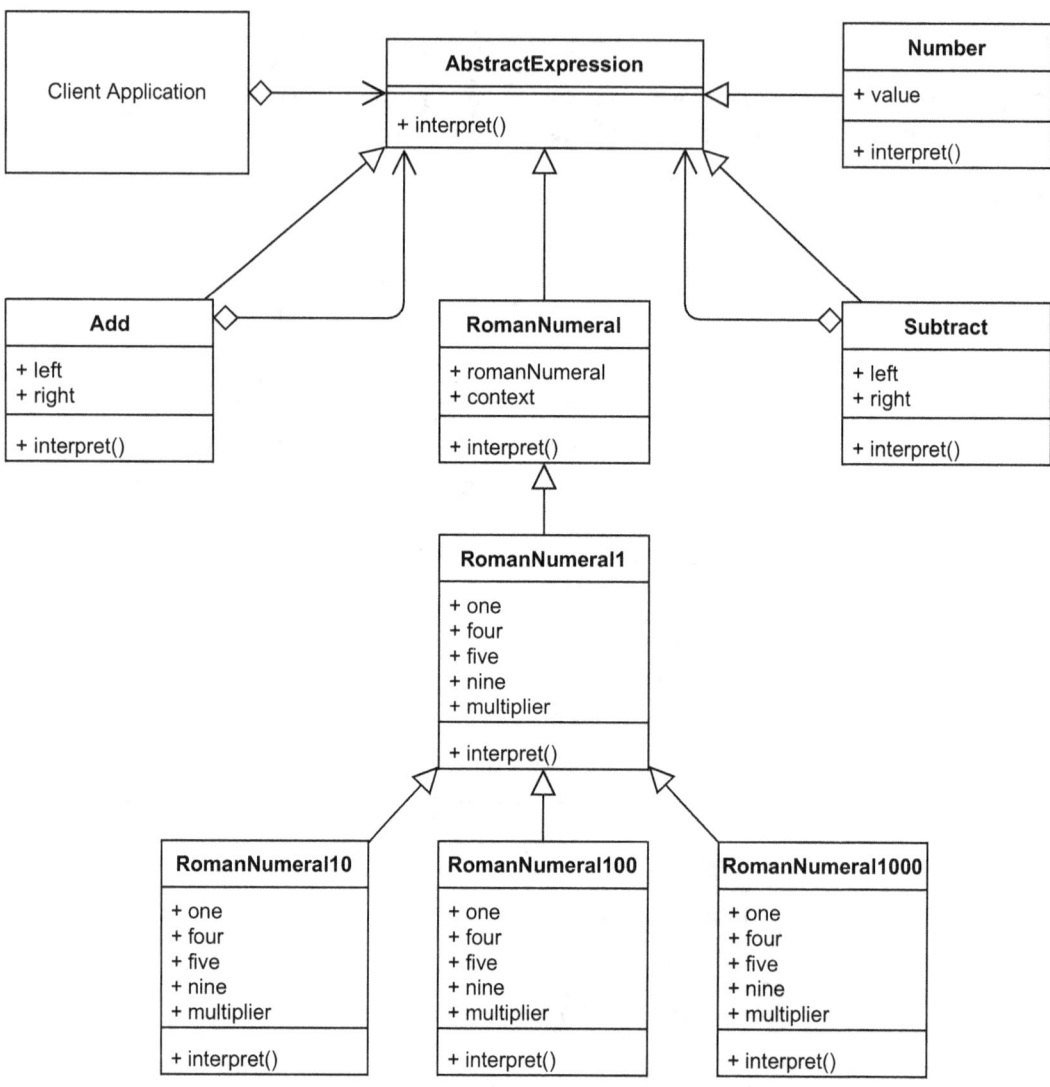

7.4.8 Source Code

./src/interpreter/client.ts

```
// The Interpreter Pattern Use Case Example
import IAbstractExpression from "./iabstract-expression"
import Parser from './sentence-parser'

// The sentence complies with a simple grammar of
// Number -> Operator -> Number -> etc,
const SENTENCE = '5 + IV - 3 + VII - 2'
// const SENTENCE = "4 + II + XII + 1 + 2"
// const SENTENCE = "5 + 4 - 3 + 7 - 2"
```

7.4.8 Source Code

```typescript
// const SENTENCE = "V + IV - III + 7 - II"
// const SENTENCE= "CIX + V"
// const SENTENCE = "CIX + V - 3 + VII - 2"
// const SENTENCE = "MMMCMXCIX - CXIX + MCXXII - MMMCDXII - XVIII - CCXXXV"
console.log(SENTENCE)

const AST_ROOT = Parser.parse(SENTENCE)

// Interpret recursively through the full AST starting from the root.
console.log((AST_ROOT as IAbstractExpression).interpret())

// Print out a representation of the AST_ROOT
console.dir(AST_ROOT, { depth: null })
```

./src/interpreter/iabstract-expression.ts

```typescript
export default interface IAbstractExpression {
    // All Terminal and Non-Terminal expressions will implement
    // an `interpret` method
    value?: number
    left?: IAbstractExpression
    right?: IAbstractExpression
    interpret(): number
}
```

./src/interpreter/numeral.ts

```typescript
import IAbstractExpression from "./iabstract-expression"
export default class Numeral implements IAbstractExpression {
    // Terminal Expression

    value: number

    constructor(value: string | number) {
        this.value = typeof value === 'string' ? parseInt(value) : value
    }

    interpret(): number {
        return this.value
    }
}
```

./src/interpreter/add.ts

```typescript
import IAbstractExpression from "./iabstract-expression"
export default class Add implements IAbstractExpression {
    // Non-Terminal Expression.

    left: IAbstractExpression
    right: IAbstractExpression

    constructor(left: IAbstractExpression, right: IAbstractExpression)
    {
        this.left = left
        this.right = right
    }

    interpret(): number {
        return this.left.interpret() + this.right.interpret()
    }
}
```

./src/interpreter/subtract.ts

```typescript
import IAbstractExpression from "./iabstract-expression"
export default class Subtract implements IAbstractExpression {
    // Non-Terminal Expression.

    left: IAbstractExpression
    right: IAbstractExpression

    constructor(left: IAbstractExpression, right: IAbstractExpression)
    {
        this.left = left
        this.right = right
    }

    interpret(): number {
        return this.left.interpret() - this.right.interpret()
    }
}
```

./src/interpreter/roman-numeral.ts

```typescript
// Roman Numeral Expression. This is a Non-Terminal Expression
import IAbstractExpression from "./iabstract-expression"
import Numeral from './numeral'
```

```typescript
export default class RomanNumeral implements IAbstractExpression {
    // Non Terminal expression

    romanNumeral: string
    context: [string, number]

    constructor(romanNumeral: string) {
        this.romanNumeral = romanNumeral
        this.context = [romanNumeral, 0]
    }

    interpret(): number {
        RomanNumeral1000.interpret(this.context)
        RomanNumeral100.interpret(this.context)
        RomanNumeral10.interpret(this.context)
        RomanNumeral1.interpret(this.context)
        return new Numeral(this.context[1]).interpret()
    }
}

class RomanNumeral1 extends RomanNumeral {
    // Roman Numerals 1 - 9
    static one = 'I'
    static four = 'IV'
    static five = 'V'
    static nine = 'IX'
    static multiplier = 1

    static interpret(context: [string, number]) {
        if (context[0].length === 0) {
            return new Numeral(context[1]).interpret()
        }

        if (context[0].substring(0, 2) === this.nine) {
            context[1] += 9 * this.multiplier
            context[0] = context[0].substring(2)
        } else if (context[0].substring(0, 1) === this.five) {
            context[1] += 5 * this.multiplier
            context[0] = context[0].substring(1)
        } else if (context[0].substring(0, 2) === this.four) {
            context[1] += +(4 * this.multiplier)
            context[0] = context[0].substring(2)
        }
        while (context[0].length > 0 && context[0][0] === this.one) {
            context[1] += 1 * this.multiplier
            context[0] = context[0].substring(1)
        }
        return new Numeral(context[1]).interpret()
    }
```

```typescript
}

class RomanNumeral10 extends RomanNumeral1 {
    // Roman Numerals 10 - 99
    static one = 'X'
    static four = 'XL'
    static five = 'L'
    static nine = 'XC'
    static multiplier = 10
}

class RomanNumeral100 extends RomanNumeral1 {
    // Roman Numerals 100 - 999
    static one = 'C'
    static four = 'CD'
    static five = 'D'
    static nine = 'CM'
    static multiplier = 100
}

class RomanNumeral1000 extends RomanNumeral1 {
    // Roman Numerals 1000 - 3999
    static one = 'M'
    static four = ''
    static five = ''
    static nine = ''
    static multiplier = 1000
}
```

./src/interpreter/sentence-parser.ts

```typescript
// A Custom Parser for creating an Abstract Syntax Tree
import IAbstractExpression from "./iabstract-expression"
import Add from './add'
import Numeral from './numeral'
import RomanNumeral from './roman-numeral'
import Subtract from './subtract'

export default class Parser {
    // Dynamically create the Abstract Syntax Tree

    static parse(sentence: string): IAbstractExpression | undefined {
        // Create the AST from the sentence

        const tokens = sentence.split(' ')

        const tree: IAbstractExpression[] = [] // Abstract Syntax Tree
        while (tokens.length > 1) {
```

```javascript
            const leftExpression = Parser.decideLeftExpression(
                tree,
                tokens
            )

            // get the operator, make the token list shorter
            const operator = tokens.shift()

            const right = tokens[0]

            if (!Number(right)) {
                tree.push(new RomanNumeral(right))
                if (operator === '-') {
                    tree.push(
                        new Subtract(
                            leftExpression,
                            tree[tree.length - 1]
                        )
                    )
                }
                if (operator === '+') {
                    tree.push(
                        new Add(leftExpression, tree[tree.length - 1])
                    )
                }
            } else {
                const rightExpression = new Numeral(right)
                if (!tree.length) {
                    // Empty Data Structures return False by default
                    if (operator === '-') {
                        tree.push(
                            new Subtract(leftExpression, rightExpression)
                        )
                    }
                    if (operator === '+') {
                        tree.push(
                            new Add(leftExpression, rightExpression)
                        )
                    }
                } else {
                    if (operator === '-') {
                        tree.push(
                            new Subtract(
                                tree[tree.length - 1],
                                rightExpression
                            )
                        )
                    }
```

```
                    if (operator === '+') {
                        tree.push(
                            new Add(
                                tree[tree.length - 1],
                                rightExpression
                            )
                        )
                    }
                }
            }
        }
        return tree.pop()
    }

    static decideLeftExpression(
        tree: IAbstractExpression[],
        tokens: string[]
    ): IAbstractExpression {
        // On the First iteration, the left expression can be either a
        // number or roman numeral.Every consecutive expression is
        // reference to an existing AST row
        const left = tokens.shift()
        let leftExpression: IAbstractExpression
        if (!tree.length) {
            // only applicable if first round
            if (!Number(left)) {
                // if 1st token a roman numeral
                tree = []
                tree.push(new RomanNumeral(left as string))
                leftExpression = tree[
                    tree.length - 1
                ] as IAbstractExpression
            } else {
                leftExpression = new Numeral(left as string)
            }
            return leftExpression
        } else {
            leftExpression = tree[tree.length - 1] as
IAbstractExpression
            return leftExpression
        }
    }
}
```

7.4.9 Output

```
node ./dist/interpreter/client.js
5 + IV - 3 + VII - 2
```

```
11
Subtract {
  left: Add {
    left: Subtract {
      left: Add {
        left: Numeral { value: 5 },
        right: RomanNumeral { romanNumeral: 'IV', context: [ '', 4 ] }
      },
      right: Numeral { value: 3 }
    },
    right: RomanNumeral { romanNumeral: 'VII', context: [ '', 7 ] }
  },
  right: Numeral { value: 2 }
}
```

7.4.10 Summary

- ASTs are hard to create and are an enormous subject in themselves. My recommended approach is to create them manually first using a sample sentence to help understand all the steps individually, and then progress the conversion to be fully dynamic one step at a time ensuring that the grammatical constructs still work as you continue to progress.

- The Interpreter pattern uses a class to represent each grammatical rule.

- ASTs consist of multiple Non-Terminal and Terminal Expressions, that all implement an `interpret()` method.

- Note that in the sample code above, the `interpret()` methods in the Non-Terminal expressions, all call further `interpret()` recursively. Only the Terminal expressions `interpret()` method returns an explicit value. See the Number class in the above code.

7.5 Iterator Design Pattern

7.5.1 Overview

SBCODE Video ID #d072b5

The Iterator will commonly contain two methods that perform the following concepts.

- **next**: returns the next object in the aggregate (collection, object).
- **hasNext**: returns a Boolean indicating if the Iterable is at the end of the iteration or not.

The benefits of using the Iterator pattern are that the client can traverse a collection of aggregates(objects) without needing to understand their internal representations and/or data structures.

7.5.2 Terminology

- **Iterator Interface**: The Interface for an object to implement.
- **Concrete Iterator**: (Iterable) The instantiated object that implements the iterator and contains a collection of aggregates.
- **Aggregate Interface**: An interface for defining an aggregate (object).
- **Concrete Aggregate**: The object that implements the Aggregate interface.

7.5.3 Iterator UML Diagram

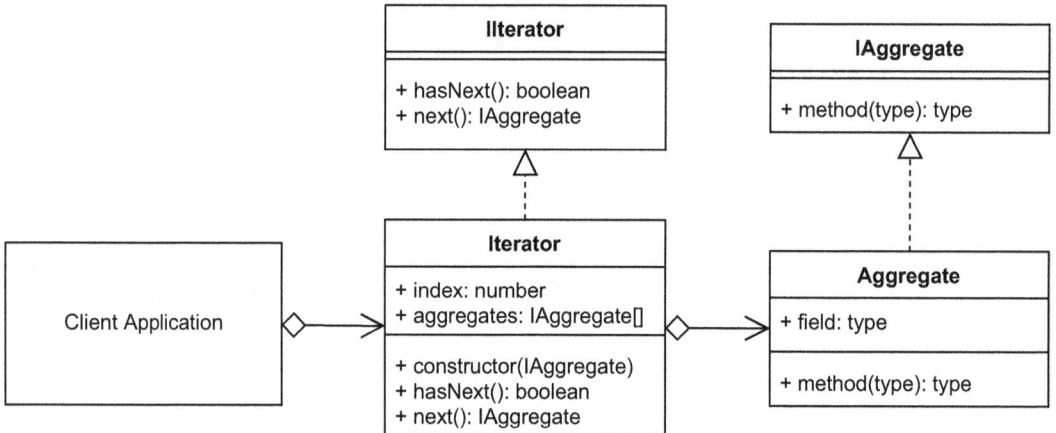

7.5.4 Source Code

In this concept example, I create 4 objects called Aggregate and group them into a collection.

They are very minimal objects that implement one method that prints a line.

I then create an Iterable and pass in the collection of Aggregates.

I can now traverse the aggregates through the Iterable interface.

./src/iterator/iterator-concept.ts

```typescript
// The Iterator Pattern Concept

interface IIterator {
    next(): IAggregate
    // Return the object in collection

    hasNext(): boolean
    // Returns Boolean whether at end of collection or not
}

class IteratorConcept implements IIterator {
    // The concrete iterator (iterable)
    index: number
    aggregates: IAggregate[]

    constructor(aggregates: IAggregate[]) {
        this.index = 0
        this.aggregates = aggregates
    }

    next() {
        if (this.index < this.aggregates.length) {
            const aggregate = this.aggregates[this.index]
            this.index += 1
            return aggregate
        }
        throw new Error('At End of Iterator')
    }

    hasNext() {
        return this.index < this.aggregates.length
    }
}

interface IAggregate {
    // An interface that the aggregates should implement
    method(): void
}

class Aggregate implements IAggregate {
```

```
        // A concrete object
        method(): void {
            console.log('This method has been invoked')
        }
    }

    // The Client
    const AGGREGATES = [
        new Aggregate(),
        new Aggregate(),
        new Aggregate(),
        new Aggregate(),
    ]

    // AGGREGATES is an array that is already iterable by default.
    // but we can create own own iterator on top anyway.
    const ITERABLE = new IteratorConcept(AGGREGATES)

    while (ITERABLE.hasNext()) {
        ITERABLE.next().method()
    }
```

7.5.5 Output

```
node ./dist/iterator/iterator-concept.js
This method has been invoked
This method has been invoked
This method has been invoked
This method has been invoked
```

7.5.6 Iterator Use Case

SBCODE Video ID #e39a6b

The iterator in this brief example will return the next number in the iterator multiplied by 2 modulus 11. It dynamically creates the returned object (number) at runtime.

It has no `hasNext()` method since the result is modulated by 11, that will loop the results no matter how large the iterator index is. Furthermore, it will also appear to alternate between a series of even numbers and odd numbers.

Also, just to demonstrate that implementing abstract classes and interfaces is not always necessary, this example uses no abstract base classes or interfaces.

7.5.7 Example UML Diagram

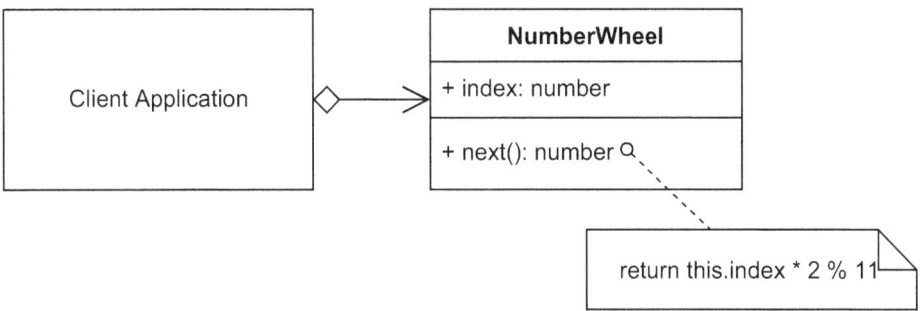

7.5.8 Source Code

./src/iterator/client.ts

```typescript
// The Iterator Pattern Concept

class NumberWheel {
    // The concrete iterator (iterable)

    index: number

    constructor() {
        this.index = 0
    }

    next() {
        // Return a new number next in the wheel
        this.index = this.index + 1
        return (this.index * 2) % 11
    }
}

// The Client
const NUMBERWHEEL = new NumberWheel()

for (let i = 0; i < 22; i++) {
    process.stdout.write(NUMBERWHEEL.next() + ' ')
}
```

7.5.9 Output

```
node ./dist/iterator/client.js
2 4 6 8 10 1 3 5 7 9 0 2 4 6 8 10 1 3 5 7 9 0
```

7.5.10 Summary

- Use an iterator when you need to traverse over a collection, or you want an object that can output a series of dynamically created objects.
- At minimum, an iterator needs a `next` equivalent method that returns an object.
- Optionally you can also create a helper function that indicates whether an iterator is at the end or not. This is useful if you use your iterator in a `while` loop.

7.6 Mediator Design Pattern

7.6.1 Overview

SBCODE Video ID #d0089f

Objects communicate through the **Mediator** rather than directly with each other.

As a system evolves and becomes larger and supports more complex functionality and business rules, the problem of communicating between these components becomes more complicated to understand and manage. It may be beneficial to refactor your system to centralize some or all of its functionality via some kind of mediation process.

The mediator pattern is similar to implementing the Facade pattern between your objects and processes. Except that the structure of the Mediator could also allow multi-directional communication between each component and provide the opportunity to add some logic to the messaging flow to make it more cooperative in some way. E.g., managing the routing behavior by serializing or batching messages, the centralization of application logic, caching, logging, etc.

7.6.2 Terminology

- **Mediator**: The coordinator of communications between the components (colleagues).
- **Colleagues**: One of the many types of concrete components that use the mediator.

7.6.3 Mediator UML Diagram

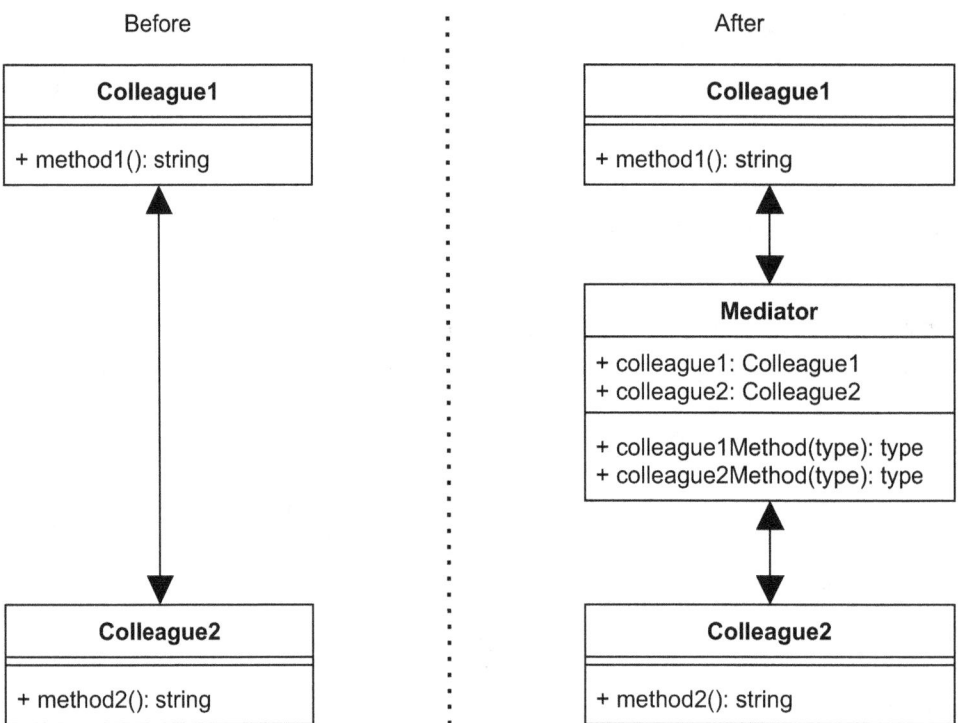

7.6.4 Source Code

In the example concept, there are two colleague classes that use each other's methods. Instead of the Colleagues calling each other's methods directly, they implement the Mediator interface and call each other via the Mediator. Each colleague is designed for a different purpose, but they utilize some related functionality from each other.

The system, in this case, would work without the Mediator, but adding the Mediator would allow extending functionality to a potential third colleague that provides a different service, such as AI analysis or monitoring, without needing to add specific support or knowledge into the two original colleagues.

In this first example the Mediator is structurally acting as a multi-directional relay between the two colleagues.

./src/mediator/mediator-concept.ts

```
// Mediator Concept Sample Code

class Mediator {
    // The Mediator Concrete Class
    colleague1: Colleague1
```

```
    colleague2: Colleague2

    constructor() {
        this.colleague1 = new Colleague1()
        this.colleague2 = new Colleague2()
    }

    colleague1Method() {
        // Calls the method provided by Colleague1
        return this.colleague1.method1()
    }

    colleague2Method() {
        // Calls the method provided by Colleague2
        return this.colleague2.method2()
    }
}

class Colleague1 {
    // This Colleague provides data for Colleague2

    method1() {
        return 'Here is the Colleague1 specific data you asked for'
    }
}

class Colleague2 {
    // This Colleague provides data for Colleague1

    method2() {
        return 'Here is the Colleague2 specific data you asked for'
    }
}

// The Client
const MEDIATOR = new Mediator()

// Colleague1 wants some data from Colleague2
let DATA = MEDIATOR.colleague2Method()
console.log(`COLLEAGUE1 <--> ${DATA}`)

// Colleague2 wants some data from Colleague1
DATA = MEDIATOR.colleague1Method()
console.log(`COLLEAGUE2 <--> ${DATA}`)
```

7.6.5 Output

```
node ./dist/mediator/mediator-concept.js
COLLEAGUE1 <--> Here is the Colleague2 specific data you asked for
COLLEAGUE2 <--> Here is the Colleague1 specific data you asked for
```

7.6.6 Mediator Use Case

SBCODE Video ID #4429bf

In this example use case, we will implement some behavior into the mediation process.

Before the mediation logic is added, consider that the below example is a series of components all subscribed to a central location being the subject. They all implement the Observer pattern.

Each component is updated independently by external forces, but when it has new information, it notifies the subject which in turn then notifies the other subscribed components.

During the synchronization of all the subscribed components, without the extra mediation, the component that provided the new information will receive back the same message that it just notified the subject of. In order to manage the unnecessary duplicate message, the notifications will be mediated to exclude to component where the original message originated from.

7.6.7 Example UML Diagram

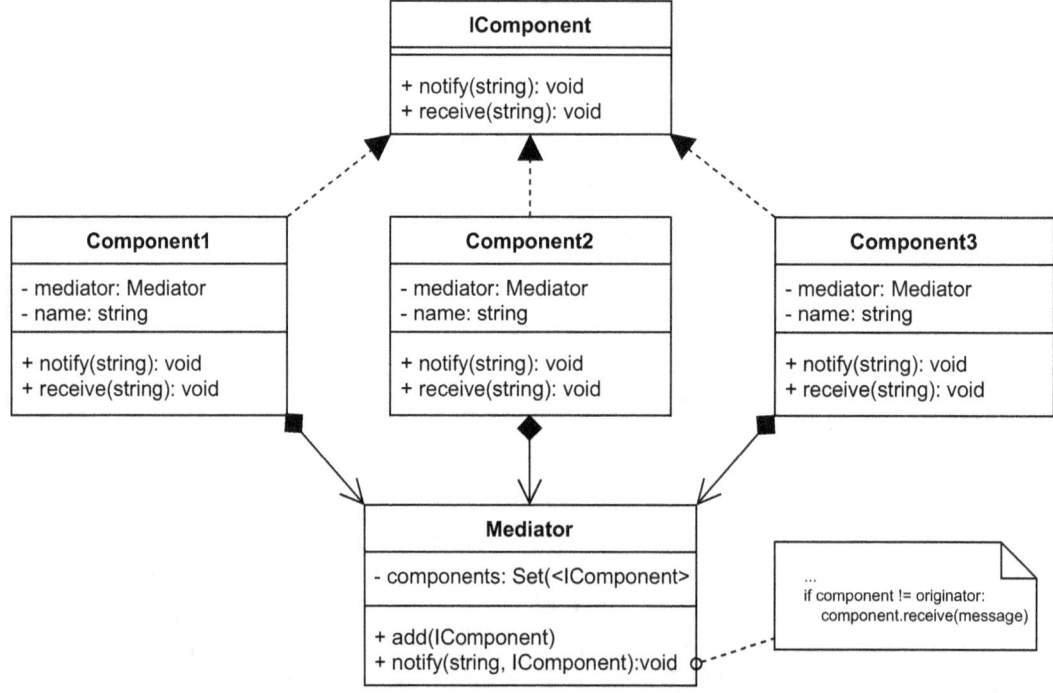

7.6.8 Source Code

./src/mediator/client.ts

```typescript
// The Mediator Use Case Example

import Component from './component'
import Mediator from './mediator'

const MEDIATOR = new Mediator()
const COMPONENT1 = new Component(MEDIATOR, 'Component1')
const COMPONENT2 = new Component(MEDIATOR, 'Component2')
const COMPONENT3 = new Component(MEDIATOR, 'Component3')

MEDIATOR.add(COMPONENT1)
MEDIATOR.add(COMPONENT2)
MEDIATOR.add(COMPONENT3)

COMPONENT1.notify('data A')
COMPONENT2.notify('data B')
COMPONENT3.notify('data C')
```

./src/mediator/component.ts

```typescript
// Each component stays synchronized through a mediator

import IComponent from './icomponent'
import Mediator from './mediator'

export default class Component implements IComponent {
    #mediator: Mediator
    #name: string

    constructor(mediator: Mediator, name: string) {
        this.#mediator = mediator
        this.#name = name
    }

    notify(message: string): void {
        console.log(this.#name + ': >>> Out >>> : ' + message)
        this.#mediator.notify(message, this)
    }

    receive(message: string): void {
        console.log(this.#name + ': <<< In <<< : ' + message)
    }
}
```

./src/mediator/icomponent.ts

```typescript
// An interface that each component should implement

export default interface IComponent {
    notify(message: string): void

    receive(message: string): void
}
```

./src/mediator/mediator.ts

```typescript
// The Subject that all components will stay synchronized with

import IComponent from './icomponent'

export default class Mediator {
    // A Subject whose notify method is mediated
    #components: Set<IComponent>

    constructor() {
        this.#components = new Set()
    }

    add(component: IComponent): void {
        // Add components
        this.#components.add(component)
    }

    notify(message: string, originator: IComponent): void {
        // Add components except for the originator component
        this.#components.forEach((component) => {
            if (component !== originator) {
                component.receive(message)
            }
        })
    }
}
```

7.6.9 Output

```
node ./dist/mediator/client.js
Component1: >>> Out >>> : data A
Component2: <<< In <<< : data A
Component3: <<< In <<< : data A
Component2: >>> Out >>> : data B
```

```
Component1: <<< In <<< : data B
Component3: <<< In <<< : data B
Component3: >>> Out >>> : data C
Component1: <<< In <<< : data C
Component2: <<< In <<< : data C
```

7.6.10 Summary

- A mediator replaces a structure with many-to-many interactions between its classes and processes, with a one-to-many centralized structure where the interface supports all the methods of the many-to-many structure, but via the mediator component instead.

- The mediator pattern encourages usage of shared objects that can now be centrally managed and synchronized.

- The mediator pattern creates an abstraction between two or more components that then makes a system easier to understand and manage.

- The mediator pattern is similar to the Facade pattern, except the Mediator can also transact data both ways between two or more other classes or processes that would normally interact directly with each other.

7.7 Memento Design Pattern

7.7.1 Overview

SBCODE Video ID #a37ae3

Throughout the lifecycle of an application, an objects state may change. You might want to store a copy of the current state in case of later retrieval. E.g., when writing a document, you may want to auto save the current state every 10 minutes. Or you have a game, and you want to save the current position of your player in the level, with its score and current inventory.

You can use the **Memento** pattern for saving a copy of state and for later retrieval if necessary.

The Memento pattern, like the Command pattern, is also commonly used for implementing UNDO/REDO functionality within your application.

The difference between the Command and the Memento patterns for UNDO/REDO, is that in the Command pattern, you re-execute commands in the same order that changed attributes of a state, and with the Memento, you completely replace the state by retrieving from a cache/store.

7.7.2 Terminology

- **Originator**: The originator is an object with an internal state that changes on occasion.
- **Caretaker**: (Guardian) A Class that asks the Originator to create or restore Mementos. The Caretaker than saves them into a cache or store of mementos.
- **Memento**: A copy of the internal state of the Originator that can later be restored back into the Originator to replace its current state.

7.7.3 Memento UML Diagram

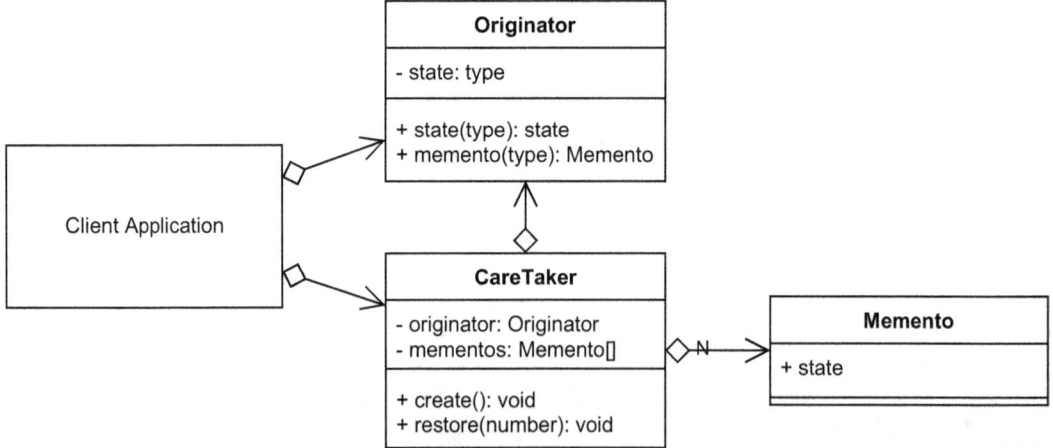

7.7.4 Source Code

In the concept code, the client creates an object whose state will be periodically recorded. The object will be the Originator.

A Caretaker is also created with a reference to the Originator.

The Originators internal state is changed several times. It is then decided that the Caretaker should make a backup.

More changes are made to the Originator, and then another backup is made.

More changes are made to the Originator, and then it is decided that the first backup should be restored instead.

And then the second backup is restored.

./src/memento/memento-concept.ts

```typescript
'Memento pattern concept'

class Memento {
    // A container of state
    state: string
    constructor(state: string) {
        this.state = state
    }
}

class Originator {
    // The Object in the application whose state changes

    #state: string

    constructor() {
        this.#state = ''
    }

    public get state(): string {
        return this.#state
    }

    public set state(value: string) {
        this.#state = value
        console.log(`Originator: Set state to '${value}'`)
    }

    public get memento(): Memento {
```

```typescript
        console.log(
            'Originator: Providing Memento of state to caretaker.'
        )
        return new Memento(this.#state)
    }

    public set memento(value: Memento) {
        this.#state = value.state
        console.log(
            `Originator: State after restoring from Memento: '${
                this.#state
            }'`
        )
    }
}

class CareTaker {
    // Guardian. Provides a narrow interface to the mementos

    #originator: Originator
    #mementos: Memento[]

    constructor(originator: Originator) {
        this.#originator = originator
        this.#mementos = []
    }

    create() {
        // Store a new Memento of the Originators current state
        console.log(
            'CareTaker: Getting a copy of Originators current state'
        )
        const memento = this.#originator.memento
        this.#mementos.push(memento)
    }

    restore(index: number) {
        // Replace the Originators current state with the state stored in the saved Memento
        console.log('CareTaker: Restoring Originators state from Memento')
        const memento = this.#mementos[index]
        this.#originator.memento = memento
    }
}

// The Client
const ORIGINATOR = new Originator()
const CARETAKER = new CareTaker(ORIGINATOR)
```

```javascript
// originators state can change periodically due to application events
ORIGINATOR.state = 'State #1'
ORIGINATOR.state = 'State #2'

// lets backup the originators
CARETAKER.create()

// more changes, and then another backup
ORIGINATOR.state = 'State #3'
CARETAKER.create()

// more changes
ORIGINATOR.state = 'State #4'
console.log(ORIGINATOR.state)

// restore from first backup
CARETAKER.restore(0)
console.log(ORIGINATOR.state)

// restore from second backup
CARETAKER.restore(1)
console.log(ORIGINATOR.state)
```

Output

```
node ./dist/memento/memento-concept.js
Originator: Set state to 'State #1'
Originator: Set state to 'State #2'
CareTaker: Getting a copy of Originators current state
Originator: Providing Memento of state to caretaker.
Originator: Set state to 'State #3'
CareTaker: Getting a copy of Originators current state
Originator: Providing Memento of state to caretaker.
Originator: Set state to 'State #4'
State #4
CareTaker: Restoring Originators state from Memento
Originator: State after restoring from Memento: 'State #2'
State #2
CareTaker: Restoring Originators state from Memento
Originator: State after restoring from Memento: 'State #3'
State #3
```

7.7.5 Memento Use Case

SBCODE Video ID #0a7255

There is a game, and the character is progressing through the levels. It has acquired several new items in its inventory, the score is very good, and you want to save your progress and continue later.

You then decide you made a mistake and need to go back to a previous save because you took a wrong turn.

7.7.6 Example UML Diagram

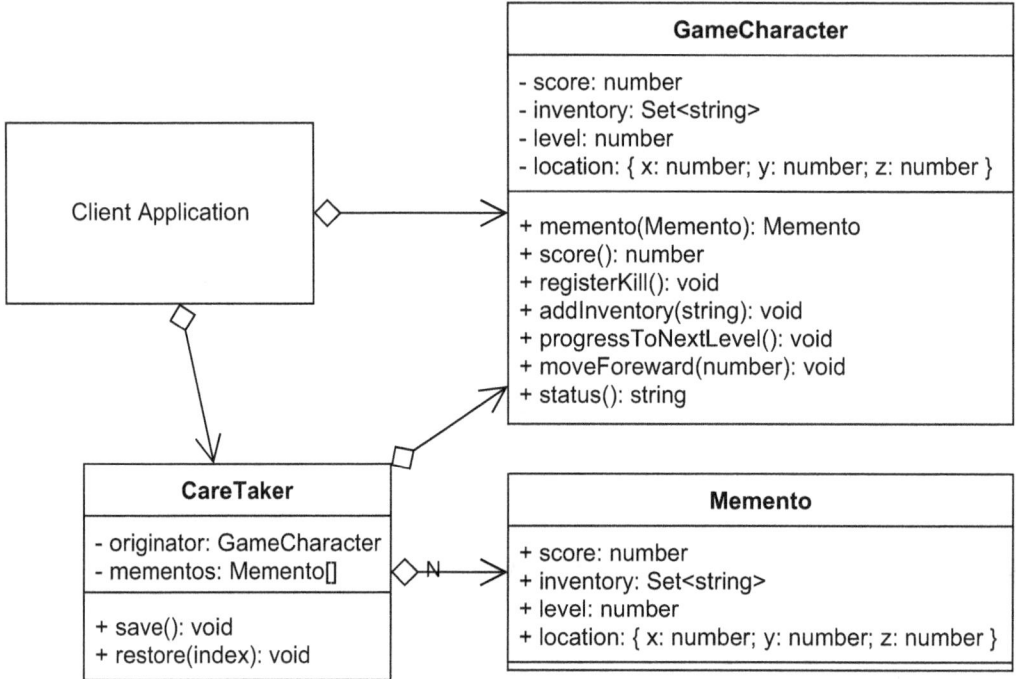

7.7.7 Source Code

./src/memento/client.ts

```
// Memento example Use Case

import CareTaker from './caretaker'
import GameCharacter from './game-character'

const GAME_CHARACTER = new GameCharacter()
const CARETAKER = new CareTaker(GAME_CHARACTER)

// start the game
GAME_CHARACTER.registerKill()
GAME_CHARACTER.moveForward(1)
GAME_CHARACTER.addInventory('sword')
GAME_CHARACTER.registerKill()
GAME_CHARACTER.addInventory('rifle')
```

```
    GAME_CHARACTER.moveForward(1)
    console.log(GAME_CHARACTER.status())

    // save progress
    CARETAKER.save()

    GAME_CHARACTER.registerKill()
    GAME_CHARACTER.moveForward(1)
    GAME_CHARACTER.progressToNextLevel()
    GAME_CHARACTER.registerKill()
    GAME_CHARACTER.addInventory('motorbike')
    GAME_CHARACTER.moveForward(10)
    GAME_CHARACTER.registerKill()
    console.log(GAME_CHARACTER.status())

    // save progress
    CARETAKER.save()
    GAME_CHARACTER.moveForward(1)
    GAME_CHARACTER.progressToNextLevel()
    GAME_CHARACTER.registerKill()
    console.log(GAME_CHARACTER.status())

    // decide you made a mistake, go back to first save
    CARETAKER.restore(0)
    console.log(GAME_CHARACTER.status())

    // continue
    GAME_CHARACTER.registerKill()
```

./src/memento/game-character.ts

```
    // The Game Character whose state changes

    import Memento from './memento'

    export default class GameCharacter {
        #score: number
        #inventory: Set<string>
        #level: number
        #location: { x: number; y: number; z: number }

        constructor() {
            this.#score = 0
            this.#inventory = new Set()
            this.#level = 0
            this.#location = { x: 0, y: 0, z: 0 }
        }
```

```typescript
    public get score(): number {
        // A getter for the score"
        return this.#score
    }

    registerKill(): void {
        // The character kills its enemies as it progresses
        this.#score += 100
    }

    addInventory(item: string): void {
        // The character finds objects in the game
        this.#inventory.add(item)
    }

    progressToNextLevel(): void {
        // The character progresses to the next level
        this.#level = this.#level + 1
    }

    moveForward(amount: number): void {
        // The character moves around the environment
        this.#location['z'] += amount
    }

    status(): string {
        return (
            `Score: ${this.#score}, ` +
            `Level: ${this.#level}, ` +
            `Location: ${JSON.stringify(this.#location)}\n` +
            `Inventory: ${JSON.stringify(Array.from(this.#inventory))}`
        )
    }

    public get memento(): Memento {
        'A `getter` for the characters attributes as a Memento'
        return new Memento(
            this.#score,
            new Set(this.#inventory),
            this.#level,
            Object.assign({}, this.#location)
        )
    }

    public set memento(value: Memento) {
        this.#score = value.score
        this.#inventory = value.inventory
        this.#level = value.level
        this.#location = value.location
```

        }
    }
```

### ./src/memento/caretaker.ts

```typescript
// The Save/Restore Game functionality

import GameCharacter from './game-character'
import Memento from './memento'

export default class CareTaker {
    // Guardian. Provides a narrow interface to the mementos

    #originator: GameCharacter
    #mementos: Memento[]

    constructor(originator: GameCharacter) {
        this.#originator = originator
        this.#mementos = []
    }

    save(): void {
        // Store a new Memento of the Characters current state
        console.log('CareTaker: Game Save')
        const memento = this.#originator.memento
        this.#mementos.push(memento)
    }

    restore(index: number): void {
        // Replace the Characters current attributes with the state
        // stored in the saved Memento
        console.log(
            'CareTaker: Restoring Characters attributes from Memento'
        )
        const memento = this.#mementos[index]
        this.#originator.memento = memento
    }
}
```

./src/memento/memento.ts

```typescript
// A Memento to store character attributes

export default class Memento {
    score: number
    inventory: Set<string>
```
```

```
    level: number
    location: { x: number; y: number; z: number }

    constructor(
        score: number,
        inventory: Set<string>,
        level: number,
        location: { x: number; y: number; z: number }
    ) {
        this.score = score
        this.inventory = inventory
        this.level = level
        this.location = location
    }
}
```

7.7.8 Output

```
node ./dist/memento/client.js
Score: 200, Level: 0, Location: {"x":0,"y":0,"z":2}
Inventory: ["sword","rifle"]
CareTaker: Game Save
Score: 500, Level: 1, Location: {"x":0,"y":0,"z":13}
Inventory: ["sword","rifle","motorbike"]
CareTaker: Game Save
Score: 600, Level: 2, Location: {"x":0,"y":0,"z":14}
Inventory: ["sword","rifle","motorbike"]
CareTaker: Restoring Characters attributes from Memento
Score: 200, Level: 0, Location: {"x":0,"y":0,"z":2}
Inventory: ["sword","rifle"]
```

7.7.9 Summary

- You don't need to create a new Memento each time an Originators state changes. You can do it only when considered necessary. E.g., an occasional backup to a file.

- Mementos can be stored in memory or saved/cached externally. The Caretaker will abstract the complications of storing and retrieving Mementos from the Originator.

- Consider the Command pattern for fine-grained changes to an objects state to manage UNDO/REDO between memento saves. Or even save command history into a Memento that can be later replayed.

- In my examples, the whole state is recorded and changed with the Memento. You can use the Memento to record and change partial states instead if required.

- When copying state, be aware of shallow/deep copying. In complicated projects, your restore functionality will probably contain a combination of both the Command and Memento patterns.

7.8 State Design Pattern

7.8.1 Overview

SBCODE Video ID #11b6da

Not to be confused with object state, i.e., one of more attributes that can be copied as a snapshot, the **State Pattern** is more concerned about changing the handle of an object's method dynamically. This makes an object itself more dynamic and may reduce the need of many conditional statements.

Instead of storing a value in an attribute, and then using conditional statements within an objects' method to produce different output, a subclass is assigned as a handle instead. The object/context doesn't need to know about the inner working of the assigned subclass that the task was delegated to.

In the state pattern, the behavior of an objects state is encapsulated within the subclasses that are dynamically assigned to handle it.

7.8.2 Terminology

- **State Interface**: An interface for encapsulating the behavior associated with a particular state of the Context.
- **Concrete Subclasses**: Each subclass implements a behavior associated with the particular state.
- **Context**: This is the object where the state is defined, but the execution of the state behavior is redirected to the concrete subclass.

7.8.3 State UML Diagram

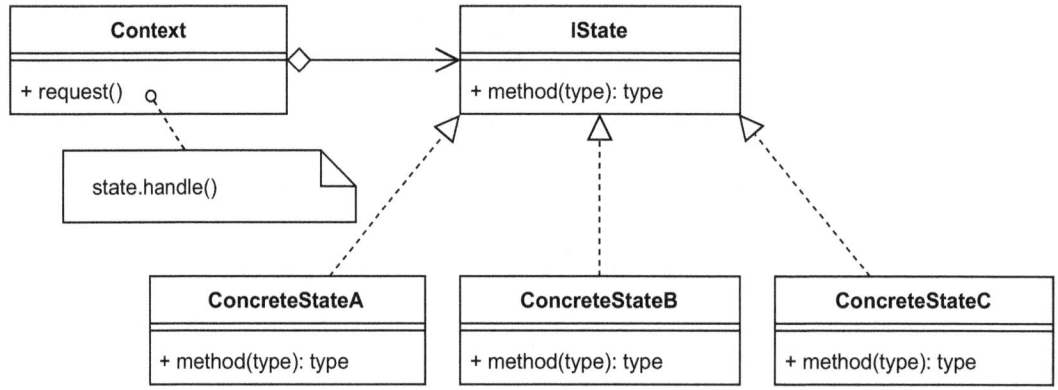

7.8.4 Source Code

In the concept example, there are three possible states. Every time the `request()` method is called, the concrete state subclass is randomly selected by the context.

./src/state/state-concept.ts

```ts
// The State Pattern Concept

class Context {
    // This is the object whose behavior will change
    #stateHandles: IState[]
    #handle: IState | undefined

    constructor() {
        this.#stateHandles = [
            new ConcreteStateA(),
            new ConcreteStateB(),
            new ConcreteStateC(),
        ]
        this.#handle = undefined
    }

    request() {
        // A method of the state that dynamically changes which
        // class it uses depending on the value of this.#handle
        this.#handle = this.#stateHandles[Math.floor(Math.random() * 3)]
        return this.#handle
    }
}

interface IState {
    // A State Interface
    toString(): string
}

class ConcreteStateA implements IState {
    // A ConcreteState Subclass

    toString() {
        return 'I am ConcreteStateA'
    }
}

class ConcreteStateB implements IState {
    // A ConcreteState Subclass

    toString() {
        return 'I am ConcreteStateB'
    }
}

class ConcreteStateC implements IState {
```

```
    // A ConcreteState Subclass

    toString() {
        return 'I am ConcreteStateC'
    }
}

// The Client
const CONTEXT = new Context()
console.log(CONTEXT.request())
console.log(CONTEXT.request())
console.log(CONTEXT.request())
console.log(CONTEXT.request())
console.log(CONTEXT.request())
```

Output

```
node ./dist/state/state-concept.js
ConcreteStateB {}
ConcreteStateA {}
ConcreteStateC {}
ConcreteStateA {}
ConcreteStateC {}
```

7.8.5 State Use Case

SBCODE Video ID #f5b4b7

This example takes the concept example further and instead assigns then next state in sequence rather than choosing the states subclasses randomly.

It also allows to set the state outside the context by using a getter/setter.

The client will set the state, and then run a request, and then change the state again, etc., and depending on the state, the behavior of the method would have changed.

7.8.6 State Example Use Case UML Diagram

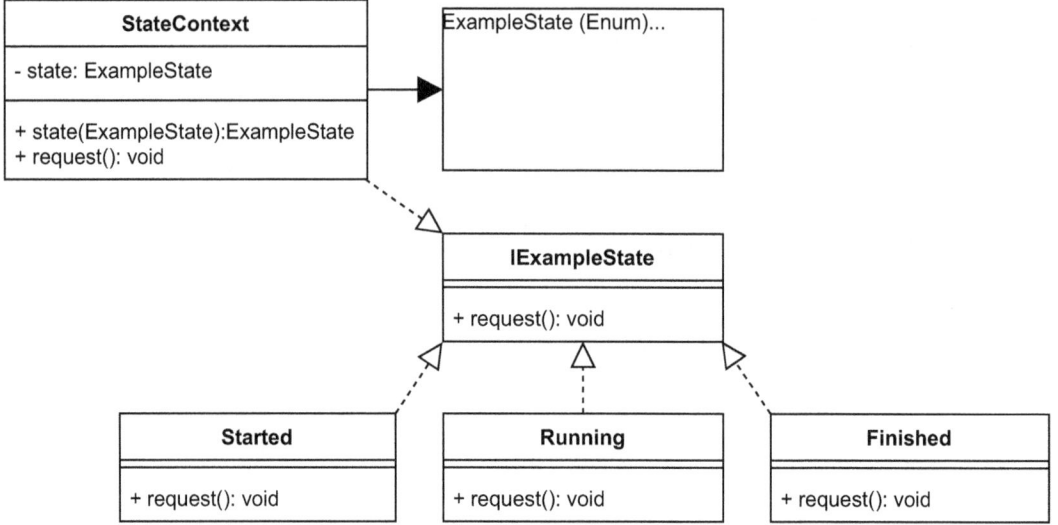

7.8.7 Source Code

./src/state/client.ts

```typescript
// The State Use Case Example

enum ExampleState {
    Initializing = 'Initializing',
    Started = 'Started',
    Running = 'Running',
    Finished = 'Finished',
}

interface IExampleState {
    // A State Interface
    request(): void
}

class StateContext implements IExampleState {
    #state: ExampleState

    constructor() {
        this.#state = ExampleState.Initializing
    }

    public get state() {
        return this.#state
    }
```

```typescript
    public set state(value: ExampleState) {
        switch (value) {
            case ExampleState.Started:
                this.request = Started.prototype.request
                break
            case ExampleState.Running:
                this.request = Running.prototype.request
                break
            case ExampleState.Finished:
                this.request = Finished.prototype.request
                break
        }
        this.#state = value
    }

    request() {
        // Does nothing until state changes, when then
        // this method handle is reassigned to a different
        // concrete states request method
    }
}

class Started implements IExampleState {
    // A ConcreteState Subclass
    request() {
        console.log(`I am now Started`)
    }
}

class Running implements IExampleState {
    // A ConcreteState Subclass
    request() {
        console.log(`I am now Running`)
    }
}

class Finished implements IExampleState {
    // A ConcreteState Subclass
    request() {
        console.log(`I am now Finished`)
    }
}

// The Client
const STATE_CONTEXT = new StateContext()
console.log('STATE_CONTEXT = ' + STATE_CONTEXT.state)
STATE_CONTEXT.state = ExampleState.Started
STATE_CONTEXT.request()
STATE_CONTEXT.state = ExampleState.Running
```

```
STATE_CONTEXT.request()
STATE_CONTEXT.state = ExampleState.Finished
STATE_CONTEXT.request()
STATE_CONTEXT.state = ExampleState.Started
STATE_CONTEXT.request()
STATE_CONTEXT.state = ExampleState.Running
STATE_CONTEXT.request()
STATE_CONTEXT.state = ExampleState.Finished
STATE_CONTEXT.request()
```

7.8.8 Output

```
node ./dist/state/client.js
STATE_CONTEXT = Initializing
I am now Started
I am now Running
I am now Finished
I am now Started
I am now Running
I am now Finished
```

7.8.9 Summary

- Makes an object change its behavior when its internal state changes.

- The client and the context are not concerned about the details of how the state is created/assembled/calculated. The client will call a method of the context, and it will be handled by a subclass.

- The State pattern appears very similar to the Strategy pattern, except in the State pattern, the object/context has changed to a different state and will run a different subclass depending on that state.

7.9 Strategy Design Pattern

7.9.1 Overview

SBCODE Video ID #545946

The **Strategy** Pattern is similar to the State Pattern, except that the client passes in the algorithm that the context should run.

The algorithm should be contained within a class that implements the particular strategies interface.

An application that sorts data is a good example of where you can incorporate the Strategy pattern.

There are many methods of sorting a set of data. E.g., Quicksort, Mergesort, Introsort, Heapsort, Bubblesort. See https://en.wikipedia.org/wiki/Sorting_algorithm for more examples.

The user interface of the client application can provide a drop-down menu to allow the user to try the different sorting algorithms.

Upon user selection, a reference to the algorithm will be passed to the context and processed using this new algorithm instead.

The Strategy and State appear very similar, a good way to differentiate them is to consider whether the state of the context is choosing the algorithm at runtime, or whether the algorithm is being passed into it.

Software Plugins can be implemented using the Strategy pattern.

7.9.2 Terminology

- **Strategy Interface**: An interface that all Strategy subclasses/algorithms must implement.
- **Concrete Strategy**: The subclass that implements an alternative algorithm.
- **Context**: This is the object that receives the concrete strategy in order to execute it.

7.9.3 Strategy UML Diagram

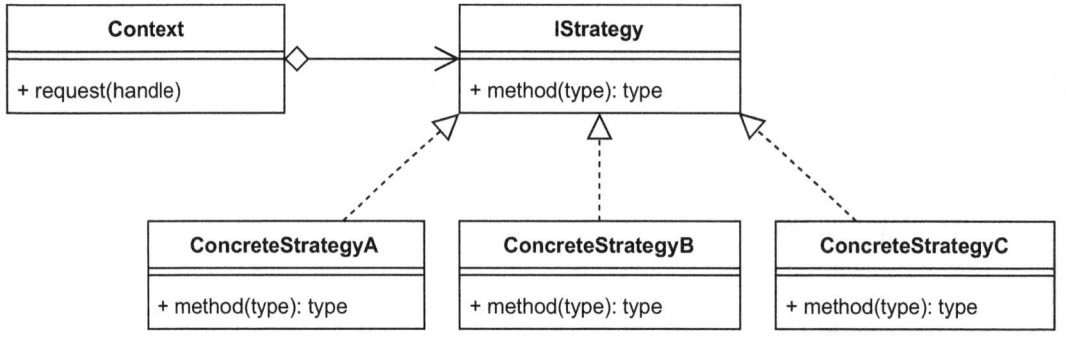

7.9.4 Source Code

There is a Context and three different strategies to choose from.

Each Strategy is executed in turn by the context.

./src/strategy/strategy-concept.ts

```ts
// The Strategy Pattern Concept

class ObjectContext {
    // This is the object whose behavior will change

    request(strategy: IStrategyConstructor) {
        // The request is handled by the class passed in
        return new strategy()
    }
}

interface IStrategyConstructor {
    // A Constructor for the IStrategy
    new (): IStrategy
}

interface IStrategy {
    // A strategy Interface
    method(): string
}

class ConcreteStrategyA implements IStrategy {
    // A Concrete Strategy Subclass

    method() {
        return 'I am ConcreteStrategyA'
```

```
        }
    }

    class ConcreteStrategyB implements IStrategy {
        // A Concrete Strategy Subclass

        method() {
            return 'I am ConcreteStrategyB'
        }
    }

    class ConcreteStrategyC implements IStrategy {
        // A Concrete Strategy Subclass

        method() {
            return 'I am ConcreteStrategyC'
        }
    }

    // The Client
    const OBJECT_CONTEXT = new ObjectContext()

    console.log(OBJECT_CONTEXT.request(ConcreteStrategyA).method())
    console.log(OBJECT_CONTEXT.request(ConcreteStrategyB).method())
    console.log(OBJECT_CONTEXT.request(ConcreteStrategyC).method())
```

7.9.5 Output

```
node ./dist/strategy/strategy-concept.js
I am ConcreteStrategyA
I am ConcreteStrategyB
I am ConcreteStrategyC
```

7.9.6 Strategy Use Case

SBCODE Video ID #89d36a

A game character is moving through an environment. Depending on the situation within the current environment, the user decides to use a different movement algorithm. From the perspective of the object/context, it is still a move, but the implementation is encapsulated in the subclass at the handle.

In a real game, the types of things that a particular move could affect is which animation is looped, the audio, the speed, the camera follow mode and more.

7.9.7 Strategy Example Use Case UML Diagram

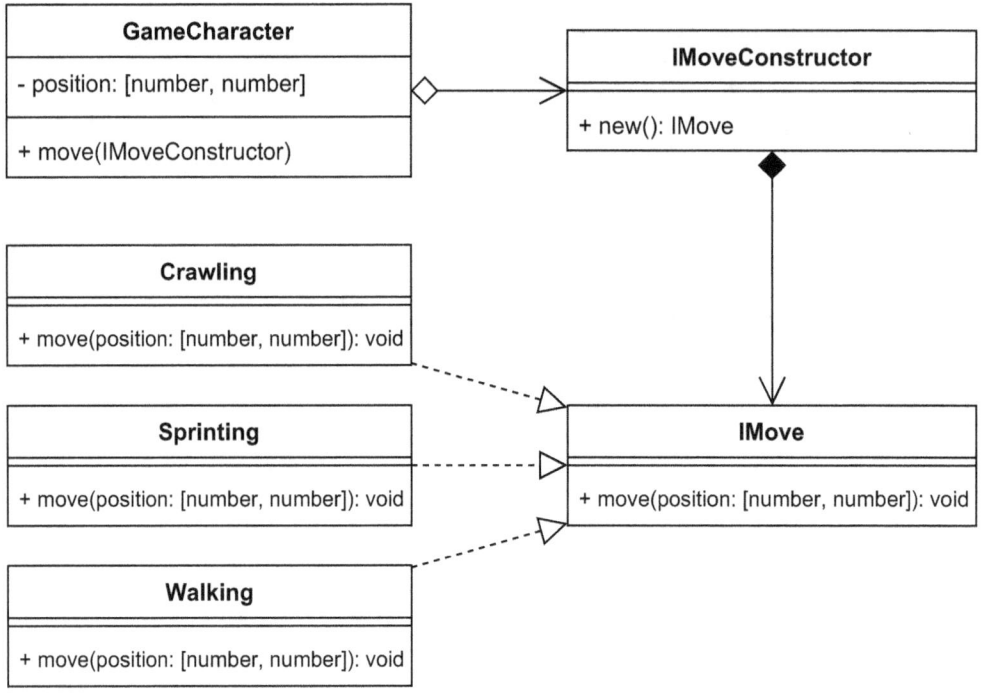

7.9.8 Source Code

./src/strategy/client.ts

```
// The Strategy Pattern Example Use Case

class GameCharacter {
    // This is the context whose strategy will change

    #position: [number, number] = [0, 0]

    move(movementStyle: IMoveConstructor) {
        // The movement algorithm has been decided by the client
        new movementStyle().move(this.#position)
    }
}

interface IMoveConstructor {
    // A Constructor for the IMove
    new (): IMove
}

interface IMove {
    // The Move Strategy Interface
```

```
    move(position: [number, number]): void
}

class Walking implements IMove {
    // A concrete movement strategy for walking

    move(position: [number, number]) {
        position[0] += 1
        console.log(`I am Walking. New position = ${position}`)
    }
}

class Sprinting implements IMove {
    // A concrete movement strategy for sprinting

    move(position: [number, number]) {
        position[0] += 2
        console.log(`I am Running. New position = ${position}`)
    }
}

class Crawling implements IMove {
    // A concrete movement strategy for crawling

    move(position: [number, number]) {
        position[0] += 0.5
        console.log(`I am Crawling. New position = ${position} `)
    }
}

// The Client
const GAME_CHARACTER = new GameCharacter()

GAME_CHARACTER.move(Walking)
// Character sees the enemy
GAME_CHARACTER.move(Sprinting)
// Character finds a small cave to hide in
GAME_CHARACTER.move(Crawling)
```

7.9.9 Output

```
node ./dist/strategy/client.js
I am Walking. New position = 1,0
I am Running. New position = 3,0
I am Crawling. New position = 3.5,0
```

7.9.10 Summary

- While the Strategy pattern looks very similar to the State pattern, the assigned strategy subclass/algorithm is not changing any state of the context that would affect which algorithm is used.
- The Strategy pattern is about having a choice of implementations that accomplish the same relative task.
- The particular strategies' algorithm is encapsulated in order to keep the implementation de coupled from the context.
- Software Plugins can be implemented using the Strategy pattern.

7.10 Template Method Design Pattern

7.10.1 Overview

SBCODE Video ID #217370

In the **Template Method** pattern, you create an abstract class (template) that contains a **Template Method** that is a series of instructions that are a combination of abstract and hook methods.

Abstract methods need to be overridden in the subclasses that extend the abstract (template) class.

Hook methods normally have empty bodies in the abstract class. Subclasses can optionally override the hook methods to create custom implementations.

So, what you have, is an abstract class, with several types of methods, being the main template method, and a combination of abstract and/or hooks, that can be extended by different subclasses that all have the option of customizing the behavior of the template class without changing its underlying algorithm structure.

Template methods are useful to help you factor out common behavior within your library classes.

Note that this pattern describes the behavior of a **method** and how its inner method calls behave.

Hooks are default behavior and can be overridden. They are normally empty by default.

Abstract methods, must be overridden in the concrete class that extends the template class.

7.10.2 Terminology

- **Abstract Class**: Defines the template method and the primitive steps as abstract and/or hook methods.
- **Concrete Class**: A subclass that extends some or all of the abstract class primitive methods.

7.10.3 Template Method UML Diagram

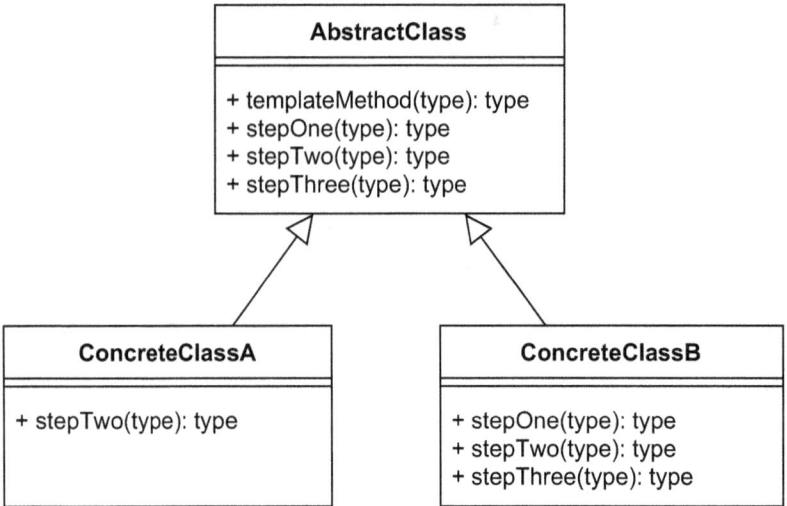

7.10.4 Source Code

Note that in both the concrete classes in this concept example, the `templateMethod()` was not overridden since it was already inherited. Only the primitives (abstract or hooks) were optionally overridden.

./src/template/template-method-concept.ts

```
// The Template Method Pattern Concept"

abstract class AbstractClass {
    // A template class containing a template method and primitive
    // methods

    stepOne(): void {
        // Hooks are normally empty in the abstract class. The
        // implementing class can optionally override providing a
        // custom implementation
    }

    abstract stepTwo(): void
    // An abstract method that must be overridden in the implementing
    // class. Note the addition of the `abstract` keyword

    stepThree(): void {
        // Hooks can also contain default behavior and can be
        // optionally overridden
        console.log(
            'Step Three is a hook that prints this line by default.'
```

```js
            )
        }

        templateMethod() {
            // This is the template method that the subclass will call.
            // The subclass(implementing class) doesn't need to override
            // this method since it has would have already optionally
            // overridden the following methods with its own
            // implementations
            this.stepOne()
            this.stepTwo()
            this.stepThree()
        }
    }

    class ConcreteClassA extends AbstractClass {
        // A concrete class that only overrides step two"
        stepTwo() {
            console.log('Class_A : Step Two (overridden)')
        }
    }

    class ConcreteClassB extends AbstractClass {
        // A concrete class that only overrides steps one, two and three"
        stepOne() {
            console.log('Class_B : Step One (overridden)')
        }

        stepTwo() {
            console.log('Class_B : Step Two. (overridden)')
        }

        stepThree() {
            console.log('Class_B : Step Three. (overridden)')
        }
    }

    // The Client
    const CLASS_A = new ConcreteClassA()
    CLASS_A.templateMethod()

    const CLASS_B = new ConcreteClassB()
    CLASS_B.templateMethod()
```

7.10.5 Output

```
node ./dist/template-method/template-method-concept.js
Class_A : Step Two (overridden)
```

```
Step Three is a hook that prints this line by default.
Class_B : Step One (overridden)
Class_B : Step Two. (overridden)
Class_B : Step Three. (overridden)
```

7.10.6 Template Method Use Case

SBCODE Video ID #313583

In the example use case, there is an `AbstractDocument` with several methods, some are optional and others must be overridden.

The document will be written out in two different formats.

Depending on the concrete class used, the `text()` method will wrap new lines with `<p>` tags and the `print()` method will format text with tabs, or include HTML tags.

7.10.7 Template Method Use Case UML Diagram

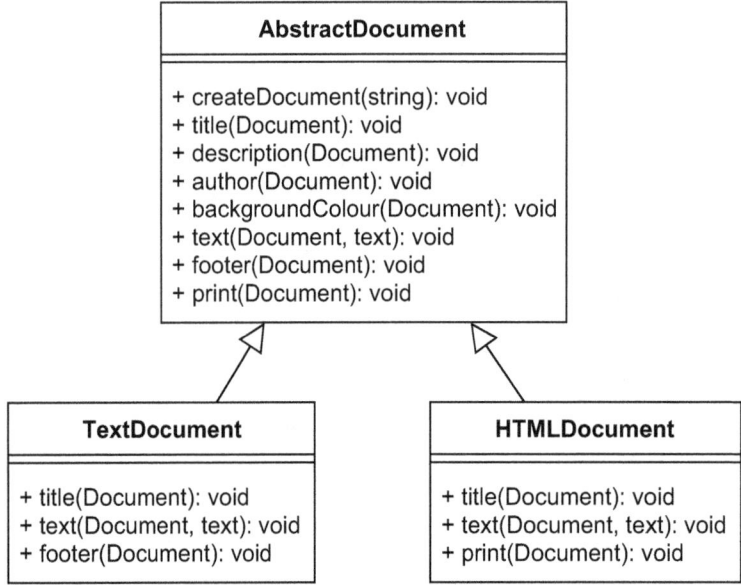

7.10.8 Source Code

./src/template/client.ts

```
// The Template Pattern Use Case Example

import TextDocument from './text-document'
import HTMLDocument from './html-document'
```

```typescript
const TEXT_DOCUMENT = new TextDocument()
TEXT_DOCUMENT.createDocument('Some Text')

const HTML_DOCUMENT = new HTMLDocument()
HTML_DOCUMENT.createDocument('Line 1\nLine 2')
```

./src/template/abstract-document.ts

```typescript
// An abstract document containing a combination of hooks
// and abstract methods

export interface Document {
    [id: string]: string
}

export abstract class AbstractDocument {
    // A template class containing a template method and
    // primitive methods

    document: Document = {}

    abstract title(document: Document): void
    // Must implement

    description?(document: Document): void
    // Optional

    author?(document: Document): void
    // Optional

    backgroundColour(document: Document): void {
        // Optional with a default behavior
        document['bg-col'] = 'white'
    }

    abstract text(document: Document, text: string): void
    // Must implement

    footer?(document: Document): void
    // Optional

    print(document: Document): void {
        // Optional with a default behavior"
        console.log('----------------------')
        Object.keys(document).forEach((attribute: string) => {
            console.log(`${attribute}\t: ${document[attribute]}`)
        })
        console.log()
```

```
        }

        createDocument(text: string): void {
            // The template method
            this.title(this.document)
            if (this.description) this.description(this.document)
            if (this.author) this.author(this.document)
            this.backgroundColour(this.document)
            this.text(this.document, text)
            if (this.footer) this.footer(this.document)
            this.print(this.document)
        }
    }
```

./src/template/text-document.ts

```
    import { Document, AbstractDocument } from './abstract-document'

    export default class TextDocument extends AbstractDocument {
        title(document: Document): void {
            document['title'] = 'New Text Document'
        }

        text(document: Document, text: string): void {
            document['text'] = text
        }

        footer(document: Document): void {
            document['footer'] = '-- Page 1 --'
        }
    }
```

./src/template/html-document.ts

```
    // A HTML document concrete class of AbstractDocument

    import { Document, AbstractDocument } from './abstract-document'

    export default class HTMLDocument extends AbstractDocument {
        title(document: Document): void {
            document['title'] = 'New HTML Document'
        }

        text(document: Document, text: string): void {
            // Putting multiple lines into there own p tags
            const lines = text.split('\n')
```

```
        let markup = ''
        lines.forEach((line) => {
            markup = markup + '    <p>' + line + '</p>\n'
            document['text'] = markup.substring(0, markup.length - 1)
        })
    }

    print(document: Document): void {
        // overriding print to output with html tags
        console.log('<html>')
        console.log('  <head>')
        Object.keys(document).forEach((attribute: string) => {
            if (
                ['title', 'description', 'author'].indexOf(attribute) > -1
            ) {
                console.log(
                    `    <${attribute}>${document[attribute]}</${attribute}>`
                )
            }
            if (attribute === 'bg-col') {
                console.log('    <style>')
                console.log('      body {')
                console.log(
                    `        background-color: ${document[attribute]};`
                )
                console.log('      }')
                console.log('    </style>')
            }
        })
        console.log('  </head>')
        console.log('  <body>')
        console.log(`${document['text']}`)
        console.log('  </body>')
        console.log('</html>')
    }
}
```

7.10.9 Output

```
node ./dist/template-method/client.js
----------------------
title    : New Text Document
bg-col   : white
text     : Some Text
footer   : -- Page 1 --
```

```html
<html>
  <head>
    <title>New HTML Document</title>
    <style>
      body {
        background-color: white;
      }
    </style>
  </head>
  <body>
    <p>Line 1</p>
    <p>Line 2</p>
  </body>
</html>
```

7.10.10 Summary

- The Template method defines an algorithm in terms of abstract operations and subclasses override some or all of the methods to create concrete behaviors.
- Abstract methods must be overridden in the subclasses that extend the abstract class.
- Hook Methods usually have empty bodies in the super class but can be optionally overridden in the subclass.
- If a class contains many conditional statements, consider converting it to use the Template Method pattern.

7.11 Visitor Design Pattern

7.11.1 Overview

SBCODE Video ID #4dffa4

Your object structure inside an application may be complicated and varied. A good example is what could be created using the Composite structure.

The objects that make up the hierarchy of objects, can be anything and most likely complicated to modify as your application grows.

Instead, when designing the objects in your application that may be structured in a hierarchical fashion, you can allow them to implement a **Visitor** interface.

The Visitor interface describes an `accept()` method that a different object, called a Visitor, will use in order to traverse through the existing object hierarchy and read the internal attributes of an object.

The Visitor pattern is useful when you want to analyze, or reproduce an alternative object hierarchy without implementing extra code in the object classes, except for the original requirements set by implementing the Visitor interface.

Similar to the template pattern it could be used to output different versions of a document but more suited to objects that may be members of a hierarchy.

7.11.2 Terminology

- **Visitor Interface**: An interface for the Concrete Visitors.
- **Concrete Visitor**: The Concrete Visitor will traverse the hierarchy of elements.
- **Concrete Element**: (Part) An object that will be visited. An application will contain a variable number of Elements/Parts that can be structured in any particular hierarchy.
- **Visitable Interface**: The interface that elements/parts should implement, that describes the `accept()` method that will allow them to be visited (traversed).

7.11.3 Visitor UML Diagram

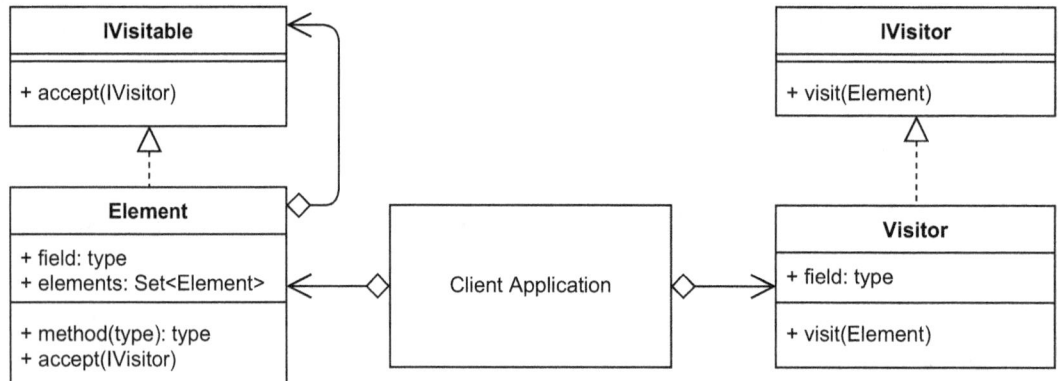

7.11.4 Source Code

In the concept code below, a hierarchy of any object is created. It is similar to a simplified composite. The objects of `Part` can also contain a hierarchy of sub elements/parts.

The `Part` class could also consist of many variations, but this example uses only one.

Rather than writing specific code inside all these elements/parts every time I wanted to handle a new custom operation, I can implement the `IVisitable` interface and create the `accept()` method that allows the custom Visitor to pass through it and access the Elements/Parts internal attributes instead.

Two different Visitor classes are created, `PrintPartNamesVisitor` and `CalculatePartTotalsVisitor`. They are instantiated and passed through the existing Object hierarchy using the same `IVisitable` interface.

./src/visitor/visitor-concept.ts

```
// The Visitor Pattern Concept

interface IVisitor {
    // An interface that custom Visitors should implement
    visit(part: Part): void
}

interface IVisitable {
    // An interface the concrete objects should implement that allows
    // the visitor to traverse a hierarchical structure of objects
    accept(visitor: IVisitor): void
}

class Part implements IVisitable {
```

```typescript
    // a.k.a Element. An Object that can be part of any hierarchy
    name: string
    value: number
    parts: Set<Part>

    constructor(name: string, value: number, parent?: Part) {
        this.name = name
        this.value = value
        this.parts = new Set()
        if (parent) {
            parent.parts.add(this)
        }
    }

    accept(visitor: IVisitor) {
        // required by the Visitor that will traverse
        this.parts.forEach((part) => {
            part.accept(visitor)
        })
        visitor.visit(this)
    }
}

// The Client
// Creating an example object hierarchy.
const Part_A = new Part('A', 101)
const Part_B = new Part('B', 305, Part_A)
const Part_C = new Part('C', 185, Part_A)
const Part_D = new Part('D', -30, Part_B)

// Now Rather than changing the Part class to support custom
// operations, we can utilise the accept method that was
// implemented in the Part class because of the addition of
// the IVisitable interface

class PrintPartNamesVisitor implements IVisitor {
    // Create a visitor that prints the part names
    visit(part: Part) {
        console.log(part.name)
    }
}

// Using the PrintPartNamesVisitor to traverse the object hierarchy
Part_A.accept(new PrintPartNamesVisitor())

class CalculatePartTotalsVisitor implements IVisitor {
    // Create a visitor that totals the part values
    totalValue = 0
```

```
        visit(part: Part) {
            this.totalValue += part.value
        }
    }

    // Using the CalculatePartTotalsVisitor to traverse the
    // object hierarchy
    const CALC_TOTALS_VISITOR = new CalculatePartTotalsVisitor()
    Part_A.accept(CALC_TOTALS_VISITOR)
    console.log(CALC_TOTALS_VISITOR.totalValue)
```

7.11.5 Output

```
node ./dist/visitor/visitor-concept.js
D
B
C
A
561
```

7.11.6 Visitor Use Case

SBCODE Video ID #f5f97b

In the example, the client creates a car with parts.

The car and parts inherit an abstract car parts class with predefined property getters and setters.

Instead of creating methods in the car parts classes and abstract class that run bespoke methods, the car parts can all implement the `IVisitor` interface.

This allows for the later creation of Visitor objects to run specific tasks on the existing hierarchy of objects.

7.11.7 Visitor Example UML Diagram

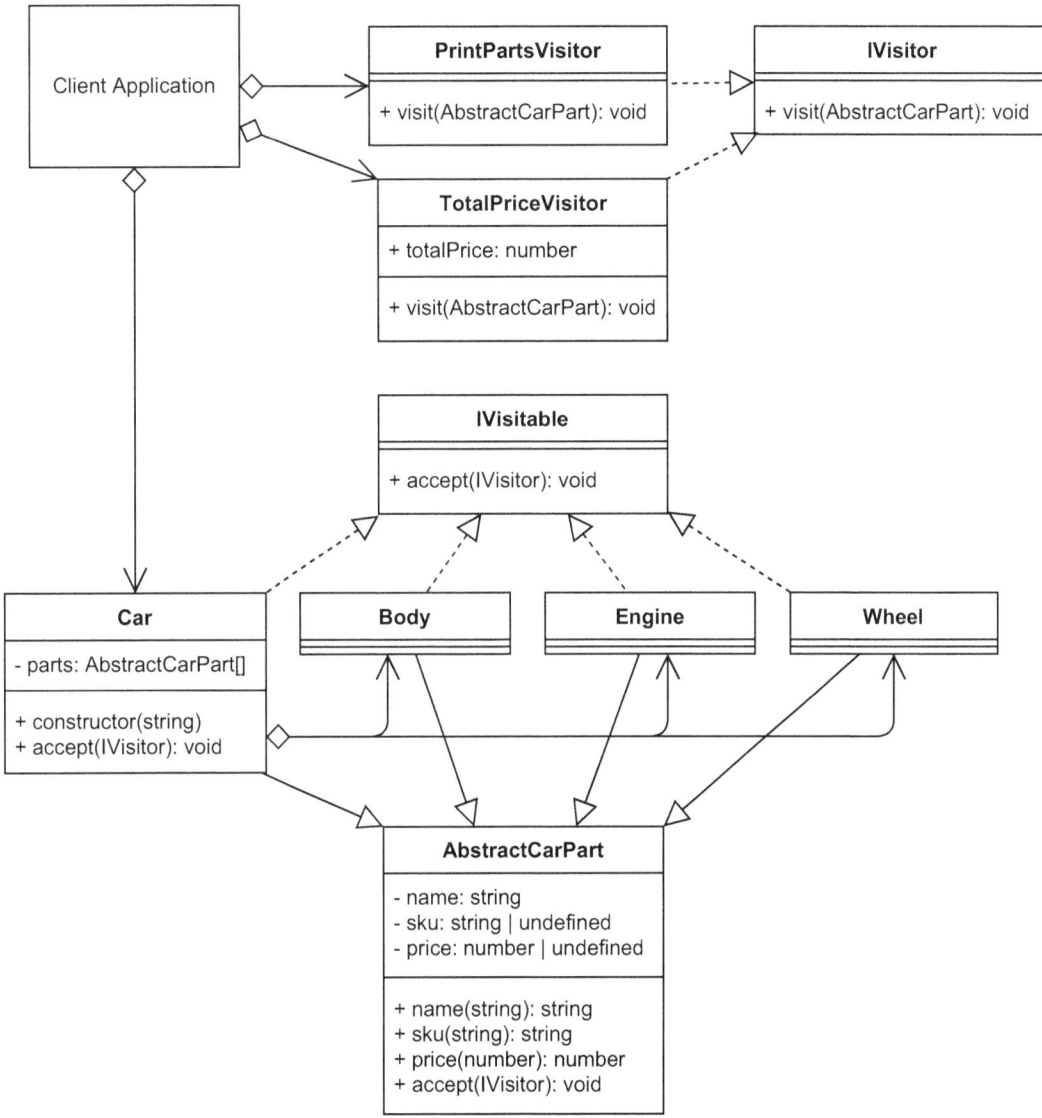

7.11.8 Source Code

./src/visitor/client.ts

```
// The Visitor Pattern Use Case Example

import AbstractCarPart from './abstract-car-part'
import IVisitor from './ivisitor'

class CarBody extends AbstractCarPart {
    // A part of the car
}
```

```typescript
class Engine extends AbstractCarPart {
    // A part of the car
}

class Wheel extends AbstractCarPart {
    // A part of the car
}

class Car extends AbstractCarPart {
    // A Car with parts
    #parts: AbstractCarPart[]

    constructor(name: string) {
        super(name)
        this.#parts = [
            new CarBody('Utility Body', 'ABC-123-21', 1001),
            new Engine('V8 engine', 'DEF-456-21', 2555),
            new Wheel('FrontLeft', 'GHI-789FL-21', 136),
            new Wheel('FrontRight', 'GHI-789FR-21', 136),
            new Wheel('BackLeft', 'GHI-789BL-21', 152),
            new Wheel('BackRight', 'GHI-789BR-21', 152),
        ]
    }

    accept(visitor: IVisitor) {
        this.#parts.forEach((part) => {
            part.accept(visitor)
        })
        visitor.visit(this)
    }
}

class PrintPartsVisitor implements IVisitor {
    // Print out the part name and sku
    visit(abstractCarPart: AbstractCarPart) {
        if (abstractCarPart.sku !== undefined) {
            console.log(
                `${abstractCarPart.name}\t:${abstractCarPart.sku}\t:${abstractCarPart.price}`
            )
        }
    }
}

class TotalPriceVisitor implements IVisitor {
    // Print out the total cost of the parts in the car
    totalPrice = 0
```

```
        visit(abstractCarPart: AbstractCarPart) {
            if (abstractCarPart.price !== undefined) {
                this.totalPrice += abstractCarPart.price as number
            }
        }
    }

    // The Client
    const CAR = new Car('DeLorean')

    // Print out the part name and sku using the PrintPartsVisitor
    CAR.accept(new PrintPartsVisitor())

    // Calculate the total prince of the parts using the TotalPriceVisitor
    const TOTAL_PRICE_VISITOR = new TotalPriceVisitor()
    CAR.accept(TOTAL_PRICE_VISITOR)
    console.log(`Total Price = ${TOTAL_PRICE_VISITOR.totalPrice}`)
```

./src/visitor/abstract-car-part.ts

```
    import IVisitable from './ivisitable'
    import IVisitor from './ivisitor'

    export default abstract class AbstractCarPart implements IVisitable {
        // The Abstract Car Part
        #name: string
        #sku: string | undefined
        #price: number | undefined

        constructor(name: string, sku?: string, price?: number) {
            this.#name = name
            this.#sku = sku
            this.#price = price
        }

        public get name(): string {
            return this.#name
        }

        public set name(value: string) {
            this.#name = value
        }

        public get sku(): string | undefined {
            return this.#sku
        }

        public set sku(value: string | undefined) {
```

```
        this.#sku = value
    }

    public get price(): number | undefined {
        return this.#price
    }

    public set price(value: number | undefined) {
        this.#price = value
    }

    accept(visitor: IVisitor): void {
        visitor.visit(this)
    }
}
```

./src/visitor/ivisitable.ts

```
import IVisitor from './ivisitor'

export default interface IVisitable {
    // An interface the concrete objects should implement that allows
    // the visitor to traverse a hierarchical structure of objects
    accept(visitor: IVisitor): void
}
```

./src/visitor/ivisitor.ts

```
import AbstractCarPart from './abstract-car-part'

export default interface IVisitor {
    // An interface that custom Visitors should implement
    visit(abstractCarPart: AbstractCarPart): void
}
```

7.11.9 Output

```
node ./dist/visitor/client.js
Utility Body     :ABC-123-21      :1001
V8 engine        :DEF-456-21      :2555
FrontLeft        :GHI-789FL-21    :136
FrontRight       :GHI-789FR-21    :136
BackLeft         :GHI-789BL-21    :152
```

```
BackRight       :GHI-789BR-21    :152
Total Price = 4132
```

7.11.10 Summary

- Use the Visitor pattern to define an operation to be performed on the elements/parts of a hierarchical object structure.

- Use the Visitor pattern to define the new operation without needing to change the classes of the elements/parts on that it operates.

- When designing your application, you can provision for the future possibility of needing to run custom operations on objects, by implementing the Visitor interface in anticipation.

- Usage of the Visitor pattern helps to ensure that your classes conform to the single responsibility principle due to them implementing the custom visitor behavior in a separate class.

8. Summary

A table of one-liners to help summarize the design patterns in this book.

Pattern	Description
Abstract Factory	Adds an abstraction over many other related objects that are created using other creational patterns.
Adapter	An alternative interface over an existing interface.
Bridge	The Bridge pattern is similar to the Adapter pattern except in the intent that you developed it.
Builder	A creational pattern whose intent is to separate the construction of a complex object from its representation so that you can use the same construction process to create different representations.
Chain of Responsibility	Pass an object through a chain of successor handlers.
Command	An abstraction between an object that invokes a command, and the object that performs it. Useful for UNDO/REDO/REPLAY.
Composite	A structural pattern useful for hierarchical management.
Decorator	Attach additional responsibilities to an object at runtime.
Facade	An alternative or simplified interface over other interfaces.
Factory	Abstraction between the creation of an object and where it is used.
Flyweight	Share objects rather than creating thousands of near identical copies.
Interpreter	Convert information from one language to another.
Iterator	Traverse a collection of aggregates.
Mediator	Objects communicate through a Mediator rather than directly with each other.
Memento	Save a copy of state and for later retrieval. Useful for UNDO/REDO/LOAD/SAVE.
Observer Pattern	Manage a list of dependents and notifies them of any internal state changes.
Prototype	Good for when creating new objects requires more resources than you need of have available.

Pattern	Description
Proxy	A class functioning as an interface to another class or object.
Singleton	A class that can be instanced at any time, but after it is first instanced, any new instances will point to the original instance.
State	Alter an objects' behavior by changing the handle of one of its methods to one of its subclasses dynamically to reflect its new internal state.
Strategy	Similar to the State Pattern, except that the client passes in the algorithm that the context should then run.
Template Method	An abstract class (template) that contains a method that is a series of instructions that are a combination of methods that can be overridden.
Visitor	Pass an object called a visitor to a hierarchy of objects and execute a method on them.

Remember that design patterns will give you a useful and common vocabulary for when designing, documenting, analyzing, restructuring new and existing software development projects now and into the future.

Good luck and I hope that your projects become very successful.

Sean Bradley

www.ingramcontent.com/pod-product-compliance
Lightning Source LLC
Chambersburg PA
CBHW080452220526
45465CB00006B/2248